T5-DID-046

New York University Studies
in Near Eastern Civilization
Number 11

General Editor
Bayly Winder

ALSO IN THIS SERIES

Number I: F. E. Peters, *Aristotle and the Arabs*

Number II: Jacob M. Landau, *Jews in Nineteenth-Century Egypt*

Number III: Lois Anita Giffen, *Theory of Profane Love Among the Arabs: The Development of the Genre*

Number IV: Lewis V. Thomas, *A Study of Naima*, Norman Itkowitz, editor

Number V: Carl Max Kortepeter, *Ottoman Imperialism During the Reformation: Europe and The Caucasus*

Number VI: Linda Fish Compton, *Andalusian Lyrical Poetry and Old Spanish Love Songs: The Muwashshah and Its Kharja*

Number VII: Peter J. Chelkowski, *Ta'ziyeh: Ritual and Drama in Iran*

Number VIII: Arthur N. Young, *Saudi Arabia: The Making of a Financial Giant*

Number IX: Donald Quataert, *Social Disintegration and Popular Resistance in the Ottoman Empire, 1881–1908: Reactions to European Economic Penetration.*

Number X: Tawfiq Al-Hakim, *The Return of Consciousness*, Bayly Winder, translator

New York University Studies in Near Eastern Civilization

The participation of the New York University Press in the University's commitment to Near Eastern Studies provides Americans and others with new opportunities for understanding the Near East. Concerned with those various peoples of the Near East who, throughout the centuries, have dramatically shaped many of mankind's most fundamental concepts and who have always had high importance in practical affairs, this series, New York University Studies in Near Eastern Civilization, seeks to publish important works in this vital area. The purview will be broad, open to varied approaches and historical periods, including the range of social scientific approaches. It will, however, be particularly receptive to work in two areas that reflect the University and that may have received insufficient attention elsewhere. These are literature and art. Furthermore, taking a stand that may be more utilitarian than that of some other publications, the series will welcome translations of important Near Eastern literature. In this way, an audience, unacquainted with the languages of the Near East, will be able to deepen its knowledge of the cultural achievements of Near Eastern peoples.

Bayly Winder
General Editor

Jerusalem and Mecca

The Typology of the Holy City in the Near East

F. E. PETERS

NEW YORK UNIVERSITY PRESS
New York and London

Library of Congress Cataloging-in-Publication Data

Peters, F. E. (Francis E.)
Jerusalem and Mecca.

(New York University studies in Near Eastern civilization; no. 11)
Bibliography: p.
Includes index.
1. Jerusalem—Religious life and customs. 2. Mecca (Saudi Arabia)—Religious life and customs. 3. Temple of Jerusalem (Jerusalem) 4. Ka'bah. 5. Jewish shrines. 6. Islamic shrines—Jerusalem. 7. Islamic shrines—Saudi Arabia—Mecca. 8. Christian shrines—Jerusalem. 9. Pilgrims and pilgrimages—Jerusalem. 10. Pilgrims and pilgrimages—Mecca—Saudi Arabia. I. Title. II. Series.
BL2345.J47P47 1987 291.3'5'09538 86-23451
ISBN 0-8147-6598-X

Book design by Ken Venezio

For Bayly Winder,
teacher, guide, friend

Contents

Preface

The present work is an immediate outgrowth of my study, *The Children of Abraham: Judaism, Christianity and Islam.* It is in a sense the translation of that work from the high tradition of ideology and institutions into the earthly vernacular of places, buildings, and streets, of buying and selling, and finding bed and board. The subject is the cities of choice of those same three religions, their primary holy cities Jerusalem and Mecca, where the claims and expectations of each had to be converted into stone and mortar; where institutions had to be housed, staffed, and supported; and where politics and religion had to come to terms or to grips. It is a book about appropriation and implementation.

It is something more, I hope. All religions have their holy places, and some even their holy cities. Judaism, Christianity, and Islam all had theirs, and in a sophisticated urban milieu that knew and cared about cities before those three monotheistic faiths took up permanent residence in such. When they finally did, the children of Abraham made certain cities their own and so produced gloriously complex examples of one of the most interesting of all urban phenomena, the holy city.

My primary interest here is not in the religions themselves, which do not lack for attention, nor in the origins, nature, and shape of the holy, though I have ventured some preliminary remarks on holy places and holy men. The focus is rather on their cities. We now know a good deal about how urban settlements worked in the preindustrial world, how they grew and declined, how they served and were served by the people who lived in them, and, finally, how best they might be studied and understood. I have tried to cast some of that understanding on the holy cities of Judaism, Christianity, and Islam.

Anyone who takes up these questions in the context of Near Eastern urbanism is deeply in the debt of Professor Eugen Wirth of Erlangen, as will be abundantly clear on the pages to follow, and here I wish explicitly to acknowledge my share in that debt. Wirth's work has been continuously stimulating to me, as has that of André Raymond of Paris and Oleg Grabar of the Fogg Museum and Harvard University. I first came to know Near Eastern cities in the "land of Sham," the best of all places for that experience, and with the best of guides, Heinz Gaube, now of Tübingen, a friend as well as a teacher; Dorothée Sack, to whom I owe other considerable debts; Michael Meinecke of the German Institute in Damascus; Dr. Afif Bahnassi of the Syrian Department of Antiquities; and in a particular way Dr. Kassem Toueir of that department, who allowed me to share not only his knowledge but his wisdom and the priceless friendship of himself and his family in Damascus.

There were many generously helpful scholars in Jerusalem, from each of whom I learned something unique and important: John Wilkinson and Michael Burgoyne of the British School there; Père Benoit of the Ecole Biblique; Yoram Tsafrir, Moshe Barasch, and Myriam Rosen-Ayalon of the Hebrew University; Moshe Gil of Haifa and Dan Urman of Ben Gurion; and Meir Ben Dov of the Israel Department of Antiquities. In Saudi Arabia I was greeted with great courtesy and warmth by Dr. Sami Mohsin Angawi, the Director of the Hajj Research Center; he and his colleagues there and at King Abdul Aziz University in Jedda generously shared their work with me and, in the mysterious manner of such things, may have planted the seeds of this present study. None of them is, of course, responsible for, or may even agree with, what I have chosen to say or to omit in the pages that follow.

We are all dependents in our work, in different ways on different people, and very little of this or other projects would likely have come about without Jack Hayes of the Mobil Oil Corporation and his quiet and deeply appreciated efforts on my behalf. I am grateful too to Ralph Minasian and the Kevorkian Fund for the support they have given to my work both abroad and at New York University. Colleagues helped too: Larry Schiffman, who supplied always useful material, and Bayly Winder, who supplied equally helpful comments and advice. I thank them both, as well as Dr. Barakat Ahmad for his always stimulating discussions and observations.

Finally I must thank the graduate students of the Near East Center of the University of Chicago for applying the stimulus to whatever faculty it is that thrusts pen into hand. All they required was that I deliver the Marshall G. S. Hodgson Lecture at the university on May 21, 1982. Life is not so simple, however. This book, and an unconscionably long lecture in the bargain, was the immediate result of their invitation, and it is intended to honor, in its own modest fashion, that scholar who taught so many of us to think in other, better ways.

Stockport, New York
January 1, 1986

INTRODUCTION

The Cities of God

We were once not so anxious to escape cities, for a weekend, a month in the summer, perhaps even permanently; over the centuries far more social energy has been expended on making and moving into cities than in getting out of them. Like the human body, they seemed like good places to live. Part of it was the mystery, surely. Their organic complexity seemed beyond comprehension, how they not only supplied what was required, but offered a glittering choice from among what might be simply desired to enhance the human condition. There were vistas of pleasure and power and enlightenment in the city; a man might become learned or rich there, and perhaps even happy.

But only rarely virtuous. A tradition as long-lived and as pervasive as the one that dreams of urban streets paved with gold has maintained that the city is also the natural habitat of iniquity, and the first suburban refuges were not gracious bedroom townships nestled across the river and amidst the trees but sun-struck deserts and dark caves that were safely remote from invincibly urban sin. Which is curious, since the gods, and even the fastidious One True God worshipped by the many children of Abraham, have also followed the well-trodden path of urban immigration and chosen to live amidst their devotees in cities. For a very long time the House of God, whether here or below or in the remotest of heavens, has had a distinctly urban cast.

As with much else, urbanism has lost many of its more obvious mysteries, and by now we know a good deal about how cities work, particularly contemporary ones. We can even reassemble the pieces of evidence long ago taken apart and studied separately by the historian under the headings of art, architecture, politics, and theology and so make some organic sense of the preindustrial city. We could do even better if we had the cities' records and archives—more real estate deeds or tax rolls, for example, which are particularly scanty in the Near East before the sixteenth century. True, we do not know very much about demography or some of the more intriguing mechanisms of self-government, but we do have a representative sample of medieval houses and public buildings, can trace some ancient street plans, and are able to follow the career lines of enough lawyers and soldiers and poets to understand how the preindustrial city worked. To speak only of the Near East, we can fashion tolerably convincing and detailed portraits of medieval Cairo and Isfahan and Aleppo, of Constantinople and Antioch of late antiquity, and of even earlier Rome and Athens.

All these cities were, and most still are, important places. More, their old cores are well preserved, and on both counts they have attracted the most prolonged and detailed attention. There are, however, two equally important places—or perhaps even more important places, at least as far as religious consciousness is concerned—that find little or no place in the consideration of urban historians: Mecca, the holiest city of Islam, and Jerusalem, the object of the love and strife of all three of the great monotheistic religions that have dominated human history.

We are plentifully served on the history of Jerusalem, of course, and with headline, polemic, and aspiration, but neither that city nor Mecca has been much studied *as a city.* Perhaps they were not very important as cities, lacking as they did many of the commercial and political advantages of those other prime exemplars of the species, or perhaps we have just gotten it wrong. If we put aside the praise and the polemic, the manifestos, claims, dreams, and imaginings that surround them, and look more closely at the "material culture" of Mecca and Jerusalem during the premodern era—roughly the period before A.D. 1800—the shape and form and substance of those places as represented by their public monuments and private homes, their pattern of walls and streets and lanes, the urban fabric that shaped and was shaped by the life that went on within them, we discover that both cities were at the same time more important than they should have been and less important than they appear to be.

The fact is that neither place conforms very comfortably to

either our historical expectations of them or even the accepted typology of the Near Eastern city of late antiquity and the Middle Ages. Mecca and Jerusalem were assuredly cities, and from the seventh century into modern times they were just as certainly "Islamic," as we understand that admittedly ambiguous term. But they were more. They were also holy cities, an urban type that transcends even the "Islamic" component in their analysis and whose understanding must be sought in some larger classification of cities. Indeed, before either of them became "Islamic," Mecca and Jerusalem were both "holy" and "cities."

Let us begin by attempting at least a provisional definition of what is meant here by a holy city. Every urban settlement has its holy places—shrines, temples, churches, or the tombs of the holy, the learned, or the martyred—and the performance of cult acts in connection with these sites is one of the normal functions of city life in Moscow or Nairobi or Tokyo. To offer prayer or sacrifice in a public or "political" mode in them is typologically little different from the market functions of a city, as contrasted, let us say, to those same acts done in a village or in one's own home.

What constitutes a holy city is not then the mere existence of such holy places, but rather the presence in the city of a *sacrum*, or perhaps several, of such an order of importance or allure that the cultus connected with it exercises an attraction not merely on the city's immediate hinterland but over an extended network. Or, to put it somewhat differently, the cult center or centers, like those at Kyoto or Lourdes or Benares or Salt Lake City, attract to the city people who would not normally resort there. The external sign that such is indeed the case is not merely the anomalies in the ebb and flow of population but the fact that the city itself is modified in an untypical manner—that it has grown new municipal organs or that its urban muscles, sinews, and conformation swell and bulge, like an athlete's, in quite unexpected places—or, that there should be a city in that place to begin with.

One may approach the holy city, then, as a distinct urban type from either of two directions: from the presence, shape, and extent of the "pilgrimage network" from which it draws its extraordinary number of visitors, or more directly from an inspection of what appears to constitute its peculiar urban morphology. Both perspectives will be investigated in turn, but first we must cast at least a passing regard at the nature of holy places themselves, to make essay of what has been called the "anthropology of the sacred," before turning to what are, even today, two of the most vital of the cities of God.

CHAPTER I

The Holy Place

What is holy and why are questions that run deeply back into history and human consciousness, but a given place is holy for the simpler reason of the numinous presence that is thought to abide there, whether in a spring or a river, a tree or a grove, within a stone or a cave, atop a high place. It is in such a place, or in such an object, that the divine suffers approach, to be entreated, to be mollified, or simply to permit man to draw upon that awesome power of the Other. "The place on which you are standing," God warned Moses, "is holy ground."[1] There must be no mistake. The place is marked; it is physically circumscribed and defined by a *temenos* or a *haram* to advise those who come there that this is indeed holy ground, which may be approached, though with all the caution associated with a taboo. In Jerusalem's Temple there was a sign: no Gentiles beyond this point; outside present-day Mecca, a checkpoint.[2]

In this manner a necessary formalization has taken place: a holy presence is defined within a holy place. A similar formalization is manifested in the *enshrinement* of the object, some architectural adaptation of the sacred object or its setting intended to adorn, to dignify, or to render symbolic the object and its place. And in some instances, though by no means all, the object or the presence within it likewise begins to undergo a process of *personification,* and in the sequel the enshrinement is understood to be the abode of the god. Spring becomes nymph; and tree, dryad. And the shrine at the place of their presence both honors and shelters them.

In the early stages of their encounter, man will almost invariably anthropomorphize the divine, and not merely in those physical and corporeal terms that speak so beguilingly from the icons of the Hellenes, but with more subtle and more social nuances.

Thus the god is not simply *enformed;* he is also *enhoused* and in the end made to dwell beside his worshippers in cities. "How awesome is this place!" Jacob exclaimed. "This is nothing else but the house of God, and this is the gate of heaven." House of God and Gate of Heaven, the earthly and the heavenly abodes of God. Heaven's Gate has its own history and geography, to be sure, but it is only God's dwelling here below—Beth El as the Israelites called it, *Bayt Allah* to the Muslims, or the "tents" that disciples wished to pitch for Jesus, Moses, and Elijah on the Mount of the Transfiguration—that we shall be entering here.[3]

Today the presence of God dwells for the Muslim in a simple and unadorned stone structure in the midst of Mecca. The Ka'ba, or "House of the Lord," has been in much its present form for as long as we have an convincing records. We may surmise, however, that the Ka'ba suffered at least one major modification in the course of its doubtlessly long history before Islam, though we cannot say exactly when. Mecca began its career of holiness as a nomadic sanctuary, and if, as seems plausible, the black rock embedded in one corner of the Ka'ba was once a *betyl,* (a sacred rock that both manifested and enhoused the deity), then we must conclude that the nomads carried about with them what was to become the stone of Mecca.[4] And further, it was only when its devotees had begun to become sedentary at Mecca that it was housed there in the Ka'ba.

A parallel to this common practice lies no farther from our hand than the Bible. The Ark of the Covenant, carried through the Sinai by the Israelites and housed at each stop in a tent designed by the Lord Himself, had temporary domiciles at a number of different places. But with the inevitable shift from nomadic to sedentary housing, we can observe two separate but converging threads of conservative reaction. First, there was David's continuing practice of keeping the Ark under a bedouin tent or tentlike structure even in unmistakably urban Jerusalem (2 Sam. 6:17). Then, when David proposed more fitting quarters than a tent—"Here I live in a house of cedar, while the Ark of the Lord is housed in curtains" (2 Sam. 7:2)—the Lord Himself warned that He did not care for the change in facilities: "Down to this day I have never lived in a house since I brought Israel up from Egypt. I made My journey in a tent . . . " (2 Sam. 7:6).

God likewise speaks out on the subject of housing in the Qur'an, but now to bid Abraham "raise the foundations" of His house in Mecca (Qur'an 2:127). Here the Lord is reconciled, as He was in Jerusalem in Solomon's day, to a proper urban house of wood and stone, but the still only recently sedentarized Quraysh of Mecca were perhaps less so. They continued, at any rate, to build round, tentlike houses in their new urban environment[5] and made symbolic pretence that God still dwelled, as of old, in a tent by draping the undeniably stone and square Ka'ba with a black cloth.[6]

"But how can God indeed dwell on earth?" Solomon mused when he built his Temple in Jerusalem. "Heaven itself, the highest heaven, cannot contain thee; how much less the house I have built!" The answer is refined and Deuteronomic: Yahweh himself does not live there, but the presence of His Name sanctifies that place and renders it a *qibla* toward which every Jew turns in prayer (1 Kings 8:27–53).

We have no way of knowing how Solomon himself would have answered his own question, or indeed if the question even occured to him in the first place. In any event he moved the Ark of the Covenant, upon which God manifested His presence between the wings of the cherubim, and brought it straightaway into the newly constructed Temple. That latter was, how else can we express it, a *Bayt Allah,* the final resting place of the nomads' God in the capital city of the promised *Eretz Israel,* and Solomon lived near to his God's House in his own richly constructed royal palace.

We cannot say how the other gods reacted to their transformation from residents upon mountains and in the depths of caves into city dwellers, but the more voluble God of Israel leaves no doubt that in the end He enjoyed the change. "I am Yahweh," He announces in the recently discovered Temple Scroll, "who dwells in the midst of the Israelites forever."[7] And no longer in a tent or some other makeshift shelter. Both the Temple Scroll and the biblical books that preceded it are redolent wth images of the city, to the point indeed that if the *Bayt Allah,* the House of the Lord, shared its sanctity with the city, the city gave shape and form and intelligibility to the Temple. In his vision Ezekiel was taken by God to the top of a high mountain, where he saw the Temple spread before him "in a form resembling a city," and that parallel continues to come easily in Scripture, as it does in the Temple Scroll. Yahweh lived in an *'ir hammiqdash,* a "Temple City," and He sternly warns, "the city of My Temple (*'ir miqdashi*) must not be defiled."[8]

By the time of the Greco-Roman occupation of the Near East, many important holy places likewise appear to have vacated their original rural settings near trees and springs, on mountain tops or deep within caves, and to have moved, either literally or by association, into the urban locales where in the age after Alexander the Great a new generation of the Hellenized elite lived in the Near East. In many instances, however, the nature of the original site and cultus can be recovered. Thus a number of the shrines of Roman Damascus are depicted on its coins, and one minted in the mid–third century shows the god Marsyas enshrined in a temple with columns and a pediment, while below a spring is personified as a river god seated in a grotto.[9] Again, the original high places of the East, now in an unmistakable urban setting, are readily discernible in the temples atop the heights of Pella and Zeugma and in Hadrian's sanctuary built over the Samaritan temple atop Mount Gerizim in Neapolis/Nablus.[10] Pan was still worshiped in a grotto at the springs of highly urbanized Caesarea Philippi, but most Near Eastern cities had transformed the cult of the woodland nymphs into a piece of urban furniture, the nymphaeum-fountain, whose symbolic and conventional nature is underscored by its artificial water source.[11]

Without being unnecessarily formal about it, we can trace in the iconographic evidence a line of development from the association of a god or goddess with an altar, then a shrine, a temple, and, finally, a holy place that has become an integrated part of the urban environment and serves specifically urban needs. A number of Near Eastern examples of this paradigm are particularly interesting for our own purposes in that the holy object, in these cases a *betyl*, was never entirely personified. We are told that it was Aphrodite who had her sanctuary at Byblos in Phoenicia, but as a matter of fact the cult centered around a large conical stone. The Byblos sanctuary is destroyed, but a coin minted by that city in A.D. 217 or 218 shows what is unmistakably a *betyl* placed either atop or behind—the numismatic convention permits either interpretation—a typical Near Eastern horned altar.[12] This was probably the original sacred composition, cult object and altar, but the coin shows how far it had progressed. *Betyl* and altar are now enclosed by a large *temenos* set off by an urban designer's colonnaded arcade.

At Emesa the sacred stone "represented" the sun god Elagabal. It is sometimes depicted with an eagle sculpted onto or attached to it, almost as a rather tentative and preliminary step toward personification. During the Roman period the stone was enshrined in a large peristyle temple within the city, and as depicted on coins, it appears atop an altar either within or just outside the temple.[13] Here the ambiguity is not so much artistic as liturgical: deities normally resided in the *adyton* within the temple, and altars were in the courtyard outside; it is not inconceivable that the *betyl* was transported back and forth between *adyton* and altar. The connection between object and cult altar remains strong and continuous, in any event, not only at Byblos and Emesa but at Adraa, now Dera'a, and Bostra, today Busra eski Sham, in the Roman Provincia Arabia. In the first city a single *betyl* and at Bostra three such were placed on an altar or a high platform approached by steps.[14]

At Emesa, Adraa, and Bostra we are clearly in the presence of local Arab cults; in the case of Bostra, probably Nabatean Arabs who had a large temple there before the Romans took over the city in A.D. 106.[15] We know a good deal about the cult of stone *betyl*s among the pre-Islamic Arabs, and at their famous shrine at Mecca the association of object, shrine, and *haram* is manifest in the pre-Islamic cult there.[16] As already noted, the black meteoric stone was incorporated into the cubelike building called the Ka'ba at some unknown point, and the entire domain was surrounded by a sacred *temenos*. The stone and the Ka'ba rested somewhat uneasily together in Islamic times, since the building was then regarded no longer as housing for the *betyl* but rather as the "House of God."[17]

As has already been remarked, the temple or shrine, and particularly its concealed inner *cella* or *adyton*, regarded as the domicile of the god was a common phenomenon in the urban centers of the Greco-Roman world, and it was frequently connected with an etiological myth, like that of Jacob and Beth El, to explain how the deity, now thoroughly personified, came to dwell in that place. In the early Muslim perception, and possibly among the pre-Islamic Arabs as well, that myth connected Mecca with Adam, for whom God built the original Ka'ba on the plan of God's own residence in heaven, a common cosmological echo in temple myths, and principally with Abraham, who rebuilt the edifice after its destruction in the Flood.[18]

The Ka'ba at Mecca continued to be a modest building down to and through its rebuilding during Muhammad's thirty-fifth year. The *Sira*, or *Life of the Prophet*, describes it as "made of loose stones above a man's height" (122). Today it is taller, and mortar holds the stones more firmly together, but essentially it is the same building. Elsewhere shrines grew to more prodigious proportions, however. We cannot say what the original cult assemblage was at highly syncretized Baalbek in Central Lebanon,[19] but by Roman times it had expanded into a large sanctuary complex. The *temenos* arcade visible on the coins of Byblos had grown at Roman Baalbek into an immense colonnaded court preceded by an entrance porch of monumental size and with flanking square towers in the Syrian fashion. The interior *temenos* court had its own shrine niches—like the *haram* at pre-Islamic Mecca, it attracted other deities to the resort of the principal god—and not one but two altars, one of which was a veritable tower.[20] And at the far end of the inner court, opposite the entry gate, was a large, raised decastyle temple of Jupiter Heliopolitanus in which the cult image was preserved.[21]

To this point it has been a question of a holy object as the generating force of a holy place and, as we shall see, eventually of a holy city. But men too have the numinous about them, living or dead. The Near East had its deified rulers from the beginning, and royal palaces and tombs from the era of the pharaohs down through Byzantine times reflect in their architectonic structure and rich decor the sacred character of the kings and autocrats who lived and died in them. In these instances, however, the holiness attached in effect to the office more than to the individual; personal and popular devotion, the kind that turns a site into a genuine holy place, was not often associated with it. But we are concerned here not so much with the deified ruler as with another type, the holy man, the saint, or the "friend of God," who in the end turned out to have far greater potency than mere rulers. In pharaonic Egypt the notables of the land huddled their tombs in the shadow of the pharaohs' grandiose pyramids; by medieval times the process had been reversed, and it was Cairo's Muslim rulers who moved their tombs to the vicinity of the graves of holy men to partake of their sanctity and perhaps even in the popular esteem that surrounded them.[22]

The intimate connection between cult and place is absolutely transparent in the case of the Christian saint. Christianity's early heroes are commemorated in the document that is their chief literary monument, the Acts of the Apostles; indeed, one of them, James, "the brother of the Lord," appears to have been the rarest of all God's creatures, a Christian *and* a Jewish saint, a *hagios* and a *zaddiq*.[23] But the true cult of the Christian holy man did not come into full flower until the third century with the liturgical veneration that began to be paid to the martyrs of the new faith.[24] And it was site-oriented: the first public veneration of the Christian martyrs took place, in either cruciform tombs or circular mausolea on the Roman style, in the traditional burial places outside the city walls.[25]

In the new Christian climate established by Constantine and his successors in the Empire, what were once simply tombs were expanded into magnificent churches where the memorial day of the saint could be celebrated in full liturgical splendor. The earliest of these appears to have been a martyrium built in 381 just outside the walls of Antioch, but during the next century the "translation" of all or parts of the relics of the saints to shrines *within* the city was in progress, and the martyrium was on the way to becoming an urban institution in the Near East. There were instances where the relics of the saint simply found a place, a special chapel perhaps, in an urban church, but there is good reason to think that many of the most typical nonbasilical churches built in Near Eastern cities in the fifth and sixth centuries, like the Church of Saint George at Ezra (A.D. 515) and that of John the Baptist at Gerasa (A.D. 531), were in fact urban martyria.[26]

The *translatio* is an overt and ingenuous demonstration of the capacity of men to transfer holiness from one place to another, in this instance from cemeteries outside a city to a shrine at its very center: the saint's remains are simply picked up and ceremoniously carried from the grave site to another, more appropriate location. It was not, of course, the only way to relocate the sacred. History and tradition could be rewritten or embroidered by sectarian groups, often with their rivals' own stories, to explain unlikely geography or events. Shrines of "Musa" and "Ayyub" are ubiquitous in the Near East, each with its appropriate haggadic tale of how Moses or Job came to be in that place. So too Abraham could be resettled at Mecca or the body of the Prophet's cousin and posthumous rival 'Ali find its final and unexpected resting place at Mazar-i Sharif in Afghanistan. One Muslim legend invoked the workings of the Flood to explain the presence of fragments of the earth of Palestine, and so of the holiness of Palestine as well, at Wasit in Mesopotamia,[27] while the Christians thought that a cortege of angels had transported by air to Loretto in Italy the holy house in Nazareth where Gabriel announced to Mary her conception of the Messiah.

We have already cast a brief glance at the chief object-oriented shrine in Islam, the Ka'ba at Mecca with its black meteoric stone. If we except the curious political totems and fetishes like the Prophet's cloak and hairs from his beard that were superstitiously carried about by later Caliph-Sultans, the veneration of objects found little official support in Islam.[28] Nor was the cult of saints, living or dead, an entirely natural development in a belief system that placed an almost infinite gulf between a transcendent Allah and His creation here below. It occurred nonetheless in Islam, and with some speed.[29] Muhammad, who never claimed to be anything but a mere mortal and who stoutly refused to produce supernatural "signs" to verify his claim to Prophethood (Qur'an 40:78; cf. 6:37, 13:7; 21:5), was soon after his death credited with miraculous powers, and those special gifts and graces (*karamat*) bestowed by God on His Prophet were quickly extended to God's "friends," His *walis,* male and female, who then became objects of a special cult, even during their lifetime.[30]

A great deal of the Islamic cultus that attached to the persons and graves of holy men and women originated in and remained on the level of folk religion,[31] and is still visible, at least in its architectural manifestations, in the shrine-tombs scattered around the countryside and suburbs in the Near East and particularly in North Africa.[32] But in other cases the cultus is robustly urban and was likely so from the beginning. The subjects of such veneration fall into a great many categories. The most recent are Sufis and founders of religious orders, but others go back to the early history of Islam: heroes of the conquest, for example, or even pre-Islamic personages who had become part of the Muslim religious heritage as early as the Qur'an itself. Thus the prophets from Adam to Jesus were memorialized at their putative grave sites, most of them quite naturally in Syria-Palestine and Mesopotamia,[33] and generated a considerable local traffic in pilgrims. Hebron in particular was a famous Muslim shrine center, as it had been for Jews and Christians previously, since it was reputed to possess the graves of the patriarchs and their wives.[34] Mecca too was rich in such patriarchal grave sites.[35]

The prevalence in Islamic times of Near Eastern grave sites associated with biblical figures immediately raises the question of whether they did not exist as cult centers in earlier Christian and even Jewish days. Their connection back to Christian piety is not difficult to make: the accounts of pre-Islamic Christian pilgrimages to Palestine leave little doubt that there was already a grave site cult of the heroes of Israel.[36] And through them we can detect—somewhat dimly, since rabbinical sentiment was strongly opposed to such practices—an earlier Jewish cultus of the same figures and at the very same places,[37] and even eventually of the rabbis themselves who, in despite of their own theology, became posthumous saints.

The reasons are not difficult to understand. Not only was Jerusalem a holy city; all of Palestine, and even parts of Syria and Mesopotamia as well, was in some sense a holy land filled with places resonant with Jewish history, an *Eretz Israel* that extended beyond Jewish political control, beyond the Talmud's wider legal parameters, to a numinous undefined horizon. It did little good to restrict the official cultus to the Temple in Jerusalem; the Bible account continued to preserve the memory of other places associated with the Jewish past, and local tradition was not slow in identifying them for the pious traveler.

Rabbi Meshullam of Volterra, who was in Palestine in 1481, was one of the many travelers and immigants who reported on the Jewish Holy Land and the burial sites there. He was perhaps surprised by their number, but another element of the cultus struck him as well:

All round Jerusalem there are many caves and in them are buried many pious and saintly people without number, but we do not know who they are except those marked; but it is a tradition among us from mouth to mouth in ancient times and there is no doubt as to their truth. And we see that the Muslims also honor all those and that they have the same traditions about them as we do.[38]

And when questioned, as Ibn Battuta did a learned shaykh in Hebron in the fourteenth century, the Muslim authenticated a holy place by appealing to the same tradition as Meshallam had:

All the scholars I have met accept as a certainty that these graves are the very graves of Abraham, Isaac, Jacob and their wives. No one raises objections to this but followers of false doctrines; it is a tradition that has passed from father to son for generations and admits no doubt.[39]

Since this was the neighborhood of Jerusalem and since the local Muslims shared both the cultus and the traditions surrounding it, these were probably patriarchal grave sites, but the Jews were not immune to the notion that more recent generations of holy men might be revered at their grave sites, as they were at Tiberias and Safed in the later Jewish holy land of Galilee, where the graves of eminent rabbis generated their own cult. Isaac ben Joseph, an Aragonese Kabbalist who migrated to Palestine and visited Tiberias in 1334, reports that there were thirteen synagogues and a great many schools and then adds,

People come from far and wide to visit the tombs of Tiberias; they are very many in number. The best known are the sepulchers of the disciples of Rabbi Akiba, Yohanan ben Zakkai and of Rab Kahana; the tombs of Jonathan ben Levi and Moses, son of Maimun, the grottoes of

Rabbi Khiya, of Rab Huna, of Rabbi Meir and of Rabbi Zemakh Gaon, upon whose memory be blessing.[40]

Safed, a Galilean town with no biblical and almost no ancient Jewish past, gives us some preliminary insight into how holy cities come about. The Ottomans took Palestine from the Mamluks at the beginning of the sixteenth century, and in that newly relaxed atmosphere Jewish immigrants from Spain and Portugal began to settle in Safed. The change in regime did in fact have a generally healthy effect on the population and standard of living in Palestine through the course of the sixteenth century,[41] but certain conditions made Safed particularly attractive to the new immigrants. It lay in Galilee, the center of Jewish life in Palestine since Hadrian's ban of the Jews from Judea in the mid-second century; it possessed in its near vicinity the tomb of a famous tannaitic rabbi, Simeon ben Yohai, whom a much later generation of Spanish Kabbalists had identified as the author of one of their primary texts, the *Zohar;* the Talmudic scholars who settled there were exempt from municipal taxation; and, finally, it was the center of an emerging wool industry in which the immigrants could play an immediate and important part.[42] The effects were already visible by the end of the century: a European traveler noted the presence of six yeshivas in Safed and "many aged go purposelie to die there,"[43] a certain sign that we are in the presence of a holy city, albeit a very commercial one.

Once established as a holy city, Safed began to display what is, as we shall see, one of the chief characteristics of such places, the multiplication of secondary shrines. Simeon ben Yohai, the primary holy man of the area, lay buried at Meron, about six miles from the city; the road between the two places is now lined with tombs of rabbis of succeeding generations, almost all of them innocent of any connection with the place, and many of their sepulchers are furnished with domed chambers, the *maqam*s and *qubba*s typical of the tombs of local Muslim holy men. Below the Jewish quarter on the western slope of the hill upon which the city of Safed is seated are the revered tombs of the newer saints of the Kabbala and the Law like Isaac Luria (d. 1573) and Joseph Karo (d. 1575), and nearby, Israel's most recent saints and martyrs, the members of Irgun and Lehi executed by the British in

Acre prison in 1947 on charges of terrorism.

The Iberian immigration did not make Safed a holy city, merely a successful one. Lower Galilee was already a densely shrined Jewish holy land in the twelfth century, when the travelers Petachia of Ratisbon and Rabbi Jacob ben Nathaniel were shown tombs and ruined synagogues there and told stories that were still being repeated many centuries later.[44] There was remembrance in Galilee, surely, diffused in an unsophisticated way over many sites, but not much prosperity. In 1489 Obadiah da Bertinoro, who had immigrated to Jerusalem and knew the country well, wrote to his brother in Europe, who had inquired about Jewish-Arab relations in Palestine. "It is said," the meticulous Obadiah reported "that the Jews live quietly and peacefully with the Arabs in Safed, in Cana and in all of Galilee, yet most of them are poor and have to live by peddling."[45] It was that poverty that the new Spanish and Portuguese immigrants, and the new Ottoman administration, finally cured in Safed and its holy Galilean hinterland.

Brief notice should be taken of an entirely contrary example, an undoubted holy place that never succeeded in generating a holy city. Despite its undeniable biblical associations, Hebron remains almost invisible to us in the centuries after the Maccabees, when it was accounted a Gentile town (1 Macc. 11:65), as well as during the Roman years that followed. Constantine, who had already taken in hand the Christianization of the holy places in Jerusalem and Bethlehem, was alerted by his mother-in-law to what he had overlooked: that Abraham's oak at Mamre "was being defiled in every possible way by certain superstitious persons. She declared that the idols worthy of utter destruction are being erected beside it, and that an altar stands near, and that impure sacrifices are continually offered."[46] Constantine directed that the offending temple be removed and a basilica be put up there as well, but in a manner quite different from that followed in the new Christian shrines in Jerusalem and Bethlehem. At Mamre the basilica was merely a smallish appendage to what was not an atrium but a genuine *haram* on the order of those in Byblos and Baalbek and Mecca: a walled enclosure around the sacred oak of Abraham and an altar that stood nearby.[47]

Despite this early imperial attention, later Christian Hebron could not even boast of a bishop and appears nowhere in the ecclesiastical *notitiae*. In the Islamic era, and early in that era if we are to believe the endowment tradition, its patriarchal grave sites made Hebron a Muslim pilgrimage center of sorts, and visitors from the tenth century onward speak of the *haram* there, the famous *Masjid Ibrahim*. Idrisi, who never visited the place, went so far as to call Hebron "a village that had become a city,"[48] a judgment that found no echo in the registers of the Ottoman tax assessors: for them Hebron was not the normal *shehir* ("city") but the unusual *madina*, a courtesy title, doubtless, for what was no more than a village, or rather an agglomeration of villages, one of which was called Bayt Ibrahim.[49]

With its massed grave sites of great antiquity, Hebron would exercise a powerful attraction on Muslims accustomed from the very beginning to the notion of pilgrimage. Indeed, among the Arabs pilgrimage long antedates Islam, and in both the greater (*hajj*) and the lesser (*'umra*) canonical versions current in pre-Islamic Mecca, it was incorporated into the heart of the Muslim liturgy.[50] The *hajj* and *'umra* are construed as acts of worship of God, however; here it is a question of the veneration paid to dead heroes and saints, an impulse strong enough to provoke a special trip (*ziyara*) to the grave site and the embellishment of that site in an appropriate architectural manner. In Islam this generally took the form of a small chapel crowned with a dome (*qubba*), perhaps, as has been suggested, in imitation of Christian martyria, though of a rural sort.[51]

If we had to rely solely on the surviving material evidence, we would probably underestimate the strength and extent of the cult of saints in Islam; Muslim sensibilities have somewhat changed in this regard, as have Christian ones. The Muslim shrine-tomb (*mashhad, maqam*), eventually to grow into a shrine-mosque,[52] has survived, however, in certain large examples of the species, like the two competing *mashhads* of 'Ali at Najaf in Iraq and Mazar-i Sharif in Afghanistan, both of which have generated genuine holy cities. But for the real breadth of the phenomenon in medieval Islam, we must turn elsewhere, to the travel diaries of inveterate voyagers like Ibn Jubayr in the late twelfth century and Ibn Battuta in the early fourteenth, and particularly to the ecumenical *Book of Pilgrimages* of al-Harawi.

The mandatory *hajj* to Mecca must have loosed an annual torrent of travelers across the face of the *Dar al-Islam*. The numbers were in any event large and the pace leisurely; it was not uncommon to spend two or three years on the journey to Mecca and back. The ebb and tide of travelers produced in its wake a substantial number of personalized travel accounts, but al-Harawi's *Pilgrimages,* written in the closing years of the twelfth century, had a more specific aim and audience: to supply the traveler with an authoritative guide to the pilgrimage sites he might encounter across the Islamic world, or at least that part of it visited by the author.[53]

Their number is astonishing. Damascus and Baghdad were literally filled with the shrines of saints, whether biblical personages, early Muslim heroes and heroines, or local religious notables, lawyers, Sufis, and the like,[54] and Jerusalem with its biblical and Christian associations was also rich in resorts for the pilgrim.[55] And once in Mecca, with his spiritual enthusiasm at its highest pitch, the *hajji* was escorted around some of the historical, and sacred, sites connected with the Prophet and the birth of Islam: the houses of 'Abbas and Abu Bakr, the house of Khadija and the place where Fatima was born, the birthplaces of Aisha, Abu Bakr, 'Umar, 'Ali and of the Prophet himself.[56]

None of this passed without remark and even strenuous opposition on the part of some Sunni Muslims who regarded such devotions as a heretical innovation. To little avail. The cult of saints in Islam was, as Goldziher remarked, the clearest possible example of the power of a popular consensus over normal orthodox belief.[57] What was particularly repugnant to religious sensibilities was the mosque-tomb, and the Muslim traditions are quite specific in condemning all and any association of a place of prayer with a tomb.[58]

It is difficult to estimate the effect of this orthodox opposition not merely to mosque-tombs but the the veneration of the dead in general. It likely had little or no success in discouraging popular cultus, but it must have exercised at least some inhibition on public and official recognition of the practice and the investment of public or private capital in the construction of large scale mosque-tombs and shrines. The great shrines of the Shi'ites at Najaf, Karbala, and Mazar-i Sharif are in fact exceptions rather than the rule. They were political as much as they were religious statements, monuments to sectarianism and to the ethnic and national sentiment that the Arabs called *shu'ubiyya* and that attracted the support of rulers who stood to profit from it. But for all that, the Christian Saint Symeon Stylites' fifth-century cathedral complex north of Aleppo and Saint Sergius' sixth-century center in Rusafa easily outshone the shrines of their Shi'ite counterparts in all but their most recent versions, and Constantine's basilicas over Jesus' traditional birthplace in Bethlehem and tomb in Jerusalem had no analogous rivals in either Mecca or Medina.

The saints' memorial days circled the Christian liturgical calendar with public and official pomp; Islam had few such,[59] and even the most important of them, the *Mawlid al-Nabi,* or Prophet's Birthday, fixed on the twelfth of Rabi' al-awwal, has always met with some opposition in Muslim circles, and except at Mecca it has no fixed abode for its celebration; indeed, it most often appears as an extremely popular street festival.[60] The tenth of Muharram was the date of the slaying of the Shi'ite protomartyr Husayn in A.D. 680, and it is commemorated with great enthusiasm by Shi'ites. There was even a type of liturgy that developed around it, the famous *tazi'eh,* or Passion of Husayn. But not at the grave site at Karbala. The processions of public mourning that were the antecedents of the fully developed Persian *tazi'eh* likewise took place in the street, notably in Baghdad, where they were first reported in A.D. 964 under the Buyids, a Shi'ite dynasty.[61]

Though the Muslims' enthusiasm for grave site cults and even the public celebration of the *mawlid* of a holy man or woman was ambivalent at best, the early Christians showed only the slightest hesitation in erecting large martyria, first at grave sites and then at the very heart of the city, whither they carried the bones of saints and martyrs.[62] And their faith was rapidly justified by miracles worked through the relics. Not only did competition develop, sometimes for cash, over the saints' remains; the remains themselves began to multiply miraculously in the form of relics, which soon appeared in all major urban centers of the Christian world. Miracles were the magnets for pilgrims, who were thus drawn into the orbit of the shrine. Tours in France and Thessalonika in Greece became famous as pilgrimage centers by reason of their possession of the potent relics of Saint Martin and Saint Demetrius, and even the Frankish kings were sufficiently intimidated by the bones of Saint Martin to grant Tours an important urban blessing of its own—immunity from taxation.[63]

In the entire Church it was probably Constantinople that had the most complete collection of Christian relics, begun in fact by Constantine himself; it included even the well where Jesus spoke to the Samaritan woman and the trumpets that brought down the walls of Jericho, most of them brought there at the emperors' insistence and expense.[64] Nor were the Muslims immune to the practice. We are given a brief insight into the purchase and collection of relics in medieval Islam by Ibn Battuta in his description of a convent in the town of Dayr Tin, two miles south of Cairo:

> It is an enormous convent built [by the vizier Taj al-Din ibn Hanna] for the sake of certain possessions of great pride and illustrious relics that he deposited in it, namely a fragment of the wooden basin of the Prophet, the pencil with which he used to apply kohl to his eyes, the awl he used in sewing his sandals and the Qur'an of the Commander of the Faithful 'Ali ibn abi Talib, written in his own hand. Taj al-Din, it is said, bought the illustrious relics of the Prophet which we have mentioned for one thousand silver dirhams, and built the convent and endowed it with funds to supply food to all comers and goers and to maintain the guardians of those holy relics.[65]

Even in the largest of premodern cities holy places can work, under special circumstances, profound changes on the urban environment. In Rome, for example, where Boniface VIII's extension to visitors to Rome during the Jubilee Year of the plenary indulgence previously granted only to those on Crusade had a remarkable effect of the population of the city all during the fourteenth and fifteenth century.[66] In a city of the size and functional complexity of Constantinople it is difficult to measure the precise social and economic impact of pilgrimages to its shrines.

Let us turn, then, to somewhat less complex examples. In the case of Tours and Thessalonika, each city had a history before it had a saint, but the miraculous remains of Christian saints and the pilgrims they attracted effectively created, with important help from the emperor, the city of Menasopolis in Egypt and another around the shrine of Saint Symeon Stylites in northern Syria—two places where once there had been little more than a crossroads and a farming village.[67]

The imperial enhancement of Menasopolis and Qala'at Sema'an was not simply a matter of piety, however. Martyrs' shrines have a particularly local character at times, and so in recognizing a local or even a national saint in Egypt and Syria, for example, the Emperor Zeno, who was the principal imperial patron of both shrine cities, was openly courting favor in two of the most religiously disaffected provinces of his empire.

Holy places are, then, a spontaneous if occasionally ambiguous growth in the spiritually fertile soil of the Near East. In countryside and city, sacred objects and the graves of the holy received their appropriate popular cultus. The urban holy place was, however, the focus of generally greater attention, more lavish gifts, a more elaborate and monumental architectural treatment, and, whether as cause or effect, greater political manipulation, interference, or encouragement. The cult shrines of the tribes may indeed have been portable, as both the Israelites and the Arabs showed in their early history,[68] but when each of those peoples became sedentary, the enshrined palladium found a permanent home in a city that was also, and not accidentally, a national capital. Tribal, national, religious, and political identity are all closely related concepts, and in the sequel national capitals were as little willing to suffer competition as were the jealous deities that were worshipped within them.

The Greeks and the Romans were generally tolerant of other peoples' cults, and though they might on occasion be induced to enhance certain cities and shrines, they made no serious attempts at eradicating indigenous religious practices—so long as the practices were not linked to treason or insurrection, as was the case with Jerusalem under Antiochus IV Epiphanes or later under Hadrian after the uprising of A.D. 135. The great monotheistic-religions had quite another view, however, and early Israelite political expansion inevitably spelled the suppression of Canaanite or Phoenician or Syrian cults native to the places newly under Jewish political control. Indeed, the Jewish monarchy subsequently suppressed its *own* cult centers to the benefit of the Temple and the priesthood in the royal capital of Jerusalem.[69]

Jerusalem is, of course, the prime example of the association of the sacred with a single place over a long period of time and under a variety of religious sponsors, but the city's long history illustrates something else as well: the mutual reinforcement of politics and the holy in an urban context. The shrine at Baalbek eventually generated a modest city, as we shall see, but Jerusalem enjoyed the enviable advantage of not merely possessing a famous shrine, and from the seventh century B.C. onward the *unique* Jewish cult center in Palestine, but also serving as the political and administrative capital of a kingdom.

Jerusalem was a city before it had a temple set down in its midst, nor does the mere possession of a famous shrine convert an urban center into a holy city. As has already been suggested, a holy city is one where the shrine, temple, or cultus plays a predominant role in urban life. This can come about in a number of ways, perhaps most obviously when the local political authority is identical or closely identified with the religious authority vested in the shrine or its guardians. Such was the Jewish case for much of the period between the return from Exile down to the Roman destruction of both the Temple and the priesthoods in A.D. 70, though at other times there were Syrians or Hasmoneans or Herodians ruling in Jerusalem, whose power and authority were by no means identical or even sympathetic with what was going on atop the Temple mount across the Tyropean valley from the citadel and the palace. Again, the Jewish monarchs were on occasion militant and expansionist, as the Temple priesthoods never were, and it seems that the longer the reach of the crown in Palestine—into agricultural Galilee, for example—the broader and more varied was the economic base upon which the policy rested. Conversely, when Jerusalem stood isolated as a simple temple-state within Judea, the more closely it approximated a single-industry enterprise, what an American would call a "company town" or, to use our own terminology, a holy city.

Throne and altar, king and priest, shah and magus do not easily coexist within the same city. Either king and court dominate temple and clergy, as the Hasmoneans would have had it or as has occurred in post-Concordat Rome and contemporary Jerusalem; or else emperor, caliph, or shah will leave the sacred precinct for other venues. The shahs deserted authentic Susa and Persepolis for the more "Gentile" environment of Seleucia-Ctesiphon, and the caliphs too departed the *Haramayn* for the more congenial Damascus no more than thirty years after the death of Muhammad. Constantine constructed his capital city to *his* liking, and the 'Abbasids Baghdad to *their* specifications.

Overwhelmed by its own secular rulers, a city might still expect to carry on as a holy city in a diminished though still distinct mode, as both Rome and Jerusalem have continued to do in their fashion; deserted by its sovereign, it would seem to be condemned to a kind of oblivion, like Thebes and Amarna and Istakhr and Persepolis. But such has not always been the case, particularly when the shrine is independent of political connection and has the power or persuasiveness to generate a substantial flow of pilgrims on its own merits, and it is to this latter question that we must now turn.

NOTES

1. Exod: 3:5.

2. These are gross judgments, and the full judicial extent of the *haram* is a more delicate matter. In Jerusalem, for example, the sanctity of the Temple was extended under certain circumstances to some, though not all, sections of the city (Jeremias 1969: 20–21; Safrai 1975: 290–91, 330; and see pp. 131, 399, and at Mecca the ritual *haram* reached as far as the points (*mawaqif*) on the outskirts of the city where the pilgrim had to don the *ihram:* Gaudefroy-Demombynes 1923: 17–25, and cf. Ibn Jubayr 1949–51: 112–13 Ar./132–33 tr.

3. Beth El: Gen. 28:17–19; Transfiguration: Mark 9:5 and parallels.

4. The wide-ranging evidence for this bedouin practice is collected in Lammens 1928. There is even a depiction of the phenomenon. A relief from Palmyra shows what must be a *betyl* being carried in a tentlike structure atop a camel; see Seyrig 1934 and cf. Seyrig 1970.

5. Jahiz, *Kitab al-Hayawan* 3:44.

6. Wellhausen 1897: 73.

7. Yadin 1977: col. 45.

8. Levine 1978: 14–17, for the complex and interesting interplay of Temple and city in both the Temple Scroll and Scripture.

9. Price and Trell 1977: fig. 433.

10. Ibid.: figs. 56, 22, 283, 303.

11. Constrast the highly conventional nymphaeum at Gerasa (Kraeling 1938: Plate 6, Plan 28) with the nearby genuine fountain whose doubtless primitive cultus survived the passage from paganism to Christianity and ended its days comfortably in the court of the city's cathedral (ibid.: 63–64). On the survival of the traditional motifs of high place, cave, spring, and tree in rural Muslim shrine-tombs down into the twentieth century, see Canaan 1927: 1–45.

12. Price and Trell 1977: fig. 271.

13. Ibid.: figs. 296–99.

14. Ibid.: figs. 442, 257.

15. Peters 1977: 272–74.

16. Lammens 1928 and compare the often overlooked and still, for a long time, mobile *second* stone in the Meccan *haram,* that in the *maqam Ibrahim:* Gaudefroy-Demombynes 1923: 103–09; Kister 1971; and chapter 5.

17. On the embarrassment of some early Muslims at the continued presence of the stone, see Gaudefroy-Demombynes 1923: 43–48 and Fahd 1973: 83–84, who also cites the continuing popular belief among Muslims that the stone is in fact "God's right hand on earth" and that by kissing or touching it one can establish direct physical contact with God.

18. Qur'an 2:127; cf. Gaudefroy-Demombynes 1923: 128–32, 156–57.

19. See Seyrig 1929: 354–55.

20. Collart and Coupel 1951.

21. Price and Trell 1977: fig. 290.

22. Fernandes 1980: 66 n. 90.

23. Eusebius, *HE* II, 23.

24. Delehaye 1923.

25. Lassus 1947: 114–20

26. Ibid.: 142–60; on the movement of churches from the periphery to the center of the city, Claude 1969: 89ff.

27. Hasson 1981: 177.

28. A number of examples are cited by Goldziher 1971: 322–32, chiefly from the domain of folk religion. For the relics of the Prophet and his early Companions kept in the Topkapi Serai in Istanbul: de Gaury 1951: 60. There is, nonetheless, one genuine "sacrament" in Islam, the Qur'an, which as an exact *physical* copy of its heavenly prototype, is precisely the embodiment of the holy in matter; see Dodd 1969.

29. Goldziher 1971: 255–62.

30. Ibid.: 261–79. On the cult of Muhammad in Islam, Andrae 1913.

31. Kriss and Kriss-Heinrich 1960.

32. Cf. Dermenghem 1954; Gellner 1969.

33. Cf. Canaan 1927: 292–95. The traditions about the grave sites of two such biblical figures have been studied in detail by Goldziher 1897 (Joshua) and Abel 1922 (Jonas).

34. See Vincent et al. 1923; Simon 1962: 168–70; and for a fourteenth-century pilgrims' guide, Matthews 1949: 43–138.

35. Goldziher 1971: 280–81, and chapter 5.

36. Simon 1962: 162; 1973: 99.

37. Jeremias 1958; Simon 1973: 101–04; cf. Torrey 1946 for what was originally a Jewish pilgrims' guide, the *Lives of the Prophets,* later retouched for Christian use and attributed to Epiphanius.

38. Adler 1966: 193.

39. Ibn Battuta 1958–62: 52.

40. Adler 1966: 146. The French Rabbi Jacob who visited Tiberias a century earlier is more specific: there were 24,000 pupils of Rabbi Akiba buried in the cemetery at Tiberias (ibid.: 124).

41. Cohen and Lewis 1978: 23–28.

42. Ibid.: 60–61.

43. Ibid.: 29 n. 38. On the earlier connections between pilgrimage and burial in Jerusalem, Safrai 1981: 16–17.

44. Adler 1966: 87 (Petachia), 94–95 (Rabbi Jacob). The same early fourteenth century traveler, Isaac ben Joseph, immigrant to Palestine and himself a Kabbalist, suggests that Safed had already set its foot on the path toward esotericism: "In this place (Safed) Rabbi Shemtob of Soria composed his numerous works. Although the wise men, followers of the truth, have much criticized this learned man, they have never ceased to copy him and receive his traditions" (ibid.: 145).

45. Ibid.: 245

46. Eusebius, *Life of Constantine III*, 52–53.

47. For the archeological evidence and a reconstruction of the Constantinian building there, Vincent et al. 1923 and Mader 1957.

48. Le Strange 1890: 316.

49. Cohen and Lewis 1978: 112 n. 19; cf. Le Strange 1890: 310n.; Massignon 1951/1963: 188; and for Hebron in more recent times, Karmon 1975.

50. Qur'an 3:90–92.

51. Pedersen 1953: 334.

52. On the architecture and terminology, Canaan 1927:11–30, and cf. Grabar 1966.

53. On the genre, see Sourdel-Thomine's introduction to her translation in al-Harawi 1956, and the interesting comparative observations in Ashtor 1981.

54. Sourdel-Thomine 1954–1955 (Damascus); Massignon 1908/1963 (Baghdad).

55. For a fourteenth-century pilgrams' guide to Palestine, Matthews 1949: 1–41; on the Christian sites; Wilkinson 1977: 33–39.

56. Al-Harawi 1956: 197–98; cf. Ibn Jubayr 1949–51: 134–36, 188–89, and, more recently, Burckhardt 1829: 171–79 and Snouck Hurgronje 1888: 21–22. In Burckhardt's day (1814) the Wahhabis had already torn down some of the shrine-tombs of Mecca.

57. Goldziher 1971: 332; on the larger question of opposition to the cultus, ibid.: 332–41.

58. Wensinck 1927: 89 s.v. "Grave," with a very direct allusion to the Christian and Jewish practice of "taking the graves of their Apostles as places of worship."

59. See, for example, the liturgical cycle associated with visits to Qarafa, Cairo's "City of the Dead" (Ibn Battuta 1958–62: 45) and described by Massignon 1958/1963: 251–54; and for the cycle of feasts at Mecca at the end of the nineteenth century, Snouck Hurgronje 1931: 39–76.

60. Snouck Hurgronje 1931: 46–48 for its celebration in Mecca. On the *Mawlid al-Nabi* in modern North Africa and the opposition, religious and secular, that it has provoked, Shinar 1977.

61. Busse 1964: 422–23.

62. Dagron 1977; on the revolutionary implications of this new handling of corpses and remains, see Brown 1981: 1–22.

63. Gregory of Tours, *History of the Franks* IX, 30; on the cult of relics in the Byzantine Empire, Jones 1964: 958–62.

64. The shrines of Constantinople are described in Janin 1969.

65. Ibn Battuta 1958–62: 60.

66. See Rapp 1973: 124–128, and Romani 1948.

67. On Menasopolis: Kaufman 1921 and Claude 1969: 210–13. On Qala'at Sema'an, see chapter 2.

68. The portable betyls of the pre-Islamic Arabs are discussed in chapter 4.

69. 2 Kings 23.

CHAPTER II

The Pilgrimage Network

Cities are born, prosper, and decline for a variety of well-defined reasons. We can even sketch a "normal" set of growth conditions for the preindustrial city in the Near East: a defensible and healthy site surrounded by a fertile and well-watered hinterland represents one typical configuration. But other circumstances, political, commercial, and military, have created cities even in the midst of arid wastes and the most inhospitable locales. Imperial favor and investment, for example, have turned villages into urban showcases; earthquakes, plagues, and invasions have reduced municipal glories to rubble, ashes, or swamp.

In the study of urban growth patterns in the Near East, considerable attention has been given to the relationship of the city to its agricultural hinterland, what the Romans called its *ager* or *territorium*.[1] The relationship between city and hinterland is indeed intimate, since most preindustrial cities had to feed themselves out of their own resources. But some cities managed something more, and if we take another step up the scale of urban success, it is equally useful to speak of another kind of hinterland: a commercial "network," that is, the extent of the mercantile reach of the urban center. The nodes of such a network are defined by the other centers where the city's merchants serve as prime commercial agents; the links are the caravan and maritime routes strung between them.

The Near East is rich in examples of such mercantile networks. The Nabateans of Petra, for example, who like the later Arab Quraysh at Mecca were only recently domesticated in from the steppe, created, by commercial activity alone and without benefit of armies or conquest, a first-century "empire" that extended from Mada'in Salih in the northern Hejaz to Gaza on the Mediterranean and Damascus in Syria, and they had a secondary trade network that reached even farther abroad, into Egypt and the European ports of the Mediterranean.[2] In the third century another Arab caravan city, Palmyra, though situated in the midst of the Syrian steppe, extended itself by trade down through Iraq to the head of the Persian Gulf, where Palmyrene merchants owned and operated "factories" for the benefit of the company headquarters in their mother city.[3] Mecca too in the sixth century had a commercial network whose main lines were strung between southern Syria and the port cities of the Yemen.[4] In all three cases political and military control were minimal; the linkage was commercial, the long-distance trade owned and operated by the city in question.

But the reach of a city might exceed its political control or even its commercial activity. Next to Rome and the caravan cities there were other cultural and religious "empires" whose urban centers possessed a special spiritual significance and so could establish a flow of people and capital across another kind of hinterland in the form of a *pilgrimage network*. Thus Athens under the Roman Empire, Jerusalem in the Second Temple period and again in the Christian era, and Mecca under Islam were all sustained and nourished as cities by their cultural and religious reputations. Each would have suffered an inevitable decline by reason of the shift in its earlier political or commercial importance had it not possessed the magnetic power of drawing "pilgrims" from across its network: for Athens, from the orbit of cultural Hellenism; for Jerusalem, from the Jewish Diaspora network and then from the limits of Christendom; and for Mecca, from the entire "Abode of Islam."

Let us begin somewhat farther back, however, with a city that should not have existed at all. Rusafa is a site on the Syrian steppe more than a hundred miles north of Palmyra and about fifteen miles south of the Euphrates; it is located in a landscape with little arable soil, little ground water, and little precipitation. Yet there stand there, even today, the extensive ruins of a large and impressive city once called, after its patron saint, Sergiopolis. Sergius, a late third-century martyr for the Christian faith, was a popular holy man in the Near East, and his tomb and cultus attracted a great number of pilgrims from across and around the steppe.[5] His remains were interred at Rusafa, and though we cannot trace the exact progress of the city's growth, we do know that by the beginning or the middle of the sixth century Rusafa, now christened Sergiopolis, was already the seat of a bishop, had large and splendid walls, and possessed a fine basilica built over the saint's remains. The entire nine acres within the city walls were filled with sturdy and elegant stone buildings, while other churches and shops were ranged along cross-axial streets. The sparse rainwater was carefully collected in large pools outside the city walls and then transferred by aqueduct to underground storage within the city.[6]

Saint Sergius and the Christian cult that attracted pilgrims to his tomb made a city at Rusafa, where there should have been, on any other conceivable urban basis, only a village or a small post station. The site had no physical attractions like the spring and oasis at Palmyra; it sat astride no major trade route, as did Mecca; and its thick, manmade walls give eloquent testimony to the fact that, unlike Petra, it was not naturally secure. Nor were there any older gods concealed and ready for conversion in those dry ravines; Rusafa *became* both holy and a city, and before our very eyes, so to speak.

It is not certain how long Sergiopolis survived the arrival of Islam; not for very long, surely, since whatever Muslim buildings survive there are set disinterestedly outside the city walls. Without its pilgrimage network the city then as now had few resources to sustain itself. Nor was it the only Near Eastern shrine city to suffer eclipse: pagan holy places like Baalbek lost population, prestige, and power with the spread of Christianity, and Christian ones like Qala'at Sema'an went into a similar decline in the face of a triumphant Islam.

Baalbek, the site in central Lebanon sacred to the "Baal of the Beqa'," was probably an old Aramaic holy place. But unlike Rusafa, it had distinct commercial and strategic advantages as well: it sat in the fertile and well-watered Beqa' valley on a major trade artery that connected Emesa, the present Homs, with both the inner Lebanon and the Mediterranean ports.[7] It was probably Baalbek's agricultural attractions that prompted Augustus to place it within the city territory of his Colonia Berytus[8]—Beirut could feed itself off the Beqa'—and strategic considerations that lay behind the city's eventual elevation to municipal autonomy as Colonia Julia Helipolitana and its being provided with a Roman garrison.

The central shrine at Baalbek-Heliopolis was enormously expanded by the Roman builder-emperors of the second century A.D.[9] We cannot tell if the city around the shrine was expanded at the same time, but it may be doubted that even a greatly enlarged Baalbek would have seriously strained its fertile agricultural hinterland in the Beqa'. And the city, for all the magnificence of its temple complex in the second century, appears to have been far more successful in exporting the cult of its deities than in attracting permanent residents to itself.[10] It is not surprising, then, that with the coming of Christianity there was an abrupt change in the fortunes of Baalbek. Constantine abolished many of the local pagan practices like temple prostitution, and Theodosius began the destruction of the temple precinct itself.[11] And with the Arab conquest the place reverted to its original and more modest secular position, that of a fortified strong point guarding the strategic Beqa' valley.[12]

Holiness, once established, does not easily desert a place, though the names may be altered and old deities converted to more current, and acceptable, ones. But a shrine city like Baalbek is a more fragile phenomenon and responds readily to religious and particularly to political changes. And there are modern as well as ancient Baalbeks. Nazareth has always been a known, if secondary, Christian shrine center in Palestine. With the establishment of the 1948 borders of Israel, however, it became, *faute de mieux,* the single most important Christian city in that new country. In 1955 the eighteenth-century Church of the Annunciation was torn down, and plans were made for a grandiose new cathedral to take its place. The project was at least in part a response to the diversion to Nazareth of Christian tourist-pilgrims to the new, politically reduced version of the "Holy Land." The Nazareth cathedral was completed in 1966, one year before the Israeli occupation of the far more important Christian holy cities of Jerusalem and Bethlehem. Consequently, Nazareth was again thrust back to the status of a minor stop on the Christians' itinerary, and the Cathedral of the Annunciation has predictably disappeared from the Israeli travel posters where it was once so prominently displayed.

Mention has already been made of the site called Qala'at Sema'an northwest of Aleppo. There was at the site a modest agricultural settlement in the midst of a fertile plain, but in the fifth Christian century the holy man Symeon took up his residence on a pillar on a nearby hillside. Even during his lifetime the fragrance of his sanctity, and perhaps the curious and fiercely ascetic mode of life he had chosen to embrace, extended his reputation across the Mediterranean as far as Rome and southward across the Syrian steppe into the remote domains of the Arab bedouin.[13] Christian pilgrims began to arrive at the pillar of the Blessed Symeon. By the sixth century the saint's cult had become so popular both at court and in the countryside that the top of the hill where he had lived boasted a large cathedral erected around the base of his pillar, an elegant baptistry, and an entire complex of ecclesisastical buildings, while the village of Telanissos (Tell Neshin) at its foot had been completely converted from its earlier agricultural pursuits to serving the now considerable pilgrim industry.[14]

The Muslim invasion brought a severe depopulation of the commercial farming area of north Syria between Antioch and Aleppo, and by drawing nearby a religious frontier between the *Dar al-Islam* and still-Christian Anatolia, it effectively shattered the spiritual network that had supported Qala'at Sema'an. The place was taken back by the Byzantines in the tenth century, and though a community of monks briefly reoccupied the site, the new importance of the area was that of a strategic frontier post rather than of a religious center. Symeon's holy city was girt round with a stout wall and converted into the prototype of a Crusader fortress to protect the approaches of Antioch against the Muslims of Aleppo.[15]

Rusafa had little reason to exist, save the presence there of the bones of a holy man; Mecca, on the other hand, had its commercial attractions. Like Palmyra, pre-Islamic Mecca lay upon a major overland trade route between eastern producers and Roman consumers in the urban markets of the Mediterranean. And again like Palmyra, that "unfruitful valley," as the Qur'an refers to Mecca, would likely not have played an important part in that trade except that it had access to the surrounding bedouin and their camel herds, the essential means of transport in the long-distance overland trade.

Palmyra was certainly holy before it was prosperous—it boasted a sacred spring and a great *haram* of Baal—and it may have been this fact, together with its natural attractiveness as a steppe oasis, that enabled its entrepreneurs to draw the bedouin into Palmyra's sacral orbit and so under its control. With Mecca we are certain. The *haram* of the Ka'ba, the *hajj,* and the pilgrimage's attendant commercial fair were all pre-Islamic institutions at Mecca, and it was the genius of its mercantile aristocracy that they could weld those religious and commercial elements into an alliance of profit to both parties—the townsmen of Mecca and the often fractious bedouin on the grazing hinterland to the east of the town.[16] The assemblage of these elements of a commercial empire was the work of Hashim, the great-grandfather of Muhammad, who, by securing the proper licenses from the Byzantine, Sasanian, Abyssinian, and Yemeni authorities, expanded the mercantile reach of Mecca into the sixth century's chief commercial markets.[17]

It is the sequel, not the mechanics, of the Meccan trade that concerns us here. The Arab Nabateans and Palmyrenes of an earlier era were middlemen for goods alone. In the seventh century Mecca exported not merely goods but a message, with enormous consequences for the world and some rather interesting long-term effects on the city itself. But first it was to undergo profound political changes. Within a brief span of time Mecca was transformed from a mere commercial entrepot to the heart of a world empire. The political promotion was as brief as it was staggering. Within thirty years after the death of Mecca's Prophet Muhammad, the imperial power he had founded shifted from Mecca and Medina to Damascus, and the enormous bureaucratic growth that had transformed the town of Byzantium into imperial Constantinople or would change the villages of Mada'in into Baghdad never occurred in the holy cities of the Hejaz.

Rusafa was a tour de force, an exemplary *creatio ex nihilo* to dazzle the urban historian; Mecca speaks more to the reality, namely, that the birth, growth, and even death of holy cities is in most instances tied either to the immediate political fortunes of a city or, perhaps more frequently, to its symbolic value in a political context. The history of holy cities is filled, for example, with cases where the ruler shows a marked disinclination to make such sacred soil his own residence but an equally remarkable willingness to invest large sums in adorning and enhancing a city whose values he wishes to identify as his own. Athens, for instance, had under Roman rule little political or commercial importance, yet in the second Christian century it was still the acknowledged spiritual and intellectual heart of Greco-Roman Hellenism and so was the beneficiary of immense private bequests from patrons like Herodes Atticus; moreover, the Roman imperial government granted that city—as it did to its other cultural shrine at Ilium in the Troad, and as the Muslims later gave their shrine city of Najaf—quite extraordinary tax immunities.[18] The other, earlier Herod, the king of Judea, supported lavish building programs in an impressively catholic array of shrine cities, not only his own Jerusalem but the Nabateans' holy place at Sia' and the Panhellenic Olympia as well.[19]

Herod, of course, did not institute the practice of pilgrimage to Jerusalem, though on all the evidence it was during his reign and the years immediately following that the practice became widespread and popular. In the Jewish manner of editing such documents, the injunction that "three times a year you shall keep a pilgrim-feast for Me," appears in the earliest books of the Bible,[20] even though the ritual has transparently to do with Jerusalem, not Sinai, and particularly with the post-Exilic Temple in Jerusalem. Indeed, though there is evidence enough that Jews went up to the Temple in discharge of this liturgical duty before the Exile—a number of the Psalms appear to be pilgrims' hymns, for example—it is clear that the pilgrimage as an act of religious and social solidarity, a community phenomenon, becomes discernible only in later Hasmonean times and that it had reached the height of its popularity precisely when the Temple was destroyed in the wake of the Jewish insurrection against Rome in A.D. 66–70,[21] after which, of course, it could no longer be performed.

Why this sudden surge of interest in pilgrimage to Jerusalem? The growth of Jewish pilgrimage to the national and religious capital of the people corresponds almost exactly to the geographical extension and numerical expansion of the Jewish community out and away from the narrow, and familiar, confines of Judea. From the time in the late fourth century B.C. that Alexander the Great and his successors changed the political and cultural face of the Near East, Judaism became a diaspora phenomenon, a community that continously read out its past as tied to a specific land and that nevertheless turned its back in increasing numbers upon that land in preference for Syria, Greece, Italy, Iraq, and, with a particular irony, Egypt, from which the Lord had so urgently bade the pharaoh to let His people go.

The reasons for this reverse exodus, this self-chosen exile from the Land of the Promise, do not directly concern us here. We simply observe that by the second and first pre-Christian centuries there were very large numbers of Jews living abroad, many of them in the great urban centers of the Greco-Roman Mediterranean, and that it was precisely at this point that the urge, or the need, to return, however briefly, to the Land of Israel manifested itself in the vitalization of a doubtlessly old custom: the Temple pilgrimage at the great feasts of Passover, Weeks, and Tabernacles.[22]

It is difficult to doubt that the Hasmoneans' refurbishing of the city in the Hellenic style, followed by Herod's even more grandiose construction program in and around Jerusalem and its climax in an enormous new Temple, encouraged the practice of pilgrimage to the holy city. When Jesus made the pilgrimage, the disciples who accompanied him were agog at the new edifice,[23] and similar impressions must have spread back and out through the Diaspora with returning pilgrims to rouse still others to worship God in this national capital that was also a national shrine. "He who has not seen the Temple of Herod," the rabbis later murmured in a still vivid recollection, "has never seen a beautiful building."

And yet it was the same Herod who began the process that eventually separated the administrative and religious functions of Jerusalem by his construction of the new city of Caesarea Maritima on the Mediterranean coast of Palestine. The Romans chose to rule their Jewish subjects from that more Gentile environment during their long centuries of hegemony in Judea, and when the Muslims conquered Palestine from the Romans, they too in the end preferred nearby Ramle to Jerusalem as a provincial capital for Judea. The Jewish Gaonate, even after it moved its seat from Tiberias back to Jerusalem, detached the primary judicial functions of the Yeshiva and settled them where the "secular" authorities were, in Ramle.

The Christian Church too, which had every reason to exalt the mother church of all Christians, had difficulty maintaining the priority of the bishop of Jerusalem, even in the Holy Land itself.[24] Finally, the Prophet of Islam was driven from his own native holy city of Mecca to Medina, from which he subsequently directed the political fortunes of his community.[25] Nor did any of his successors choose to rule the Abode of Islam from Mecca; indeed, after Harun al-Rashid's *hajj* in 804, no caliph even so much as made the pilgrimage there. Even its Turkish governors, like the Romans ensconced in Caesarea, preferred the view of Mecca from Jedda or Medina.

Herod's career as a builder provides us with some clues as to why a holy city, for all its symbolic value, might be an unattractive site for an imperial or national capital. Herod felt no more secure in Jerusalem than the Romans did. He filled the city with strong towers and the countryside with redoubts furnished to serve as both palace and refuge.[26] Both he and the Romans preferred to observe the Temple in Jerusalem from the safe parapets of the Fortress Antonia, just as the Israeli army presently does from its own "Antonia," the Tankiziyya *madrasa*, which was built in 1328 as a law school and from whose rooms soldiers now watchfully regard the troubled Haram al-Sharif. Jerusalem was and is quite simply an inflammable and explosive place where dissent, agitation, political tempers, and religious emotions come too quickly to a boil.

Mecca and Medina were much the same kind of environment

in early Islam, and so too were their Iraqi alternatives at Kufa and Basra. And though the ʿAbbasids might have called their new capital at Baghdad *Madinat al-Salam*, "City of Peace," we can more readily identify it for what it really was: a new Herodium.[27] Or nearly so. Baghdad had other attractions, as the Babylonians, Greeks, and Persians had all earlier observed by building their own capitals in the vicinity. It was strategically situated in the midst of a rich agricultural hinterland and at the nexus of important trade routes. And more important, it was a place where a new dynasty could create its own political image in architectural and urban terms without competition from a House of God or its servants.[28]

One consistent element in that imperial image is reverence for the past, particularly the religious past. If Herod built Caesarea, he also rebuilt the Temple in Jerusalem, and in a religiously impeccable manner.[29] Constantine, a new man in a new world, affirmed his Roman legitimacy in Constantinople, the New Rome whither he transported many totems of the Old. But he was equally careful to establish his Christian piety by adorning both Jerusalem and the old Rome with shrine churches of a magnificence that the new faith had never previously experienced. And the same Muslim dynasty that built Baghdad was exemplary in its regard for Mecca and its pilgrims. Intention and effect are graphically illustrated in Ibn Battuta's judgment on the contemporary ruler of Egypt, Al-Malik al-Nasir (sultan 1293–1341):

> He was a man of generous character and great virtues, and sufficient proof of his nobility is furnished by his devotion to the service of the Holy Cities of the Hejaz and the works of beneficence which he does every year to assist the pilgrims, in furnishing camels loaded with provisions and water for those without means and the helpless, and for transporting those who cannot keep up with the caravan or are too weak to walk on foot, both on the Egyptian pilgrim road and on that from Damascus.[30]

The sultan's benevolence was no more than standard Sunni piety perhaps, repeated time and time again from the early days of Islam down to the present. Less standard, and more interesting from the perspective of urbanism, is the growth and support of what may be regarded as Mecca's rivals and competitors as

Islam's holy cities, Najaf and Karbala in Iraq. 'Ali, the fourth caliph of Islam, was assassinated in Kufa in A.D. 661. For the next century and a half there were conflicting reports about his grave site until Ibn al-Hayda, the Shi'ite ruler of Mosul (A.D. 905–926), constructed a domed tomb over a site about six miles from Kufa and so enshrined al-Najaf, as it was called, as the authentic burial place of 'Ali.[31] Ibn al-Hayda's architectural gesture was as political as it was pious. A half century earlier the Caliph al-Mutawakkil, who was himself reacting to the 'Alid piety of his predecessors, had ordered destroyed the shrine tomb of that other early Shi'ite martyr, 'Ali's son Husayn, located not far away at Karbala.

The former village of Karbala and the even more obscure Najaf were by the mid–tenth century not simply holy grave sites; they were the shrines of an increasing active Shi'ite Islam, destroyed by Sunni reactionaries, rebuilt by Shi'ite rulers, destroyed again by orthodox puritans, and finally rebuilt and glorified by other Shi'ite princes.[32] Their safety and enduring prominence was probably guaranteed by the Shi'ite Adud al-Dawla, who ruled Iraq and parts of Iran from A.D. 949 to 983, built sumptuous tombs and other public buildings at both sites in 979, and was buried together with two of his sons at Najaf.[33] Many subsequent rulers, both Shi'ites like the Safavid Shah Ismail and Sunnis like the Ottoman Sultan Sulayman, made pilgrimages there, and by the end of the late premodern period Karbala with 50,000 inhabitants had become, after the capital of Baghdad, the second-largest city in nominally Sunni Iraq.[34]

Premodern Karbala and Najaf were both holy cities as we have defined that term, urban settlements whose chief economic and political importance lay in their shrines, in both cases monumental and expensively adorned shrine-tombs of early Shi'ite eminences. The economy of both cities turned in large part on the influx of pilgrims,[35] not only to pay homage at the tombs but as a regular stopping-off point on the Iranian pilgrimage route to Mecca. More, they were emblematic holy places of Shi'ite Islam in the face of an overwhelming Sunni majority and, at least from the sixteenth century, rallying centers and occasionally even refuges for an officially Shi'ite Persian Islam in the face of an equally overwhelming Arab majority in the *Dar al-Islam*.

There is, nonetheless, a distinctly *catholic* quality about the holy cities of Islam, even distinctly Shi'ite ones like Karbala and Najaf and officially Sunni one like Mecca. Sunnis visit the 'Alid shrines without theological or liturgical consequence, while Mecca, the foundation of Abraham and so a certifiably pan-Islamic shrine, imposes its ritual obligation upon all Muslims, a duty from which very few have excused themselves on grounds of sectarian difference.[36] Indeed, Mecca, precisely because it lies open and inviting to all Muslims, has often served as the ideal place to air—or fight over—religious and political differences within the Islamic community, from the contemporary supporters of the Shi'ite Ayatollah Khomeini, who can display his portrait with a kind of uneasy impunity in the Meccan *haram*, back to the pitched and bloody battles that occurred at Mecca between pilgrim adherents of the 'Alids and 'Abbasids on an almost annual basis during the early decades of the tenth century.[37]

If Mecca lay exposed to its own diaspora, so too did Jerusalem. The allure of sanctity, which spread outward from the city and drew pilgrims to it, also attracted thither all the religious, social, and political tensions that afflicted the community. We have little sense that the Jews of the Second Temple era fought out their internecine battles in Jerusalem, perhaps because dissidents were already excluded from the Temple precincts; Jewish schismatics like the Samaritans, whose half-shekel tax was refused on religious grounds, were treated as the legal equivalent of pagans,[38] while the Essenes appear to have withdrawn voluntarily from a Temple and a ritual whose validity they could not accept.[39] The Christians too, though they continued to frequent the Temple before its destruction, would almost certainly have been eventually excluded from it, just as they were from the synagogue.[40]

Where the festival pilgrimages did reveal tensions in Jerusalem was in the relations between Jewish subjects and their Hasmonean, Herodian, and Roman masters. Josephus cites a number of occasions when trouble brewed in Jerusalem or the Temple during the pilgrimage season,[41] and the New Testament supplies its own illuminating commentary. In addition to the already cited case of Paul, there is Jesus himself, whose entry into the city during the Passover pilgrimage was greeted with an extraordinary popular fervor[42]—the same pilgrimage that ended with his execution on charges that had, to put it in the mildest possible manner, political overtones.

The large crowds, the religious enthusiasm of the occasion, the presence of foreign troops, and the perceived social and evils they represented—all these explain why the pilgrimage feasts were exciting and even dangerous times in Jerusalem in the days of the Second Temple. Three centuries later both the times and the Temple were quite different. The political auspices were then Christian, as were the pilgrims, now much reduced from the number seen in Herod's day. There were still grievances, to be sure, but they were much more likely to be aired in more popular forums, in the hippodromes of the Empire, for example, rather than in Byzantine Judea.[43]

Under Islam the circumstances of Jerusalem changed once again, particularly after the Crusades, when Muslim hostility to Christian pilgrims became palpable to even the most innocent visitor. Christians now had their own major schisms, and the various competing groups were thrown together willy-nilly in the narrow confines of the Church of the Holy Sepulcher. Here was a new "catholic" Jerusalem, a sad place indeed for any Christian community that considered itself orthodox, as of course they all did. The German Dominican Felix Fabri was appalled at this forced cohabitation, which he suspected the Muslims were manipulating for their own ends. "At the present day," he wrote in 1480, "if there were to come any sect polluted with so atrocious a heresy that none of those already in that holy church [of the Holy Sepulcher] would be willing to admit it to its services, yet the Sultan would assign the same sect a choir and an abiding place of its own in the church." How different from the days of the Crusader kingdom, Felix continued, "when Catholic Christians were able to enter it free . . . nor was any heretic or schismatic admitted into that church."[44]

The sequel was perhaps predictable in all its terrible yet comic effect. The reporter is Henry Maundrell, Anglican chaplain of the English Levant Company in Aleppo, who was in Jerusalem in 1697:

What has always been the great prize contended for by the several [Christian] sects is the command and appropriation of the Holy Sepulcher, a privilege contested with so much unchristian fury and animosity, especially between the Greeks and Latins, that in disputing which party should go in to celebrate their Mass, they have sometimes proceeded to blows and wounds even at the very door of the sepulcher, mingling their own blood with their sacrifices. As evidence of which fury the [Franciscan] Father Guardian showed us a great scar upon his arm, which he told us was the mark of a wound given him by a sturdy Greek priest in one of those unholy wars . . .[45]

This was merely the opening scene in the tragedy of mutual Christian incivility in Jerusalem. Act Two began with the arrival of still another Christian sect on the scene. Sometime after 1600, under the impulse of growing British mercantilism, the first Protestants began arriving in Jerusalem, and here too they imported with them all the religious suspicions and fears and hatreds of the larger world of Christendom. The new visitors were of course disdainful of the infidel Muslims whom they encountered, but their deepest disdain was reserved for their fellow Christians and particularly the Latin Catholics—and this attitude they took very few pains to disguise.[46]

As we have already seen, Jewish pilgrimage was tied, like the formal Muslim *hajj*, to a liturgical season and the discharge of a ritual obligation, while the Christian impulse to visit the Holy Land was no more than that—a pious desire to see where Jesus had lived and the Gospel had been preached. At first the piety appears to have been mixed with a certain scholarly curiosity as well, and the clerics who went to Palestine in the early third century were all somewhat like the bishop Alexander, who, according to Eusebius, went there "to worship and investigate the holy places."[47] Those are innocent and even edifying motives, but something else must have been at work, since by the fourth century influential voices were being raised (Gregory of Nyssa's and Jerome's, for example, both of whom knew of what they spoke since they had been to Palestine) that assured the prospective pilgrim that there was no great loss in not visiting the Holy Land. Nor did they rest there: Jerusalem was a difficult and even a dangerous place, they warned the would-be visitor, and especially for women who would be exposed to a great many uncomfortable situations.[48]

The warnings did little good, particularly after Constantine's architectural definition of the sacred geography of Palestine. Thenceforward there was a steady flow of Christian pilgrims to Jerusalem, not in the seasonal torrents that had once fallen upon the Jewish city and would later descend on Mecca, but regular nonetheless, leaving behind a trail of literary reminiscence to enkindle the interest of the next generation.[49] A number of factors contributed to encouraging the movement. The first was simply an outgrowth of the original pious impulse to visit the places connected with the Gospel narratives. The pilgrim found in those places physical and material remains of the very scenes he had imagined, souvenirs perhaps to the modern sensibility, but to that generation relics or "blessings" (*eulogiae*) as real to the early Christian as the *barakat* of the Muslim tradition; indeed, more real for the Christian, who in the fourth and fifth centuries was in the full grip of a passion for relics that could be fully satisfied in the Holy Land simply by stooping down and picking up a stone or a handful of earth.[50]

Arculf, speaking of the shrine marking Jesus' Ascension from the Mount of Olives, says,

> Moreover the dust on which God stood provides a testimony which is permanent, since his footprints are to be seen in it, and even though people flock there, and in their zeal take away the soil where the Lord stood, it never becomes less, and to this day there are marks like footprints in the earth.[51]

What had once been simply a passion became in the end a mania. By the fifteenth century Arculf's simple pilgrim helping himself to some holy dust had turned into an almost professional vandal. On their arrival in Palestine Christian pilgrims were warned against defacing holy places under pain of excommunication, and the point of the warning became clear once the pilgrims were locked in the Holy Sepulcher for the night. Some of the visitors contented themselves with writing, daubing, or scratching their names on everything in sight, but others, who had brought in chisels for precisely this purpose, fell to chipping or breaking off large pieces of the rock of Calvary and even the slab covering the Holy Sepulcher itself.[52]

The second factor encouraging pilgrimage to the Holy Land was the growth of hospices and other hostel facilities for the benefit of the pilgrim.[53] The sixth century in particular witnessed the founding of a great many charitable institutions in the Empire—some of local use, like orphanages and almshouses, but others, like the *xenones* and *xenodocheia*, specifically for the use of Christian pilgrims and travelers, as was the new facility of the hospital, or *nosokomeion*.[54] These facilities were owned and run by the Church, but the imperial government carefully regulated both their financing and their administration.[55]

To these comforts of the body there soon began to be added certain spiritual goods for the pilgrim. In the eighth century, even after the initial fall of Jerusalem to Muslim armies, the pilgrimage to the Holy Land took on a new allure when European confessors began assigning it as a penance for certain sins, a custom that not only encouraged pilgrimage but brought it, at least as far as Western pilgrims were concerned, under ecclesiastical control. Unlike the Muslim or Jew, who was fulfilling a duty in going to Mecca or Jerusalem, the Christian had to seek formal permission (*licentia*) to do so, at least if he intended to gain the spiritual benefits attached to the act.[56] Those benefits were at first simply forgiveness (*indulgentia*), but in the course of time, particularly during and after the Crusades, specific indulgences were attached to visiting specific places in Jerusalem.[57]

Pilgrimage, benefit, and protection were all closely linked in the minds of the pilgrims who required them and of the spiritual and temporal authorities who had the power to grant them. The rabbis declared the official pilgrimage routes leading to Jerusalem to be ipso facto free of ritual impurities, even though they passed through notoriously pagan areas outside the Land of Israel,[58] and those same routes were provided with various forms of ritual assistance.[59] In Europe the pope, in addition to granting indulgences, pronounced the "Truce of God" on behalf of Christian pilgrims, who were protected by other legal and spiritual devices as well.[60] And in pre-Islamic Arabia a similar truce in the sacred season of *hajj* protected both the pilgrimage and the commerce that went on during these periods.[61]

In the end it was protection that the pilgrim most needed in a Holy Land that had become a hostile place, now to Christians, now to Muslims. Muslim orthodox fervor often converted itself into the oppressive regulation of religious minorities under their political control, as when Nur al-Din and Salah al-Din began to turn their thoughts to a holy war against the Crusaders,[62] who had themselves raised the political temperature in Palestine. When the contest of Crusade and Counter-Crusade ground down into a stalemate in the early thirteenth century and both sides, Franks and Muslims, turned to negotiation, free access to the holy places became an important treaty provision. This is particularly apparent in the notorious treaty negotiated by al-Malik al-Kamil and Frederick II Hohenstaufen at Jaffa in 1229. The Ayyubid sultan surrendered sovereignty to the German emperor on provision that visitors of both faiths could pray in the appropriate holy places and that the Muslims continued to administer the Haram al-Sharif and its shrines.[63]

It may be doubted, however, how effectively such provisions could be enforced in the midst of mutually antagonistic populations. A somewhat more effective form of protection, at least for the later European pilgrims in a Holy Land without any Christian political presence, was the appointment of certain Muslim dragomans who had the officially delegated responsibility for the regulation and protection of Christian pilgrims in the midst of what was by the fifteenth century a terrifyingly hostile Palestinian environment.[64]

It is curious that most of our information on Christian pilgrimage to Jerusalem comes from the Western Diaspora, the European *Outremer.* It was so from the beginning, and hence in our eyes at least the Christian pilgrim experience, with its inevitable sea voyage across the Mediterranean, appears to have been quite different from the Muslims' going to Mecca. The latter went overland in great government-supervised caravans that formed in Cairo, Damascus, and Baghdad. The Christians collected in Mediterranean ports like Marseilles, Genoa, Pisa, or Venice. There they began a four- to six-week sea voyage to Acre or Jaffa, the Christian's equivalent of Jedda; new difficulties awaited them there, particularly after 1187, when Jerusalem was once again in Muslim hands and the Christian pilgrims had to be registered, taxed for admission and safe conduct, and given elaborate instructions by the local Christians on how to deal with the newly raised cultural and religious sensibilities of the Muslim population.[65]

Though we are fairly well informed about the medieval *hajj* to Mecca, we assume more than we really know about Muslim pilgrimages to Jerusalem. The evidence suggests that pilgrimage there was not very general until the era of Saladin and the Counter-Crusades, when a well-orchestrated effort was made to underline the sanctity of the city, sometimes even by pointing to the Christians' own devotion to Jerusalem and *their* custom of making pilgrimage to it.[66] Such seems to be point of the great outpouring of literature promoting the virtues of the Holy City and explicitly connecting it with the *hajj* to Mecca.[67] And such too was the point of the places of board and lodging that began to be constructed in Jerusalem, the well-documented *khanaqa*s, *ribat*s, and *zawiya*s, all with boarding facilities and all the product of the post-Crusade era.

There are numerous accounts of Muslim Jerusalem, but unlike the parallel Christian descriptions, all are written by travelers and not pilgrims. And Muqaddasi's city "full of strangers" may well refer to Christian visitors and pilgrims, since a few lines later he complains, in the manner of native sons, that there are too many Christians by far in Jerusalem,[68] and we know as a matter of fact that Christians did come to the city, sometimes in considerable numbers, continuously down to the sixteenth century.[69] Even the literature encouraging Muslim pilgrims to come to Jerusalem had its own equally insistent countercurrent of tradition that early and late deplored the cult of this rival to Mecca and Medina.[70]

The evidence, then, is at least ambiguous that large numbers of Muslims made formal pilgrimage to Jerusalem either before or after the Crusades. What seems far more likely (again on the evidence of the monuments, supported by that of the texts) was that the city had a very large resident community of foreigners who had been drawn to Jerusalem by reason of its sanctity and who settled there for a time as either scholars or Sufis, the former in the city's many endowed *madrasas*, or law schools, the latter in one or the other type of convents. From an urban point of view, immigration into the city under such circumstances is quite different from the *seasonal* arrival and departure of Christians at Jerusalem for the feasts of the Encaenia or Easter or of Muslims at Mecca for the *hajj*, when the city was suddenly swollen with a large number of transient visitors and then just as quickly emptied afterward.

In the seventh century the Christian Holy Land in the Near East was abruptly severed from both the western and the eastern regions of the Christian Roman Empire, and after that date pilgrimages to Jerusalem had necessarily to be made with the cooperation and at least the assent of the new Muslim masters of Palestine. In Islam, however, Mecca, Medina, and, until very recently, Jerusalem have all been under Muslim political control since the seventh century. They were at least in theory available to the pilgrim, though in the case of Mecca and Medina, only with formidable difficulties from the terrain and from the bedouin who frequently robbed and assaulted the traveler en route.[71]

Nor was Jerusalem immune to these difficulties. In 1480 that year's small band of Christian pilgrims to the Holy Land was harassed by bedouin between Ramle and Jerusalem and again between Jerusalem and Bethlehem; in 1508 it was reported that because of the bedouin it had been ten years since a *hajj* caravan had dared leave Jerusalem for Mecca. Felix Fabri, who was a member of the Christian group, describes the marauders as "a naked, miserable, bestial, wandering people, who alone can dwell in the desert which is uninhabitable to all others, attack, harry and conquer all men alike, even to the king himself, the most puissant Sultan of Egypt."[72]

Thus the religious calender, topography, and ill-disposed neighbors have all conspired to make the *hajj* a caravan experience entailing long and dangerous overland travel in large groups at fixed times, while the history of the Islamic community, and particularly of Mecca, has disposed it to become a political experience as well. That history may be resumed in one word: 'Alidism. As has already been noted, political power deserted

Mecca and Medina early on in Islam, and as soon as it did, the Holy Cities, now remote religious totems of Islamic origins and Islamic legitimacy, became what they remained until modern times: places of political dissent and political refuge.

The Umayyads (A.D. 661–750) had to fight pretenders at Mecca, and at the rise of the 'Abbasids in the eighth century, with all the disappointed 'Alid hopes they carried in their wake, the profile of dissent becomes more clearly defined. By then the descendents of 'Ali had become entrenched in Mecca, and the new 'Abbasid caliphs responded with ever more public signs of generosity and esteem toward their doubtless more legitimate rivals. From Mansur to Ma'mun the early 'Abbasid caliphs paid frequent personal visits to Mecca and lavished gifts upon the city. Ma'mun went so far as to appoint an 'Alid, the son of the Imam Ja'far al-Sadiq, as governor of Mecca.

The tenth century was a rising Shi'ite era throughout the *Dar al-Islam,* with the aggressive Fatimids spread across Egypt and North Africa and the Buyids in control of Iran and Iraq and even of the Sunni caliph himself. In 930 Isma'ili Shi'ites from the Gulf seized Mecca and removed the black stone from the Ka'ba to Bahrayn.[73] It was not entirely unexpected, then, when in the sixties of the tenth century an 'Alid line took over the rule in Mecca itelf. They were the most legitimate of the legitimate, sharifs, descendants of the Prophet by way of Fatima and 'Ali and their son Hasan, and they held power there down to the nineteenth century.[74]

The sharifs brought neither peace nor prosperity to Mecca, only a vague and phantom stability. Like the holy city they ruled, they were redolent with legitimacy: the sharifs were the closest thing the Islamic world possessed to a nobility of the blood. They could be bought, sold, coerced, threatened, and even killed, but they could not easily be removed, even by larger and more powerful rivals who inevitably suffered from Islam's endemic political disease, illegitimacy. Nor could they be ignored. The religious obligation of pilgrimage tied Mecca and its rulers to every Muslim, and every Muslim prince, in the *Dar al-Islam*, a tie that was probed and exploited through the instrument of the annual *hajj* caravan.

We have a great deal of information about those caravans, particularly from the High Middle Ages. Some of it comes from travelers' reports, accounts of men like Ibn Jubayr, Ibn Battuta, and Evliye Chelebi and, at the beginning of modern times in the Near East, of non-Muslim Westerners like Johann Burckhardt and Richard Burton, all of whom made the pilgrimage themselves and described the experience. Historians have likewise commented in passing upon extraordinary displays, like the spectacular *hajj* of the Baghdad princess Jamila in 977 or of the African king Mansa Musa who passed through Cairo in 1325 with a personal train of 15,000 people.[75] Finally Mecca's own chroniclers generally signaled the arrival in the city of each year's pilgrimage caravan from Syria, Iraq, Egypt, and the Yemen, its size and makeup and the invariable financial and political consequences that arose from its brief stay in the Holy City. And eventually we will doubtless know far more. Since the annual *hajj* caravan was an important economic and political event, they have left their considerable traces in the archives of the Ottoman Empire, where they are now in the course of being sought out.[76]

Today, in the age of air transport, Mecca's pilgrimage network extends over an immense area and each year delivers millions of *hajjis* to the holy city.[77] Earlier the extent was likely almost as broad, though the numbers of those involved were obviously far smaller.[78] The immediate overland collection points for the caravans were at Damascus,[79] Cairo,[80] the Yemen, and, less certainly after the Mongol destruction of 1258, Baghdad. Each of these had in turn feeder routes along which came other caravans that either joined the larger groups collecting at those centers or kept their own identity as far as Mecca. Cairo drew to it caravans from the Maghreb and Central Africa; Damascus then as now collected all the pilgrims from Turkey as well as from Syria itself; Baghdad was the marshaling point for Iraqi and Iranian pilgrims, who also visited the Shi'ite holy cities en route;[81] the pilgrims from India and Southeast Asia preferred the sea route as far as Aden, where they joined the Yemeni caravan assembling at Sana'a.

For the individual Muslim the pilgrimage was an act of personal piety or perhaps of Islamic solidarity, as well as a substantial expense.[82] But it meant considerably more to others. The safety and even the comfort of pilgrims was always a concern to the sovereign. In the Jewish instance that responsibility was certainly assumed by Herod, who made provisions in unsafe parts of southern Syria for pilgrims coming to Jerusalem from the "Babylonian Diaspora" in Mesopotamia.[83] In the case of the *hajj* to Mecca, that responsibility carried along with it some transparent political gain. When the 'Abbasids replaced the Umayyads as the rulers of the *Dar al-Islam* in 751, among the earliest of their projects was the improvement of the pilgrimage route from Iraq to Mecca. Water cisterns, watchtowers, and milestones were installed along this "Pilgrims' Way" (*Darb al-Hajj*), work in which Zubayda, the wife of Harun al-Rashid, was particularly prominent.[84] The objective was clearly to open access to Mecca from 'Abbasid Baghdad.

For the later Mamluk sultans in Cairo or the Ottoman ones in Istanbul, the annual *hajj* caravan departing from their realms was a staggering expense, a conduit for benefactions, and, not coincidentally, a display of sovereignty often accompanied by quite specific commands and programs. Thus, for example, the Damascus *hajj* caravan of 1672, which was led in person by the Ottoman governor of Damascus and in which Evliye Chelebi took part, had as its stated objective the removal and replacement of the then sharif of Mecca who in the previous year had massacred just another such *hajj* mission.[85] Again, for the officials along the caravan route, the *hajj* meant the responsibility of safeguarding and provisioning an enormous number of people carrying an enormous sum of money,[86] to say nothing of the opportunity for lining their own provincial coffers.[87] Finally, for the merchants of Damascus, Cairo, and all the stops along the way, the *hajj* was nothing short of a bonanza,[88] as it would later be for their counterparts in Mecca.

The cash payments carried by the caravan to the sharif, his family, and the residents of Mecca were primary instruments of Mamluk and Ottoman *Machtpolitik* in the Holy City, as we shall see, but the sign and symbol of the sovereignty the sultans were trying to impose upon Mecca was the person of the caravan leader, the *Amir al-Hajj*. From beginning to end a political appointee, the amir enjoyed almost ambassadorial powers once he arrived in Mecca[89] and, as the Ottoman archives have revealed, was from the seventeenth century onward the chief single beneficiary of the *hajj* from Cairo to Mecca, since it was he who was charged with the organization of the caravan, its passage across Sinai and down through the Hejaz to Mecca and back, and the delivery of both the pilgrims, and, more important, the endowment funds and subsidies to the Holy Cities.[90] It was an enormous and expensive operation, but it is difficult to explain the rise in his expenses from 400,000 silver *paras* in 1595 to nearly 21,000,000 in 1798 save by a massive *spoliatio Aegyptorum*, chiefly for the benefit of the amir himself.[91]

Whether performed in fulfillment of a ritual obligation or as an act of personal piety or even as a political gesture, the pilgrimage was an important part of the religious and economic life of Near Eastern cities and thus became a political consideration as well. Both the piety and the political posture of a ruler could be measured by his generosity in supporting and adorning not only the Holy City itself but the shrines and way stations that lay long the routes there. Jewish rulers had little authority outside of Palestine and European kings even less within the Muslim version of the Holy Land, though Herod, as we have seen, did manage to reach out to the Diaspora on occasion to ease the way, and Christian rulers from Charlemagne to Constantine IX successfully intruded themselves into Christian affairs in Muslim Jerusalem.[92]

The ability of a ruler to declare himself the protector of those of his "coreligionists"—an obviously elastic term—residing *in partibus infidelium* has of course been enormously enhanced by the extended reach of the modern state. In the post-Crusader era the European powers unashamedly intervened on behalf of the Latin—and European—presence in the Holy Land of Palestine. By the nineteenth century the Ottoman sultan was no longer equal to the contest and more and more frequently resorted to a legal expedient: the *juridical* definition of a holy place, already present in Islamic religious law and now extended to international law and treaty. If this new and secular extension of the sacred did not always enhance the holiness of the place in question, it did spell out the respective rights and privileges attached to it and, more to the point, rendered it a subject of *negotiation*.[93]

Christian rulers, whether they sat in Constantinople, Aachen, or, later, Rome and Paris, had grounds for intervening in the affairs of Jerusalem only after that city had passed into the hands of others, or, to put it somewhat more pointedly, after Jerusalem had been wrested from Christian sovereignty by the infidel hands of the Muslims in A.D. 638. On the face of it the situation of Mecca might appear very different since it has known no other than Muslim political authority from the Prophet's day to this. But until the establishment of the House of Saud as its rulers, Mecca had been governed in a quite ambiguous fashion: it has rested under the larger sovereignty of distant political centers like Damascus, Baghdad, Cairo, and Istanbul and at the same time had its own local dynasts whose authority was both more immediate and considerably harsher than that of its distant masters.

With the advent of each new dynasty abroad, invariably in the course of events that had little bearing on Mecca, the new rulers of the Hejaz had, in effect, to reassert their claim to their remote but important Holy City and, in addition, from the tenth century onward, to assert that authority in the face of the local sharifs who passed as kings in Mecca. Those distant caliphs and sultans generally won and controlled their shrine city by buying it. The later Muslim rulers of Jerusalem made a handsome profit on occasion by selling privileged access to the same Christian holy places to one sect after another in rather rapid succession,[94] but the custom was not entirely unknown in Mecca, where the prize was a legitimizing mention in the Friday prayer at the *haram* and the price was whatever the traffic would bear. In 1070 the enterprising sharif of Mecca Abu Hashim dropped the name of the 'Abbasid caliph from the prayers and substituted that of Alp Arslan, the new Turkish sultan on the scene in Iraq. The effect was immediate and predictable. A large gift arrived from the caliph, whose name was piously mentioned in the following years. But only until an even larger gift for the sharif arrived from Cairo in 1075 and the name of the Fatimid caliph went up to heaven. This politico-liturgical blackmail went on for some years, one name succeeding another at a price, until a body of Turkish troopers was despatched from Baghdad to settle down the fickle sharif, and the prudent and by now wealthy Abu Hashim took to his heels.[95]

Abu Hashim's game had simply found some willing and gullible players at a critical political time in Islamic history. This kind of mockery apart, it is nonetheless true that Mecca—the city, the shrine, its rulers, officials, and simple citizens—was endowed and gifted, whether in buildings, foodstuffs, or cash, on a scale never approached in Jerusalem. If the Ayyubid Salah al-Din and the Mamluk Qa'it Bay were generous in Jerusalem, they were lavish in Mecca;[96] those Ottoman paragons of giving, Selim II and Murad I, gave Jerusalem but passing notice and spent immense fortunes in Mecca.

There is no need to view the imperial donors with undue cynicism: all these rulers dealt lavishly in other parts of their domains as well—Qa'it Bay left a veritably Hadrianic trail of foundations across his dominions—and their gifts to Mecca were doubtless provoked in large measure by their esteem for the place of that holiest of cities in Islam. But this same lavishness, particularly when translated into specie rather than buildings, certainly won the at least temporary support of the notoriously volatile population of Mecca and their invariably needy and greedy rulers. And the pilgrims were surely impressed.

If the *haram,* the sacred place, was the heart of the Holy City, pilgrims were its life-giving blood, and the network of economic and political arrangements that carried them to and from the shrine were its veins and arteries. The worshipper living abroad had not only to perceive the city as holy; he had also to have the desire and means to go there. For Temple Jerusalem and Muslim Mecca that desire was translated into a *ritual obligation;*[97] the Christian, on the other hand, was provided with a number of incentives to visit Jerusalem, some of them spiritual, like the indulgences attached to the pilgrimage, others physical and psychological, like Constantine's enshrinement of the Jerusalem holy places and his and other Christian emperors' construction of facilities to assist the pilgrim on what was, under any conceivable circumstances, a difficult journey. In pre-Islamic Mecca there had been a sacred truce during the pilgrimage season; in Jerusalem the Christian traveler found bed and board, and the Jew a sometimes straitened community that in medieval times was still willing to take him in, help find him work, and even pay his poll tax.

But it remained a dangerous venture, even for the Muslim traveling through his own abode. Mecca was a long way from anywhere—some pilgrims were away from their homes for two or three years—and the way was slow. Nor was the pilgrim safe once he had arrived in the Holy City. Fanatic Qarmatians descended on it during the pilgrimage time in A.D. 930. Before the day was over 1,900 pilgrims lay dead in the *haram* itself, and another 30,000 were slaughtered in the streets of the city.[98] Even in the course of the ritual itself death might descend with terrible suddenness. In the close quarters of the *haram* and particularly at Arafat, where all the pilgrims had perforce to collect at one time in one rather constricted place, party and religious politics, and even the most trivial of incidents, sometimes provoked bloody combats among the Meccan, Syrian, Egyptian, or Iraqi contingents, or the sharif might choose that particular occasion to show his disdain for or disapproval of some distant caliph or sultan.[99] Mecca, remote from any truly effective authority and with little internal equilibrium, was quite simply a politically more violent place than Jerusalem.

Jews and Muslims had some of the same incentives to visit Jerusalem, though in the Jewish case much of the spiritual and psychological enhancement of Jerusalem took place after the destruction of the Temple in A.D. 70, when Jewish pilgrimage to the city took on a markedly different quality. With the Temple gone there could no longer be any question of Jews, either priests or laymen, performing any of the Temple rituals that were understood to lie, in one form or another, at the heart of Jewish worship of God. Moreover, in the wake of a second insurrection in A.D. 132–135 Hadrian's legislation forbade the Jews so much as to live in Judea.

There was one exception to the prohibition against approaching Jerusalem, however. We do not know when this particular privilege began, but in the fourth century Jews were being permitted to enter Jerusalem on the ninth of the Hebrew month of Ab to mourn the destruction of the Temple at the site itself. We have two different witnesses to the scene: a Christian pilgrim from Bordeaux who reports that on this occasion the Jews went up what seems to be the Temple mount and anointed a "pierced stone,"[100] and the Christian Father Jerome who offers this painful theological commentary on the lugubrious scene:

> Right to this present day those faithless people who killed the servant of God and even, most terribly, the Son of God himself, are banned from entering Jerusalem except for weeping, to let them attempt to buy back at the price of their tears the city they once sold for the blood of Christ and that not even their tears be free. You can see with your own eyes on [the anniversary of] the day that Jerusalem was captured and destroyed by the Romans a piteous crowd come together, woe-begone women and old men weighed down with rags and years, all of them showing forth in their clothes and their bodies the wrath of God . . . A soldier asks money to allow them to weep a little longer . . . They groan over the ashes of the sanctuary, the destroyed altar, over the high pinnacles of the Temple from which they once threw down James, the brother of the Lord.[101]

This is pilgrimage in some terrible new sense of the word for the Jews. And yet one must not think that, whether such visits had been permitted or not, or even if the Muslims had not allowed them to resettle Jerusalem after A.D. 638, the Jews of what was now only a Diaspora would have been likely to forget either Jerusalem or its Temple. Prayer for its speedy rebuilding was incorporated into the synagogue ritual, and even as the anonymous wretches of Jerome's meditation were weeping at the Temple site, rabbis in Tiberias and Babylon were painstakingly recalling or reconstructing every minute detail of the ceremonies of the long disappeared Temple and the circumstances of the earlier pilgrimages to it.[102]

When it was permitted to visit or live in Jerusalem, as it generally was between A.D. 638 and the Arab-Israeli falling out in 1947, Jewish pilgrims still went up to Jerusalem, as the letters preserved in the Cairo Geniza testify for the eleventh century. But they went now in the manner of Christians, to *visit* the city, since all the liturgy there had become, with a single exception, private synagogue ritual, while for the rest, Jewish sentiments about the holy city were discharged in public and private prayer, as nostalgia, longing, sadness, and hope, that complex of sentiments that contituted prepolitical Zionism—that is, before there was any expectation that an eschatological and apocalyptic goal might be converted into an actual and historical restoration of the city into Jewish hands.

These spiritual expectations toward Jerusalem, which may have been generated in the days of the first (Babylonian) Exile, guaranteed an almost continuous Jewish presence in the city from the lapse of the Hadrianic legislation down to the present day. For most of that time it was simply a presence, converted in urbanistic terms into a Jewish quarter sandwiched in between the Christian Armenians and the Muslim Moroccans in the southern part of the city;[103] the Jewish Yeshiva, or court-cum-school, which served the orthopractic needs of the "western" Jewish communities;[104] and a slowly evolving liturgical life in the city.

The Crusades, though not directed against the Jerusalem Jews, nonetheless deeply affected their presence there. Thereafter a brighter future seemed to beckon the Jews from Muslim Egypt, Spain, and even the Galilee they had so hastily abandoned for Jerusalem in 638. And the Muslims' attitudes, which had certainly altered toward the Christians in their midst as a result of the Crusades, may also have changed toward the Jews as well. The Jewish community in post-Crusade Jerusalem was poorer, less vital, and less visible than its predecessor. It was a twilight time, sketched in all its dark lines by the Jewish visitors who continued to come to Jerusalem and who showed much the same longing but perhaps somewhat less of the earlier hope. Economic and social survival were the issues of the day, not under the same pressures that were being exerted upon the more troublesome Christians, to be sure, nor faced, until the nineteenth century, with the Christians' external resources for support and resistance. And during this era between the thirteenth and sixteenth centuries Jewish liturgical practices remained within the synagogues of their quarter until there began to emerge, as we shall see, a movement toward the so-called Western Wall of the Temple platform, which from the sixteenth and seventeenth centuries gave a new liturgical and psychological focus to Jewish life in Jerusalem.[105]

Under Islam Jerusalem was undoubtedly a holy city, though it had to share its claim to that status with Mecca and Medina, and the polite rivalry that resulted is reflected in early Muslim traditions about the comparative merits of the three cities.[106] As a shrine Jerusalem's "Noble Sanctuary," the *Haram al-Sharif*, never attained the stature of Mecca's holy place, to which every Muslim was obliged to make pilgrimage at least once in his lifetime. Indeed, the Jerusalem Haram may have been a shrine only by courtesy, since the strict ritual taboos, including the exclusion of non-Muslims, that prevailed at Mecca from the beginning and were stretched to include Medina and even outlying sections of the Hejaz at times, were never extended to Jerusalem. But from a purely urban perspective, the contest was somewhat more equal. If Muslim Jerusalem possessed a somewhat lesser shrine than Mecca, it was, as we shall now see, considerably more of a city.

NOTES

1. Chevallier 1974: 762–79.
2. Starcky 1964: 916–18.
3. Seyrig 1941: 253–62.
4. Wolf 1951: 330–37; Paret 1958; Kister 1972: 77–78.
5. Charles 1936: 29–34; Peeters 1947; Higgins 1955.
6. Claude 1969: 213–16.
7. Dussaud 1927: 397–98.
8. Jones 1971: 461 n. 59.
9. Seyrig 1929; Dussaud 1942–43.
10. Hajjar 1977.
11. Eusebius, *Life of Constantine* III, 58; Socrates, *HE* I, 18; Malalas 344.
12. Cf. Le Strange 1890: 295–98.
13. Theodoret, *HR* XXVI, 13–19; cf. Nau 1933: 38.
14. Tchalenko 1953–58: 1, 220–22. Claude 1969: 208–10, underlines Telanissos' exclusively religious character after its transformation; it was lacking in almost all the civil amenities and institutions of contemporary cities.
15. Tchalenko 1952–58: 1, 242–46.
16. Serjeant 1962.
17. Kister 1972: 61–62.
18. Graindor 1927, 1930, 1931; on the tax and duty immunity of Najaf, which made it a kind of free-trade zone, Ibn Battuta 1958–62: 258.
19. Schürer 1973: 304–10. Though Herod's intentions were not entirely pious, they were always perversely intelligible. Building a theater and a full gladiatorial arena and instituting Greek games would have been a generous gesture in any city in the Mediterranean world except his own holy city of Jerusalem; cf. Schürer 1973: 313–15 and the

discussion initiated by Netzer 1981. On attendance at the theater as grounds of ritual defilement, see 2 Macc. 4:10–12; Josephus, *Ant.* XV, 8, 1 ff.; and cf. Safrai 1981: 189.

20. Exod. 23:14; 34:23 ("Three times a year all your males shall come into the presence of the Lord"); Deut. 16:16.

21. Safrai 1981: 7–8.

22. Though not only then. John 10:22 shows that there was pilgrimage made even at the new, Hasmonean-inspired Feast of Lights—that is, Hanukka.

23. Mark 13:1.

24. Beck 1959; 197–98.

25. Medina continued to be the preferred political center of the Hejaz down to the beginning of the twentieth century, when the Ottoman governor and garrison were located there. On the relative importance of Mecca and Medina as reflected in their "allotments" out of government funds and *waqf,* see p. 331 and n. 43 below.

26. Schürer 1973: 306–08; Netzer 1981.

27. Lassner 1980: 158–60.

28. Ibid.: 163–69.

29. Josephus, *Ant.* XV, 390.

30. Ibn Battuta 1958–62: 52.

31. It was not entirely secular terrain; at Najaf and nearby Kufa were sites associated with the life and death of Adam, Noah, and Abraham: Ibn Battuta 1958–62: 256, 323, and cf. Busse 1966.

32. According to Ibn Battuta (ibid.: 258), "In this town [Najaf] there is no royal governor but its authority is exercised soley by the Grand Marshal of the 'Alid Family" (*Naqib al-Ashraf*); on the history of Karbala; Nöldeke 1909.

33. Busse 1969: 427.

34. Most recently Najaf (128,000) has overtaken Karbala (82,000) in population, but both have been surpassed by the more industrialized Basra, Kirkuk, and Mosul.

35. In Ibn Battuta's day the cult at Najaf had generated a ten-day commercial fair, and as has already been noted, there were no taxes or dues levied on the city: Ibn Battuta 1958–62: 258.

36. Most notable among them the radical Isma'ili Qarmatians, some of whom carried off the *betyl* from the Ka'ba for ransom (see chapter 4) and who otherwise had scant regard for the traditional forms of Islam.

37. Wuestenfeld 1861: 201–30.

38. M. Shekalim 1:5; jShekalim I, 46b; cf. Safrai 1981: 117–18. Josephus, *Ant.* XVIII, 2, 2 does mention one incident of Samaritans' attempting to disrupt Temple ritual, and it is clear from other passages (*Ant.* XX, 6, 1; *BJ* II, 12, 3) that encounters elsewhere between Jews and Samaritans could lead to bloodshed.

39. Damascus Rule VI.

40. The signs of future trouble are already manifest in Acts 21, which describes the disturbance stirred up by the suspicion that the Christian Paul had brought a Gentile into the Temple precinct.

41. *BJ* I; 4, 3; VI, 5, 3; *Ant.* XVII, 9, 3; 10, 2 etc.

42. Mark 11:9 and parallels.

43. Which is not to say there were no more disturbances. The fanatic Syrian monk Barsauma, for example, found little difficulty in igniting passions in Jerusalem in the fifth century; see Peters 1985: 158–61.

44. Felix Fabri 1893: 1, 428–29.

45. Maundrell 1963: 94.

46. So, for example, the Englishman John Sanderson in 1601, who ignored the Franciscans in Jerusalem and thought an old friar took a shot at him with a musket in retaliation (Peters 1985: 513–14), and the American Edward Robinson in 1838 who could not resist taking his own aim on the Franciscans in Jerusalem (ibid.: 584–85).

47. *HE* VI, 11; Eusebius' own biblical gazetteer, the *Onomasticon*, is a testimony to that same scholarly impulse.

48. Windisch 1925: 126–27; Wilkinson 181: 19–22.

49. Runciman 1969; texts in Geyer 1898 and Tobler and Molinier 1872; new translations in Wilkinson 1977 and 1981.

50. Jones 1964: 959–62, and cf. Bagatti 1949.

51. Wilkinson 1977: 101.

52. Felix Fabri 1893: 1, 249; ibid., 2, 89–90; see Peters 1985: 446–49.

53. Wilkinson 1977: 16–17.

54. See Philipsborn 1961.

55. Justinian's legislation paid particular attention to hostels (*xenones*), poorhouses (*ptocheia*), and hospitals (*nosokomeia*); see *Nov.* CXX #6 (544 A.D.), and cf. Brehier 1949: 524–25. The *pandocheia*, another Byzantine institution, or perhaps just another version of the *xenodocheia*, survived into Islamic times as the *funduq*, which in Jewish communities was a kind of guest house attached to the synagogue: Goitein 1971: 113–14.

56. The *licentia* may have begun in an attempt to keep gyrovague monks closer to home (Brundage 1969: 10), but in the post-Crusade era the ban had taken on an overt political meaning: the pope was trying to curb not only close association and even intermarriage between Christians and Muslims but also the arms trade being conducted by Europeans with the Muslim powers of the Near East; so Felix Fabri 1893: 1, 248.

57. There is a fourteenth-century list summarized in Savage 1977: 55–56, but our best on the ground witness is Felix Fabri, who punctiliously notes the type and extent of each indulgence he acquired in Jerusalem and environs during his pilgrimage in 1480. The growth of both penitential pilgrimages and the extension of Crusader indulgences is traced in Brundage 1969: 7–8, 153–54. Nor were the Muslims themselves immune to the notion of "indulgence." Sivan (1968: 118) cites a post-Crusade tradition that "Whoever makes his ritual ablutions and prays in Jerusalem obtains a total absolution of his sins and becomes as innocent as on the day of his birth."

58. The pertinent texts are collected in Safrai 1981: 68, 128.

59. M. Shekalim 1:1; cf. Safrai 1981: 127–31.

60. Brundage 1969: 12–13.

61. Wellhausen 1897: 88–69.

62. Sivan 1968: 71, 98.

63. Ibn Wasil's account of the terms of the treaty are translated in Gabrieli 1969: 269–70.

64. Felix Fabri supplies abundant details on the work of this official, whom he calls the "Calinus," possibly *Khalil*, "friend," and whose work must have been as difficult as the experience of the pilgrims whose welfare he was attempting to oversee.

65. Felix Fabri (1893: 1, 248–54) reproduces the entire set of twenty-seven articles that were read to the pilgrims at Ramle by the Franciscan Guardian of the holy places; see Peters 1985: 427–31. On the sea voyage, Prawer 1972: 196–204.

66. Sivan 1968: 118–19.

67. On the *Fada'il al-Quds*, see Sivan 1971, Hasson 1981, Ashtor 1981, and Matthews 1949: 4–13, the latter from Ibn al-Firkah (d. 1329), who indicates (ibid.: 14) that in his day one of the *hajj* caravans assembled in Jerusalem.

68. Ibid.: 188.

69. Cf. Runciman 1969 and Savage 1977.

70. Kister 1969, and see the treatise of Ibn Taymiyya studied in Ibn Taymiyya 1936. There was even a Shi'ite attempt at substituting Kufa for Jerusalem: Hasson 1981: 170 and n.7.

71. The last decades of the tenth century may have been the most difficult era of all for the *hajji,* particularly if he was coming from Iraq. The breakdown of 'Abbasid power and the rising tide of Shi'ism among the tribes gave the bedouin free rein across the steppe, and in many years no caravan arrived from Iraq; see Wuestenfeld 1861: 218.

72. Felix Fabri 1893: 1, 258.

73. Wuestenfeld 1861: 212.

74. The medieval history of Mecca is essentially the history of the sharifs and their uncertain political fortunes in the face of more powerful though distant neighbors in Baghdad, Cairo, Istanbul, and eventually Riyadh; see Wuestenfeld 1861, Snouck Hurgronje 1888, and de Gaury 1951, passim.

75. See Wuestenfeld 1861: 216; Ankawi 1974: 150–51.

76. Ansary 1979 for Arabia; Barbir 1980: 108–77 for Syria; and in extraordinary detail for Egypt, Shaw 1962: 239–52.

77. See Bushnak 1978. His study is one of the first published by the Hajj Research Center newly established (1975) at King Abdul Aziz University in Jedda for the investigation of problems arising out of the *hajj.*

78. For the spread of the *hajj* network at the dawn of the modern era, see Burckhardt 1829: 247–60. In what was not a particularly notable *hajj* year (1814), Burckhardt (ibid.: 189, 269) estimated the total number of pilgrims at from sixty to seventy thousand. Rafeq's figures put the size of the Damascus caravan in the eighteenth century at anywhere between twenty and sixty thousand (Barbir 1980: 155), and Ludovico Varthema of Bologna, who was in Mecca sometime between 1503 and 1508, estimated the number of pilgrims at thirty thousand (de Gaury 1951: 118).

79. Tresse 1937; Barbir 1980.

80. Jomier 1953; Ankawi 1974.

81. After the rise of a professedly and officially Shi'ite dynasty in Iran at the beginning of the sixteenth century, the presence of Persian pilgrims in Mecca began to trouble the Ottoman sultans, and so necessarily the sharifs; see Burckhardt 1829: 251–52; de Gaury 1951: 166–67; Kortepeter 1979: 239.

82. Barbir 1980: 155–56, citing an unpublished paper by Professor Abdul Karim Rafeq of Damascus University.

83. Peters 1977: 269–70.

84. Tabari 3:81, 486; and for Harun and Zubayda, Mas'udi, *Muruj* 8:294. This route, thenceforward called the *Darb Zubayda,* is the present object of a Saudi archeological survey; see Knudstad 1977 for the preliminary report. The Sinai stretch of the *Darb Misri* has likewise been surveyed in Tamari 1982. Both of these are rather novel projects since most earlier studies of the *hajj* routes were literary and used almost exclusively the rather elaborate accounts of the routes in the medieval Muslim geographers and travelers. So, for example, Musil 1928: 205–12 on the *Darb Zubayda.*

85. Chelebi's account of the affair is in Kortepeter 1979. For his description of Jerusalem, see Chelebi 1980.

86. Barbir 1980: 133–50.

87. The governors of both Cairo and Damascus, both nominally the tributaries of the sultan in Istanbul, pleaded ever increasing pilgrimage costs as grounds for deeply cutting

their own tribute to the sultan: Gibb and Bowen 1950–57: I/2 45–46, 64.

88. Ibid.: I/1 301–02; Ankawi 1974: 146–47; Barbir 1980: 164–66.

89. Ankawi 1974: 151–57.

90. On the complex finances surrounding the office of the Cairene *Amir al-Hajj* in Ottoman times, Shaw 1962: 239–50.

91. On the annual budget of expenses, Shaw 1962: 246–47, and for Shaw's own assessment of the role of the Amir, ibid.: 248. One of the larger items on the caravan's expense sheet was the payoffs to the Bedouin tribes along the way. Embezzling this particular item often led to death and mayhem along the way, but these sums too tempted the greed of the amirs, and with predictable results for the pilgrims: ibid.: 249–50.

92. Constantine and the Holy Land: Wilkinson 1977: 11–12; Constantine IX: Runciman 1969: 74.

93. Cf. Zander 1971; Wardi 1975.

94. The situation in the seventeenth century, when the practice was at its height, is described in Wardi 1975: 289; cf. Peters 1985: 506.

95. Fasi 1857: 253–54; cf. Wuestenfeld 1861: 222–23, and Snouck Hurgronje 1888: 63–64.

96. On their work in Jerusalem: Peters 1985: 350–60, 406, 413–14; and in Mecca: Wuestenfeld 1861: 228–30, 291–96.

97. Expressed in the Bible, not entirely by coincidence, in lexicographically identical terms: "Three times a year," God commands, "celebrate for Me a *hag*." (Exod. 23:14). On the Islamic *hag* obligation of "pilgrimage to the House," Qur'an 3:90–92, and cf. von Grunebaum 1958: 15–49.

98. Wuestenfeld 1861: 211.

99. Wuestenfeld 1861: 277 for one example—this from A.D. 1415—among many.

100. His testimony is considered in another context in chapter 4.

101. Jerome, *In Sophoniam* I, 15–16; on the Ninth of Ab, M. Taanith 4:6.

102. Chiefly in the Mishna and Talmud and the complementary Tosefta and Baraitas but even in homiletic works like Lamentations Rabbah; for the rabbinic writings on the defunct Jerusalem pilgrimage, see Safrai 1981: 11–13.

103. See Gil 1982; Hopkins 1971; Peters 1985: 531–33.

104. Peters 1985: 232–33.

105. See chapter 5.

106. Kister 1969.

CHAPTER III

The Holy City

Holy cities are in the first place cities and so possess all or most of the municipal functions that characterize urban centers in the Near East.[1] But as was suggested at the outset, they also constitute a special subtype of the class because they display either peculiar functions or normal urban functions put to extraordinary uses and so discernible on an extraordinary scale.

Though it is possible to take up the various holy cities of the Near East in turn and describe the urban shape and functions of each, we are already in a position on the evidence to sketch, at least in a preliminary fashion, a typology that characterizes all of them to some degree. Holy cities, as it turns out, had common urban problems and rather standardized means of adjusting to them. Indeed, they share a common historical tradition, or perhaps a mythology, and one could compare, for example, the legends of their founding or their first possession, the growth of a stereotyped "merits" literature on the virtues of each, the sectarian strife arising out of the contests for possession of both the primary and secondary shrines, and even the eschatological expectations that were associated with the city. We shall leave these inquiries aside here, however, and concentrate, with particular reference to Jerusalem and Mecca, on a *common urban typology,* those forms and functions of city life that are immediately and remarkably affected by the fact that each was a holy place.

Let us begin with a few general remarks about the two holy cities that will chiefly concern us here, Mecca and Jerusalem during the premodern era. For all the difficulties attendant upon its investigation, Mecca is a relatively straightforward urban case study, a city with a single and continuous religious tradition and an evolutionary development from the seventh century to the present. Jerusalem, however, presents no such prospect of religious continuity. Its sacred charter has been written and rewritten by Jews, Christians, and Muslims in turn, and each new set of terms of the covenant was converted into the normal urban language of buildings and institutions. Possession and dispossession, appropriation and reappropriation are writ large across the history of Jerusalem, not in the normal political sense in which those acts might occur and recur in nearby Damascus, Beirut, or Amman, and indeed in all cities, but in the far more profound context of a religious revolution. Jerusalem too has been occupied on occasion as a simple political act and has suffered the normal succession of dynasties and their delegates and governors. But it has been more often *possessed,* taken by rights that transcend the sword or the lance and that have been chartered by a revelation and a sacred history shared, as it turns out, by all the heirs of Abraham.[2]

From this perspective it might appear that we are dealing with not one but three Jerusalems: the city of the Jewish Temple that lay at the heart of what was sometimes a Jewish state and always a Jewish nation; the Christian city in the Christian Holy Land whose definition was begun by Constantine and whose life was later and briefly resurrected by the Crusades; and finally *al-Quds*, the Muslims' "Holy Abode" whose chief monuments still stand in splendor above the city. But the city of Jerusalem is not identical with its history. Whatever religious transformations Jerusalem may have undergone over the centuries, from an urbanistic point of view we are dealing with one city, at least from the third century B.C. down to the beginnings of modern times in Palestine—one Jerusalem evolving slowly out of a single, well-defined, and stable matrix.

With the arrival of the Hellenes in the Near East, Jerusalem was drawn, not always gracefully or willingly, into a varied but nonetheless homogeneous urban network that eventually stretched from Egypt to Indus. In Jerusalem as in many other places appropriated by Hellenism, a substantial fabric of walls, streets, and public buildings was laid down over the older settlement,[3] and there came into being in the city a rich urban bourgeoisie whose wealth, attainments, and political power were now independent of the priestly corporation of the Temple. We hear of these "first men of the people" from the days of Antiochus Epiphanes right through the Roman annexation. They were present in court and council, and they shared in the political and so also the economic decisions affecting the city.[4].

The royal court too, with its Hellenized style and tastes, was a counterweight to the priestly and Temple institutions, and however disagreeable their "royal splendor" might appear in the eyes of the religious parties in Judea,[5] the enormous revenues and conspicuous consumption of Hasmonean and Herodian crown and court doubtless promoted manufacturing and craft industries eager to serve their appetites.[6] Out of the royal coffers came the investment funds for Jerusalem's building programs: the Jewish kings built on a grandiose and, more importantly for the continuity of the city, on a permanent scale.

Reports of Herod's Jerusalem, most of them from the hostile witness Josephus, sometimes make the city sound like an imperial enclave, as perhaps parts of it were in the light of the king's security problems. But it should also be recalled that the earlier Hasmonean palace and those other new organs of Jerusalem's Hellenized municipal life in the first and second pre-Christian centuries, the Council Chamber and the gymnasium called the Xystus, lay close to the Temple and the popular quarters of the town,[7] while the municipal archives, where the tax receipts were kept, was located in the Lower City itself.[8] And the violence of the class strife unleashed by the Romans' final onslaught against the city in 70 A.D., its spilling from quarter to quarter, neighborhood to neighborhood, is an eloquent testimony to how socially and physically complex a place was that Jerusalem of the first century.

But it likewise possessed an urban unity that made it more than a collection of armed camps. That the city had an integrated pattern of streets all the way from the western side of the Temple precinct to Herod's palace on the western edge of the Upper City is suggested by both the logic of the admittedly scanty archeological evidence and by the Emperor Hadrian's later city plan for his own "Aelia Capitolina." Both are to some extent reflected on the Madaba mosaic map, where two paved and colonnaded streets are traced across the city from north to south, the one along the ridge of the Upper City, the other through the Tyropean valley and the Lower City below.[9]

The Madaba mosaic tells us a geat deal about the stability of the urban fabric of Jerusalem during the four hundred years that had elapsed between Hadrian's confirmation of the even older outlines of the Greco-Roman city and the time that the map was designed. When we compare the evidence of the sixth-century map with Josephus' description of the city, we can conclude that Jerusalem had not deteriorated topographically in any obvious or substantial way in the interval,[10] and indeed Hadrian's, or perhaps even Herod's, city plan of Jerusalem is still distinguishable in the main streets of the present Old City. Much of the city wall constructed by the Ottoman Sultan Sulayman I in 1539–41 followed that built by Herod Agrippa fifteen hundred years before, and the same water facilities were in use throughout ancient and medieval times. From the Herodian kingdom through the Crusades down to the Ottoman era, the political ruler of Jerusalem has taken up his residence in the vicininty of the city's ancient citadel,[11] and it was from the steps of this same complex that General Allenby, one of Jerusalem's more recent secular liberators, announced the occupation of the city by the Allies in 1917.[12]

Mecca entered history as a small town and remained a modest-sized city down to the beginning of the twentieth century. The *haram* apart, the city's public architecture was unremarkable, and the urban consequences of the fact are significant.[13] Public buildings both shape and stabilize urban development by becoming the endpoints of the axial streets that serve as the city's skeleton; they establish a polarity that draws certain urban activities away from all-devouring shrine and so create an urban field. Roman Damascus spread its city life between a military citadel at one end of the city and a commercial agora at the other, with a large temple complex between them; the same polarity may be discerned in Aleppo, Jerash, and Palmyra. At Petra a theater stood at one end of the central way and a temple at the other. In Jerusalem the king and his court observed the city from the eminence of the western hill and the Temple establishment from another on the east, and the view was not very different in 'Abbasid Baghdad or Mamluk Cairo.

There was no such urban polarity in Mecca. Its pre-Islamic rulers, always a group rather than an individual, lived around the Ka'ba and its *haram*, and to the end of the medieval period the city's most important buildings continued to cluster around the periphery of the sanctuary. Indeed, they intruded into it, since the galleries that from the time of 'Abd al-Malik in the late seventh century marked the limits of the *haram* were pierced with windows let into the private houses that surrounded it, and, as we shall see, the commerce of the city streamed in and around this porous barrier between the sacred and the profane and established itself within the sanctuary.[14]

Mecca is already holy when it first comes to our historical attention, a western Arabian shrine-city run not by priests but by an aggressive merchant aristocracy, and the city never quite lost that dual quality, even though the proportions of the two ingredients have undergone occasionally dramatic revision. We have a graphic modern portrait of the pre-Islamic commercial life of the city from the hand of Henri Lammens,[15] but it is an account assembled from the recollections of a later generation of Muslims, with an understandably somewhat inflated sense of the importance of the cradle of Islam, and glossed by a modern scholar equally overanxious to make Mecca seem like an exceedingly wordly place. That Mecca was a commercial and worldly place need not be doubted, as the Qur'an itself testifies, but how prosperous it was or could have been in the sixth century's international economic system probably stands in need of recalculation in the light of what we know of parallel or comparable places.

Petra and Palmyra were two earlier cities that grew rich on a caravan trade built on the twin pillars of the mastery of bedouin and the possession of a religious center of sorts. As in the case of Mecca, the luxury goods in which they traded were neither produced nor consumed in the cities in question but came from East Asia and were transshipped for the eventual benefit of urban consumers of the Roman Empire in the first- and second-century heyday of their prosperity. By the sixth century the producers may not have much changed, but the consumers assuredly had, and not greatly for the better from the point of view of a middleman in the international luxury trade. There is a conclusion implicit in that fact, and the same conclusion leaps from the cities themselves. At Petra and Palmyra at least part of the profits of the enterprise was reinvested in the urban embellishment of the center. There is no sign of such capital reinvestment in pre-Islamic Mecca, no architectural celebration of its glory or its prosperity. It was not in fact until the Caliph Mu'awiya (A.D. 661–80) that the buildings of Mecca were constructed of baked rather than mud brick or that mortar was first used.[16]

We do not know when Mecca was first walled. There were certainly no walls in pre-Islamic times, and the first mention of such fortifications occurs at the time of Muqtadir at the beginning of the tenth century.[17] Perhaps here was little need of them. Mecca is steeply hemmed in by mountains, and the only real entries to the city are passes at its upper and lower ends, narrow defiles that could be easily closed, one imagines, as necessity require. There was some effort at repair in A.D. 1413, but it was not very successful, and by the beginning of the sixteenth century there was scarcely a trace to be seen of the walls of Mecca.[18]

The Nabateans and the Palmyrenes too had once been bedouin only recently converted to urban life, and though the pagan population of pre-Islamic Mecca shared with their earlier merchant relatives a taste for the cult of the dead,[19] they did not convert it into the kinds of funerary monuments that characterize Palmyra and the chief Nabatean sites, nor did they indulge in any of the other forms of Arabian urbanism that have been revealed by the recent Saudi excavation of one of Mecca's nearby commercial competitors at Qaryat al-Faw.[20] We do not know its ancient name, but a city was there, with extensive and well-planned commercial facilities for the caravan trade, none of which are attested at pre-Islamic Mecca.

The Ka'ba too, whatever its local prestige and however large it loomed in the minds of later Muslims, was a modest building at best whose decor came from the scavenged debris of other constructions, and it must be judged a minor and petty domicile for a god when set next to Baal's great sanctuary at Palmyra. The comparison is of course unfair; Palmyrene silver was mixed with Roman denarii and poured in great profusion into Palmyra. But there was silver at Mecca too, and the allowances for differences in location and life-style we might have made on behalf of Mecca have become far less persuasive since the unveiling of Qaryat al-Faw (itself no Palmyra but infinitely more impressive than the little we know for sure of the Prophet's city before the Prophet), and the absence of *any* form of monumentality there must raise some doubts about the absolute prosperity of the Meccans' commercial enterprise. Mecca was a frontier town, raw and unfinished, a commercial boom town that would likely have soon become an urban ghost had it not found a new and extraordinarily successful export item of its own manufacture.

Mecca's trading position was destroyed by the spread of Islam: the routes to Asia lay open in easier and better directions than through the Hejaz, and what once passed through Mecca now went through, and to, Alexandria and Cairo, Basra and Baghdad. Islam's holy city passed from the credit to the debit side of the ledger, becoming a city of expensive tastes and prodigious prestige that had to be supported, continuously and expensively, from the surplus of other parts of the *Dar al-Islam*, and particularly from that of Egypt, which became and remained the granary of the Hejaz.

Mecca never was an immense urban center. As we have seen, the city was only occasionally walled but relied on the natural barrier of mountains that pinched the city at its waist near the *haram*. But if nature protected the city, it also confined it. Neither the topography of the site nor the environment was greatly conducive to expansion, but the city had inevitably to grow, if for no other reason than the number of pilgrims who came there every year and were either unwilling or unable to leave. Recent calculations have put the built-up area of the city at 40 acres in A.D. 661, when Mu'awiya acceded to the caliphate, at more than double that within the next century, and double the area again (147 acres) at the beginning of the sixteenth century. By 1924 Mecca covered 350 acres, and it reached 1,750 acres in 1955.[21] During Burckhardt's visit in 1814 the city still stood close to its maximum premodern extension, and though we do not know what the population was in 1700, Burckhardt put it near 30,000 permanent residents in 1814 and calculated that the *hajj* tripled that number.[22]

Even now we can in places trace the outlines and street plan of Roman Damascus and Aleppo under the lineaments of the modern city, just as we can discern the face of Roman or perhaps even Herodian Jerusalem through the features of the Muslim city. The reason is physical: the lines of Roman settlements were fixed externally by walls and gates and internally by a characteristic grid plan, held in place by monuments at fixed points—the intersections of important streets, for example—and by street fronts lined with columns and columns and stone shop facades and anchored by stone paving.[23]

In Mecca we can make a similar identification with the *haram*, since from the eighth century onward it too was fixed by a colonnaded gallery. But we can proceed no further: we cannot confidently draw the city plan of tenth- or even seventeenth-century Mecca. Memory had preserved the sites of the house of Muhammad's wife Khadija, of those at Abu Bakr and other early Companions, and even of the birthplace of the Prophet himself. These isolated points were not, however, integrated into a city plan, as Constantine's Church of the Resurrection was in Jersualem,[24] nor were they ever important enough in the Islamic scheme of things to attract interest, and so investment, away from the central Meccan Ka'ba and its *haram*.

Mecca grew to urban maturity in the age of the camel, not that of the wheel, and its streets were still unpaved in the early nineteenth century.[25] Grow it assuredly did, but slowly and only in terms of its own somewhat uncertain inner dynamic. Mecca was never deliberately remade under the impulse of wealth or power, as Constantinople was, or Cairo or Isfahan. Its real rulers lived elsewhere, and its richest citizens, merchants most of them, often preferred Jedda on the Red Sea or al-Ta'if in the mountains, where life was easier and more expansive. Mecca certainly possessed local wealth and international esteem, but little of either was actually invested in the city, as it is today, in the form of substantial public or private buildings or facilities that might serve as the basis of the city's future growth.

Another difference between the two holy cities is a matter of ideology, but it had, when it was operative, a practical effect on everyday life in Mecca and Jerusalem. Both Islamic Mecca and Second Temple Jerusalem had large and carefully defined sanctuaries within which common Semitic forms of ritual purity were normally observed. But as has already been noted, there was in Mecca a larger zone, again marked with visible boundaries, where the pilgrim was obliged to maintain himself in a higher degree of purity—to put it somewhat differently, where and when the sanctity of the principal shrine spread out and over the very act of pilgrimage and effectively rendered the *hajji* himself a taboo object. Once within that zone, which began at the outskirts of Mecca, the pilgrim donned a special garment that signaled his *ihram* state and had thenceforward to guard himself from ritual defilement until the formal completion of the *hajj*.[26]

Something similar occured in Jerusalem, though not so much to the pilgrim as to the city that was his ritual environment. Already in the days of Solomon the king was at pains to remove his somewhat profane bride—she was the pharaoh's daughter—from the part of the city where the Ark of the Covenant had been installed to another, less sanctified quarter.[27] And in Temple Judaism, as in most of the contemporary religious systems, sanctity was measured not so much in its own terms as by the more reliable index of the absence of impurity. Ritual impurity was a pollution, a *miasma* as the Greeks called it, a condition that could be defined, diagnosed, measured, graded, and avoided with the kind of precision that unfolds from the pages of the Mishna.[28] And save for the impurities arising out of the performance of certain highly ritualized and occasional acts like the burning of the red heifer, they were not extensions of the Temple taboo but were part of the conditions of human life. Some, like the impurities arising out of sexual contact, were social acts that most often occurred in private circumstances, but others, like the "touching," often many degrees removed, of corpses, carrion, and reptiles, had not merely social but public implications.

Every Jew everywhere had to avoid these taboo contacts with the sources and carriers of pollution, the so-called Fathers of Uncleanliness, but as in the case of the Muslim *hajji,* there were certain times and places that required special care, like the great holy days and the Temple precincts. And it was in this connection that the rabbis attempted to extend that particular care beyond the Temple itself to the entire juridically defined city of Jerusalem.[29] Their rulings scattered through the Talmud in a great variety of different contexts constitute a kind of municipal code for the city, and though they were laid down in the name of ritual purity, those regulations—for instance, the prohibition against balconies and overhangs along the public streets, the requirement that excrement be removed straightway from the city and that no corpse be permitted to rest in the city overnight, the remark that Jerusalem markets were washed down daily and that the dirty business of kilns and accountants was banished outside the walls—all had an effect on the quality of life in the Second Temple Judaism.[30]

Jewish ritual is once again being celebrated in Jerusalem, but now in the public but essentially synagogue liturgies that developed in the wake of the destruction of the Temple, and most prominently on the holy ground at the foot of the Herodian platform where generations of Jews had remembered the end of the Temple and its cult. But that is merely the medieval *mawaqif* of the sanctity of the place; a few yards beyond lies the Temple site itself, now physically open and available to the Jews as it has been at no time since A.D. 614.

In 1967 the magnetism of the holy prevailed: some of the Israeli troops that had burst into the Old City, the chief rabbi of the Israeli Defense Forces among them, went up onto the Haram and prayed where Soloman's Temple had stood. But only until the countermagnetism of politics and a revised Jewish tradition prevailed. The Israeli government was unwilling to face the political consequences of the occupation of the central Muslim holy place of Jerusalem, albeit the Jewish one as well, and the rabbinate was incapable of ruling counter to a tradition that had long since adjusted itself to the absence of a Temple in Jerusalem and had cast its prescriptions for holiness in other directions. Close to where a sign once stood advising Gentiles not to enter the taboo area of ritual purity there is now a new announcement:

Notice and Warning
Entrance to the Area of Temple Mount is Forbidden to Everyone by Jewish Law Owing to the Holiness of the Place.
The Chief Rabbinate of Israel

The priests of Second Temple Jerusalem do not appear to have made any special efforts at restricting the access of Gentiles to the city as a whole;[31] rather, they concentrated their energies on maintaining the ritual purity of the Temple proper, of certain quarters perhaps, and certainly of the Jewish population living there. Since Jerusalem was a national capital and an often occupied city as well, its "haramization" was a politically unlikely project in any event. But not so the more insular Mecca. As early as the caliphate of 'Umar (A.D. 634–44) Christians and Jews were banned from the Hejaz, and a Prophetic tradition was often cited to the effect that "No two religions must remain in the land of the Arabs," or, more revealingly, "If I live, God willing, I shall certainly expel the Jews and Christians from the land of the Arabs."

Where this tradition and its parallels occur in the classic Muslim collections of *hadith* the context is invariably Muhammad's expulsion of the Jews from Medina, but the legal issue in the eighth century was the expulsion of the Jews from their oasis of Khaybar and the Christians from the city of Najran. In all three cases, Medina, Khaybar, and Najran, the grounds for the expulsion was sedition and had nothing to do with ritual purity.

How the ban operated in the early fourteenth century is described by Ibn Battuta apropos of his visit to al-Ula, a town on the northern frontier of the Hejaz: "This is the limit to which Christian merchants of Syria may come and beyond which they may not pass, and they trade in provisions and other goods with the pilgrims here."[32]

Though the "Eretz Arab" mentioned in these traditions is interestingly suggestive of other parallel discussions on the topic of ritual purity, both the tradition and the ban were palpably political. The extension or, rather, the duplication of the Meccan *haram* at Medina, in this instance by the Prophet himself, may likewise have had political motives, but its consequences were both political and social: non-Muslims would henceforth have no part in the urban life of the so-called Twin *Harams,* the *Haramayn,* as they continuously did as Damascus, Baghdad, Cairo, Istanbul, and, of course, Muslim Jerusalem.

The restrictions on the *Haramayn* were tolerably clear—no Gentiles might enter there, even to seek asylum[33]—but those for the rest of the "land of the Arabs" were much less so. No jurist ever suggested that Jews and Christians might be permitted to live in that territory, but the ban was not construed as absolute. Non-Muslims might be permitted a three-day stay in certain other areas of the Hejaz, the jurists explained, for the purpose of "commerce and manufacture."[34] Envisioned in such discussions were commercial calls at a Red Sea port like Jedda, though certainly not at Mecca or Medina, a distinction that opened at least the possibility of Jedda's entry into the competitive world of international trade (where even before the Crusades a good deal of the business was conducted by European Christians and eastern Jews) and effectively excluded Mecca from any share in it. The ban assuredly protected the ritual purity of the Meccan *haram*, but it also guaranteed a notable insularity in Islam's premier holy city.[35]

Though these elements—the occasional ritual purification of Jerusalem and the permanent ritual isolation of Mecca—were factors in the evolution of each city, the principal physical difference between the two places was the substantiality of the physical fabric of Jerusalem, which has persisted for over a millennium, and the lack of a similar foundation in preindustrial Mecca. In part the difference goes back to the beginnings, Jerusalem's early inclusion in the Greco-Roman *polis* network and Mecca's untended growth out of a morphologically unstable caravan town.

The absolute stability of Jerusalem from Herodian days onward and the relative physical instability of a Mecca unanchored by street or building lines, walls, or permanent monuments—in short, by anything save its *haram*—carries us into a profound methodological problem. Jerusalem has an archeology; Mecca has not. There are problems of archeological accessibility in both cities—religious authorities have never shown any great enthusiasm for having their holy places dug up, particularly by notoriously profane archeologists—but even if leave to excavate were granted, as it is occasionally and topically in Jerusalem, the results would be predictably and inevitably uneven. We know a good deal about the material culture of Jerusalem from people who inspected it, even though we cannot, and the urban historian can reconstruct a kind of literary archeology that is at times brilliantly and reassuringly confirmed by actual excavations. The most recent example of such a confirmation is that of the New

Church of Saint Mary. It was built by the Emperor Justinian, whose court historian Procopius gives a detailed account of both the construction and the building in his monograph *On Buildings* (v.6). There was no trace of this immense building in Jerusalem, not at least until it was unearthed by Professor Nahum Avigad, whose excavations confirmed the accuracy of Procopius in a quite remarkable fashion.[36]

For Mecca we have no such expectations. Archeological exploration, if possible, might cast additional light on some of the Ottoman or even Mamluk buildings put up between the fifteenth and eighteenth centuries around the *haram,* but it is doubtful, on the witness of visitors there, that there is much beneath them. Secondary building in Mecca was unsubstantial from the beginning, and so there is little hope that we would be greatly enlightened by even the unlikely event of major excavations in Mecca.

Why unlikely? The great excavations—or, more accurately, archeological surveys—of Jerusalem were undertaken by Westerners, from the American Edward Robinson in 1838 down to the French Dominican Père Vincent early in this century.[37] The English engineers Wilson and Warren and the Frenchman Clermont-Ganneau had what amounted to an archeological *droit de seigneur* over Jerusalem in the nineteenth century, a privilege they exploited to the fullest in the face of Turkish carelessness or bemusement—the Turks had not yet learned to connect archeology with imperialism.[38] But once that connection had been made, the rate of archeological exploration notably declined, except in those places where foreign scholarly or religious corporations had managed to buy property. In what were literally their own backyards, the work could continue in a proprietary yet guarded fashion. With the passage of sovereignty over Jerusalem to the Israelis, both the archeologists' zeal and the religious authorities' protectionism regarding holy places have increased, and in the end inevitably clashed, around the Temple mount and more recently at excavations at the City of David.[39]

In Mecca there has been no Muslim carelessness and no Western intrusions to exploit it in the name of archeological science. Snouck Hurgronje, who lived in the city in 1885–86, could observe but not survey. Indeed, the haramization of Mecca has had the effect of rendering the entire city as inaccessible to archeologists as is the platform of the Haram al-Sharif in Jerusalem. But there is perhaps another element at work. Mecca is a still-living holy place, the site of an immense annual pilgrimage that continues to infuse new degrees of religious vitality into the city, and it is precisely that ongoing vitality that renders it difficult to achieve the distance or detachment from the city that makes scientific archeology, or history, possible. This kind of detachment is visible, for example, in the excavations at the southern end of the *haram* in Jerusalem: the Israeli archeologists, finally free to dig at one of the primary Jewish sites in the city, found not Herodian or Maccabean installations but a *Muslim* palace, an even more important find, perhaps, than what they expected, and one they have treated with the scholarly respect due to it.

Even if archeological exploration were possible in Mecca—and it is not difficult to foresee the day when Saudi archeologists themselves might prudently begin to test the waters—there is little likelihood that it would produce very worthwhile results outside the *haram* proper. There were, of course, buildings, and often substantial ones, put up around the periphery of the *haram,* like the law school erected at the command and expense of the Mamluk Sultan Qa'it Bay in 1480.[40] This *madrasa,* called after its founder al-Ashrafiyya, had a similarly named counterpart on the *haram* in Jerusalem,[41] and the fate of the two contemporary buildings seems to illustrate a major urbanistic difference between the two holy cities. The Meccan school, by all accounts as sumptuous as the Jerusalem foundation, had within seventy years of its construction been taken over for political purposes—the *Amir al-Hajj* and other visiting notables resided there—and its library was reduced to a mere fraction of what it had once been.[42] Eventually the building itself disappeared, torn down or so transformed as to lose its identity. The Jerusalem Ashrafiyya suffered its own hard times, but it has remained sufficiently intact to provide evidence of its original construction and is in fact being restored.

One reason for the instability of Mecca's buildings, and so of its material remains, is the collapse of their endowments. But another potent factor in rendering the best intentioned and most substantially constructed Meccan enterprises ephemeral was the monotonously frequent flooding that plagued the city during most of its history. Every four or five years, according to the chroniclers, rainfall anywhere east of the city ended as a torrent sweeping down the watercourse in the midst of which Mecca was set. The entire center of the city was often under water, and when the waters receded they left behind an enormous deposit of mud, rubbish, and debris. Little wonder, then, that most of the buildings of premodern Mecca are merely a literary memory, and not merely to us but to a generation or two after their construction. Tradition may have perserved in some cases the sites of those former monuments, but the buildings themselves were undermined and soon collapsed and were swept away, or else they lay buried—and destroyed—deep beneath successive layers of debris.[43]

Unlike Mecca, in Jerusalem the pilgrim has been palpably replaced by the visitor, and, in fact, by the tourist;[44] holy places have declined—the word is chosen advisedly in the present context—into the secular status of historical sites. The transformation is visible in the city as early as the seventeenth century, when the Jerusalem of piety showed its first signs of yielding to the Jerusalem of curiosity, of skepticism, and thus inevitably of investigation and analysis. Contemporary visitors to Jerusalem do not lack for piety on occasion. But very few of them are there, as is every *hajji* present in Mecca, in fulfillment of a religious obligation. Mecca is far indeed from being converted into a museum or a historical landmark, as Jerusalem has to some extent already been, and it is precisely that distance that separates the archeologist's spade, a Muslim archeologist to be sure, from the sacred soil of Mecca.

Mecca too has had its occasional nonpilgrim visitors, those curious or adventuresome or perhaps suicidal Westerners who chose to share in the pilgrimage and inspect the Holy City of Islam. That they had to do so in disguise does not surprise, nor does the fact that their observations were often confused or inaccurate and their conclusions incorrect or biased. But we are deeply reliant on them, just as we are on the non-Muslim or foreign visitors to medieval Jerusalem. In both places the alien observers in the holy city were, unlike other more familiar and so more blasé narrators, in the presence of something unspeakably exotic and so deserving of comment and reflection. Wonder, as Aristotle sagely remarked, is the beginning of science, and it is certainly so in the matter of the urban life of Jerusalem and Mecca. It is the outsiders—strangers to mosque and *madrasa,* for example, to bazaars, to the goods available there, and to the Muslims, Jews, and eastern Christians who frequented them—who tell us most about such places. Most visitors to Jerusalem and Mecca intended to describe the holy places there, as they themselves assure us; but enough of them were moved by the sheer novelty of what they saw to turn their gaze somewhat further afield and so provide us with priceless data on the urban life and institutions of those cities.

This is particularly true of Mecca. Many Muslims had already imagined that sacred terrain in their mind's eye and contented themselves with reinforcing their own expectations; the secular aspects of the city, save perhaps personalities and politics, were of little or no interest to them. Western interlopers, on the other hand, were seeing everything afresh, and though dazzled or puzzled or revolted, they managed to get their impressions down on paper for our illumination. Those daredevil Europeans were of course the vanguard of the modern "orientalists," the often condescending scholars who judged and at times despised the East and Islam. But they were also, happily, the heirs of Herodotus, curious and persistent and intelligent, with prejudices in their meager luggage but with compass and notebook there as well.

The pages that follow, then, are filled with the insights of visitors—the archeologists will be found in their accustomed place in the notes—and only rarely with those of chroniclers, whose chief interest is generally the political history of the cities, though with two major exceptions that should be noted. The Meccan chronicler Azraqi (d. 837) has left us in his work a full-scale survey of the distribution of individual families and their residences across that city both in Muhammad's day and his own, while Mujir al-Din, whose history of Jerusalem written in 1496 is the most considerable consecutive account we possess of that history, has likewise provided a detailed overview of the city's streets and quarters, where they were located and how they were named when he lived in Jerusalem.[45]

Oddly, Mecca has had far more chroniclers than Jerusalem,[46] while the latter has generated a far richer travel literature, where information for the urbanist abounds.[47] It is this fact, in addition to the imbalance of archeological data, that has introduced the noticeable lack of proportion in the treatment of these two holy cities. But the disproportion is not, I hope, fatal to my purpose here. What is being sought is neither exhaustive data nor a nicely balanced treatment but enough evidence to establish in these two places parallel and analogous urban functions and so the conviction that we are in the presence not of coincidence but of a genuine typology.

We can come to that typology by way of a dramatically postponed conclusion to an induction, but it is preferable perhaps to proceed more directly, to enumerate, at the outset, the chief areas of urban function or development where the holy city shows characteristics that are anomalous to those of other urban settlements of comparable size and importance, and then in the subsequent chapters to consider each area in detail as it applies to Jerusalem and Mecca.

1. Since the city and its primary holy place have an enormous symbolic value for both the ruler and the community, there is persistent and heavy investment, most of it from imperial coffers, but some individual as well, in the *enlargement and adornment of the central holy place*.
2. The holiness of the central place, the chief shrine, inevitably extends itself over the city. This extended sacralization, taken in conjunction with the pragmatic reality that the pilgrim will spend some time in the city, leads to a *multiplication of secondary shrines* in the city and its environs.
3. Shrines require acolytes, from priests to offer sacrifice to sweepers to clean out the sanctuary, and these members of the *primary service industries* constitute an urban group or class that has an important role in both the economic and political life of the holy city.

4. The construction and continued financing of both the primary and secondary shrines, as well as a number of other public facilities in the city, takes the characteristic form of *transferred income or endowment,* usually perpetual in intention, and whose inalienable and untaxable nature is protected by law.
5. All cities possess some kind of public facilities. Those of the holy city reflect both its special religious and political importance and its peculiar urban needs. Some of the holy city's *public institutions and facilities* respond to the physical and spiritual requirements of the pilgrim population, while others, like the adornment of the city's shrines, flow from a more secular impulse to enhance and glorify both the holy city and the polity of which it is part.
6. Among the other beneficiaries of the central shrine of the holy city are the *secondary service industries,* whose income derives directly from providing lodging, food, and other nonsacral goods and services to the pilgrims. Some of these services remain informal in their organization, but others develop into a distinct *retail trade sector* that caters specifically to the pilgrims' needs and wants.

NOTES

1. Wirth 1975; cf. Wirth 1974–1975.
2. On the ideological and institutional bonds that link Jews, Christians and Muslims, Peters 1982.
3. 2 Macc. 4:9; 1 Macc. 14–15; cf. Avi-Yonah 1975: 236.
4. 1 Macc. 14:28; Josephus, *Ant.* XII, 138; *BJ* II, 411; Luke 19: 47; cf. Jeremias 1969: 222–32.
5. Josephus, *Ant.* XIV, 45 and *Ant.* XIII, 427 for the objectionable *kosmos basileios.*
6. Jeremias 1969: 87–99.
7. Josephus, *BJ* II, 344; V, 144.
8. Josephus, *BJ* II, 438; cf. Avi-Yonah 1975: 239.
9. On the tentative reconstruction of the Herodian city plan, see Wilkinson 1975; and on the Madaba map, Avi-Yonah 1954 and Milik 1961. Parts at least of the Byzantine version of the Upper City *cardo* have been unearthed in the Jewish quarter of the Old City (Avigad 1983: 213–28), and the pavement of the valley street has been found by Meir Ben-Dov emerging south of the Turkish city wall just west of the present Dung Gate.
10. The southern side of the city, where the growth rate was more pronounced in the fifth and sixth centuries for reasons that will appear below, does appear to have been breaking down into smaller and more irregular streets: Milik 1961: 174–175.

11. The only exception was the first Crusader king of Jerusalem, who initially used the Aqsa mosque on the Haram as his royal residence before moving into a citadel palace like all his predecessors and successors: Benvenisti 1970: 52–53.

12. When the Israelis repeated virtually the same act in 1967, it had a quite different significance, and so they celebrated the event not at the secular citadel where the profane Allenby had stood fifty years before, but on what was for them the far more appropriate ground at the western base of the Temple platform.

13. On the absence of large public buildings in Mecca, see Ibn Jubayr 1949–51: 127 Ar./148–49 tr. The Muslim traveler attributed the lack to overly restrictive building regulations.

14. On the many gates in and out of the Meccan *haram*: Gaudefroy-Demombynes 1923: 131–54.

15. Lammens 1924: 250–67 and elsewhere and often by the same author. For a new assessment, see Patricia Crone, *The Commerce of Mecca and the Rise of Islam*, Princeton: Princeton University Press, 1987.

16. Kister 1972: 85, and for the general poverty of the buildings of early Mecca, Lammens 1924: 219.

17. The evidence for the walls of Mecca is chiefly in Qutb al-Din 1857: 272–73, 298, 309.

18. Wuestenfeld 1861: 276; Snouck Hurgronje 1888: 2.

19. Goldziher 1969–71: 1, 209–38.

20. First report in Ansary 1982.

21. Makky 1978: 24–29.

22. Burckhardt 1829: 132–33.

23. On the case of Aleppo and Damascus, Sauvaget 1941, 1949; for the paved streets of Jerusalem, which date from the time of Herod Agrippa II at the very latest, Jeremias 1969: 12–13. They were still paved in the eleventh century: Le Strange 1890: 88, citing Nasir-i Khusraw.

24. The Madaba mosaic map shows the church, whose location was fixed by the site it commemorated, joined to the *cardo* by a kind of stepped esplanade, somewhat in the manner of the Temple of Artemis at Gerasa. The Nea, which was not connected with any particular holy place, was likewise oriented to the *cardo* toward its southern end.

25. Burckhardt 1829: 105, and on the disappearance of wheeled vehicles in the Near East in late Roman times: Bulliet 1975: 8–21. Wheeled vehicles were noticeably rare when Arculf visited the Holy Land ca. A.D. 670–60: Wilkinson 1977: 116, 12.

26. On the donning of the *ihram* and the taboo condition that it signaled: Gaudefroy-Demombynes 1923: 168–91. The wider juridical extension of the *haram* notion can be seen in the traditions clustering around the interpretation of Qur'an 9:28: "The idolators [*mushriqun*] only are unclean so let them not come near to the *Masjid al-Haram.*" The extension of the restriction to Medina, which had no Qur'anically—or biblically—authenticated claim to sanctity, was later furnished from the mouth of the Prophet himself: "Abraham declared Mecca sacred and made it a *haram,* and I declare Medina to be sacred throughout the area between the two mountain paths . . ." (*Mishkat al-Masabih* IX, 16).

27. Chr. 8:11.

28. This is the legal matter of the Mishnaic tractate Tohoroth, the euphemistically called "Cleannesses," which are of course exactly the opposite.

29. The rabbinic extension of the Temple order to the city as a whole, though not always easy to discern in the earlier visionary ambiguities of Ezekiel and the Temple Scroll, may in fact have been a consequence of the growing popularity of pilgrimage, which made the performance of certain rites physically impossible in the Temple itself;

so Safrai 1981: 194–95; and on the geographical limits of the extension, ibid.: 95–97, and p. 399 below.

30. Some of these regulations, often in the form of aphorisms and sometimes of wishful thinking, are collected in Vilnay 1973: 135–36.

31. Entry to the Temple itself was another matter, of course, and here there were prohibitions ranging from physical deformity through various grades of ritual defilement to prior excommunication; see Safrai 1981: 188–91.

32. Ibn Battuta 1959–62: 163.

33. There was, however, a rather interesting minority opinion expressed by the jurist Abu Hanifa, who read the prohibition implicit in Qur'an 9:28, and cited in n. 26 above, as forbidding non-Muslims to make the *hajj* or the *'umra* but not to enter Mecca for other purposes; cf. Heffening 1925: 48 n. 3.

34. Ibid.: 48–49, citing Ghazali and Mawardi.

35. For the commercial life of Islamic Mecca, see chapter 9.

36. Avigad 1983: 229–46, and cf. chapter 5.

37. The sites and dates of these nineteenth-century excavations in Jerusalem are set out in Gilbert 1978: 45, map #24.

38. The story is told in detail in Ben-Arieh 1979 and Silberman 1982.

39. The confrontation at the Temple mount is described in Benvenisti 1976: 305 ff.

40. Qutb al-Din 1857: 225.

41. Peters 1985: 413–16.

42. This from the chronicler Qutb al-Din (loc. cit), who attempted to save some of the remaining books.

43. Snouck Hurgronje 1888: 18–20, who cites the effect of the flooding in the case of Safa and Marwa, once distinct hills next to the *haram* but now in effect nothing more than two known points. Jerusalem suffered this same effect, though not nearly so dramatically. The Tyropean Valley running southward through its midst was also a natural draw and so has been filled in and up over the course of the centuries—this in addition to the natural rise of the urban landscape due to progressive demolitions and reconstructions, a phenomenon that did not escape the medieval visitor to the city: Peters 1985: 617 n. 36.

44. Peters 1985: 437 and n. 11.

45. Azraqi's description is rehearsed in Wuestenfeld 1861: 58–82, and Mujir al-Din's is analyzed in Schaefer 1985.

46. An unbroken chronicle line leads from Azraqi, who begins with the pre-Islamic history of the city, to Qutb al-Din (d. 1592) in early Ottoman times; it has been published in the first three volumes of Wuestenfeld 1857–58 and summarized in the form of a running narrative in German in Wuestenfeld 1861.

47. Most of the major sources on premodern Jerusalem, literary and archeological, are presented and analyzed in Peters 1985.

CHAPTER IV

The Holy of Holies

Since the city and its primary holy place have an enormous symbolic value for both the ruler and the community, there is persistent and heavy investment, most of it from imperial coffers, but some individual as well, in the enlargement and adornment of the central holy place.

1. THE TEMPLE

Solomon's Temple in Jerusalem is no more than a dream, set out in the typically bright detail of dreams in the Israelites' books of Kings and Chronicles; in professedly visionary terms by the prophet Ezekiel, and in ideal ones by the anonymous author of the Temple Scroll and the rabbinic Tannaim whose reflections are preserved in the Mishna. That there was a building, the "House of the Lord" as it was called, set atop a ridge north of David's city, that it was built by David's rich and successful son Solomon, and that it dazzled the worshippers who gathered there is surely beyond doubt, but also beyond retrieval. What is left of Solomon's shrine to his God beyond those old literary reminiscences lies buried beneath another, far more concrete ruin, that of Herod's Temple, another place of dreams, though now too of sober observation. Josephus, who witnessed both the building and its destruction, has laid it out for us in his histories: stones and circuit, courts, porticos and altars, the royal buildings along its southern side, and the ominous fortress called Antonia that looked down upon it from the north.[1] It took eighty-two years to build, and its *haram* was, on Josephus' testimony, twice as large as that of Solomon's House. That too is worth belief: we can still see and marvel at the enormous stones of Herod's platform, the immense labor of planing and adzing and filling that leveled off the living rock to provide the Temple's seat atop Mount Moriah.

Solomon's Temple was the primary consecration of a holy place, the threshing floor of Ornan or Araunah the Jebusite where God held the hand of His pestilential angel in David's day. David revered the place and may even have planned its enshrinement, though he never achieved it. What was denied to the father was granted to his son, however, and so it was to Solomon that belonged the honor of housing, then and for all time, the God of the Israelites. So it was built, of cedar and unhewn stone, four-squared like the Ka'ba, and Israel's sacred palladium, the Ark of the Covenant, was then transferred thither. So too was the growing religious and political cult that was coming to characterize the Jewish people: the holy Temple and the royal palace were joined together atop Mount Moriah in a single complex within the national capital of Jerusalem.[2]

Temple and palace were destroyed by the Babylonians in 587 B.C., and when the Jews were permitted by the Shah Cyrus to return from their Babylonian exile, the holy place at least had to be reconstructed—though not the palace, that other, more obvious symbol of political authority. More obvious, perhaps, only to us; contemporaries judged holy places as dangerous as palaces, and there was opposition and delay and oracular urging from the prophets Haggai and Zechariah that the work go on.[3] Finally the second Temple was finished, and in 516 the newly enshrined holy place atop Moriah was reconsecrated under the political auspices of Zerubbabel, the Jewish consular for Judea, and with the *aedificari licet* of the high priest Joshua. "Is there anyone among you," Haggai hopefully asked, "who saw the House in its former glory? How does it appear to you now?"[4] Under the circumstances a close resemblance seems unlikely, but the place was undoubtedly authentic, as were the rites once again being celebrated there.

In the case of Herod's Temple, there was no discontinuity. Zerubbabel's building still stood while its successor was constructed around it; ritual went on without interruption on the Temple mount. The new Temple begun in 20 B.C. was, then, a replacement of the older, much battered, and patched-up sixth-century building of a people just returned from exile. The new project was Herod's initiative purely and simply, done for reasons of piety according to Josephus, or for what is judged megalomania by some more modern and less sympathetic observers, but surely well within the style and limits of Hellenistic kingship.[5] Some of Herod's many building projects were imaginative and even daring, but the Temple complex, like most of the king's public buildings, was traditional-contemporary, and the entire ensemble—composed of a stoa-lined precinct with a podium and cult building in its center and a type of basilica on its south side, the "royal stoa" in which the king took a personal and natural interest—had a number of Roman parallels in Libya, Egypt, and Anatolia.[6] By all contemporary accounts the construction had a breathtaking effect, particularly in that still somewhat parochial environment and in a city where the very scale of the Temple complex dwarfed everything around it.[7]

However large it was, there is good reason to doubt that the Herodian platform at least was not as large as the present day Haram enclosure. Both Josephus and the tractate Middoth supply dimensions, and though they differ—Josephus says it was about 600 feet on each side; Middoth about 750—both sources agree that the Herodian platform was a square, as the present Haram, which is nearly twice as long as the measure of its southern side, is assuredly not.[8] If we accept the ancient witnesses about the square Herodian platform, we can easily make our own calculations, since the southern side, corner to corner, is transparently Herodian. By rotating the approximately 930-foot southern side through 90°, we can reconstruct the Herodian square and begin to confront some of its consequences.[9] The new northern wall of the Herodian precinct would run just north of the Dome of the Rock but somewhat south of the Golden Gate, a position that would effectively remove the Herodian Temple—and presumably the Solomonian as well; both of them would have been situated well south of the Dome of the Rock—from any connection whatsoever with the Rock under the Muslim dome. More, it would reopen the question of the function of the Golden Gate and enlarge and extend the early Muslim share in the leveling the Temple mount to its present dimensions.

Herod's Temple was not in use very long. If, as Josephus says, the work went on, by fits and starts, until A.D. 62, long after the king's own death, its mature life lasted no more than eight years.[10] But from its inception in 20 B.C., it was surely in the eyes and imaginations of the people of that city, Jesus among them, long enough to have made a powerful impression on the rabbinical tradition and the literature that eventually began to flow from it. Its memory lies behind the Mishnaic tractate Middoth,[11] and it was likely a recollection of that building and the impression it made on the Herodian generation that is echoed in later Jewish wonder and reflection over the lost Temple. "He who has never seen the Temple of Herod," it was later said, "has never seen a beautiful building."[12]

After A.D. 70 Herod's work lay in ruins. The Temple ritual may have gone on somewhat longer, though evidence for that is highly circumstantial, but the memory of what had once been there certainly lingered.[13] When Hadrian visited the city in his imperial progress through the Near East in A.D. 129 or 130, he "decided to rebuild the city, but not the Temple," according to one account; according to another, "on the site of the temple of the god he raised a new temple to Jupiter."[14] There is no easy resolution to this apparent contradiction, but since no one of the later visitors to Mount Moriah ever mentions seeing there what must have been, on the numismatic evidence, a considerable temple in Jerusalem to Jupiter Capitolinus,[15] one should perhaps follow Jerome, who was first in Palestine in 372 and who seems to place Hadrian's temple to Jupiter on the site of the Roman forum near the place of Jesus' earlier execution and burial.[16] As for the Temple mount, Jerome sustains what the Bordeaux pilgrim saw there in 333, one or two statues, probably of the Emperor Hadrian himself.[17]

The unnamed Christian pilgrim from Bordeaux, who was in Jerusalem shortly after Constantine began his building projects there; Cyril, the bishop who gave a round of catechetical lectures in the city in 348; Egeria, on pilgrimage in 381; and finally Jerome, who lived in Palestine from 385 to his death in 420—all are witnesses to the Christian disinterest in the hilltop site of what once had been the Jewish Temple, where "not one stone stood upon another," except perhaps as a stunningly literal fulfillment of that prophecy of Jesus regarding it.[18]

There were some minor Christian shrines there, or better, some interesting sites shown to the Bordeaux pilgrim: the "stone rejected by the builders" referred to by Jesus (Matt. 21:42); the "pinnacle of the Temple" where Jesus was tempted (Mark 4:4) and from which his brother James was later thrown to his death; and below it, what later came to be known as "Solomon's stables" and what the fourth century Christian was already told had been Solomon's palace. On the Temple mount itself, though the exact sites are not specified, an altar that still had upon it the blood of Zacharias, "murdered between the sanctuary and the altar" (Matt. 23:25). Finally, and most interesting of all, "a pierced stone [*lapis pertusus*] where the Jews came and which they anoint each year. They groan and rend their garments and then depart."[19] The day was the Ninth of Ab, the anniversary of the destruction of the Temple.

With the Bordeaux pilgrim we are suddenly and unexpectedly in the presence of a ritual stone—unexpectedly because Josephus, for all his detail on the Temple, makes no mention of it and because the size and shape of the Herodian platform make it unlikely that the Temple stood on or near the rock (for it is part of the bedrock and not a detached stone) that now rests enshrined beneath the center of the chief Muslim monument on the mount, the Qubbat al-Sakhra, or Dome of the Rock. It is difficult not to think they are the same, the fourth-century Christian pilgrim's *lapis pertusus* and the pierced *sakhra* under the Muslim dome. Both Jerome and the pilgrim's text suggest that some sort of identification had been made, possibly by the Jews themselves, of the place where the high altar of the sanctuary had been and that it was connected with a visible rock. Just when this took place is hard to guess: after Josephus certainly, possibly when Bar Kokhba moved away some of the debris of A.D. 70 to rebuild his own Temple in 132–35.[20] And if we can trust the pilgrim's account, before 362 there was another attempt at rebuilding the Temple (though on this occasion with the encouragement of the anti-Christian Emperor Julian), a task that involved clearing away the old foundations.[21]

A rock connected with the Temple shows up in the Jewish rabbinic tradition. It makes its first appearance in the Mishna treatise Yoma in connection with the ritual celebrated on the Day of Atonement. "After the Ark was taken away a stone remained there from the time of the early prophets, and it was called 'foundation' [*shetiyah*]. It was higher than the ground by three fingerbreadths."[22] The plain sense of this somewhat abrupt text at least suggests that the Ark of the Covenant had been placed atop this stone,[23] which, in the days of the "early prophets"—that is, David and Solomon—was already on the site. The site, as we know from Kings and Chronicles, was the "threshing floor of Araunah the Jebusite," a place that in the biblical accounts had nothing sacred about it until David saw there the avenging angel of the Lord. The presence of this "foundation stone" in Mishna Yoma, however, suggests something quite different: that we are already in the presence of an autochthonous holy place.

And that was precisely the way the later Jewish tradition understood the matter of the stone on the Temple mount. The literature of piety and mysticism made a great deal of the Shetiyah and its cosmological associations: this "stone of foundation" was in fact the foundation not merely of the Temple but of the very world.[24] But there was still no connection between this stone and the annual recollection of the events of the Ninth of Ab, and so no assurance for us that the *lapis pertusus* of the Bordeaux pilgrim or the sad rites described by Jerome had anything to do with the "stone of foundation." One must in fact advance as late as the *Pesiqta Rabbati,* a tract written in A.D. 845, for the first suggestion that the Shetiyah was a surviving remnant of the Jewish Temple,[25] an identification that may already have been influenced by Muslim traditions about the rock under the ornate dome that already stood on the Temple mount.

2. THE ROCK AND THE DOME

The problem of the rock on the Temple mount is almost intractable at this remove,[26] as is the more general question of what was occurring on that hill between Titus' destruction of the Temple and the Muslims' decision to build their remarkable shrine there. All that is certain is that the rock—neither the one anointed annually by the Jews nor, if it is different, the one meditated by the rabbis who stand behind the Mishna—meant nothing at all to the contemporary Christians and that the Temple mount itself was at most a place of some curious, though minor, sites for the Christian tourist. A pilgrim from Piacenza who was in Jerusalem in 570, only seventy years before the Muslim takeover, did not even visit the place. He was shown the altar upon which Abraham intended to sacrifice Isaac, but it was far away across the city, at the place of Jesus' crucifixion on Golgotha.[27]

The pilgrim from Piacenza knew where the Temple had been, of course, and he noted it briefly in passing. "We climbed by many steps up from Gethsemane to the [city] gate of Jerusalem. The gate of the city is next to the Gate Beautiful, which was part of the Temple, and its threshold and entablature are still in position there."[28] This latter was one of Herod's gates surely—a companion piece to the two Huldah Gates still visible on the south side of the Herodian platform, which also lead up into the *temenos* from below through a kind of portico with steps[29]—and it appears from the pilgrim's account that it was mostly in ruins.

Parts of Herod's construction are still in fact visible on the site, but the rest of the rather elaborate structure of what is now called the Golden Gate is certainly neither Herod's nor even Justinian's, since the latter imperial builder was already dead by 570. There have been attempts at dating the Golden Gate on stylistic grounds, but a rather commonsensical question presents itself in the midst of such discussions. If the Temple mount was nothing more than a field of ruins from A.D. 70 onward, why should anyone, Christian emperor or Jerusalem patriarch, build an obviously expensive and grandiose processional gate—and perhaps rebuild the two Huldah Gates as well—that leads from nowhere to nowhere? The Golden Gate as it now stands makes sense only if there was *something* on the Temple mount, something that required a monumental approach from the eastern or Kedron side of the enclosure.

One time that might fit these circumstances is the reign of the Umayyads, the Muslim princes who ruled Jerusalem from 661 to 750 and who releveled the mount and erected where there had once been ruins both the Dome and the Rock and the Aqsa mosque. In that architectural context the construction of the

Golden Gate would make good, if not perfect, sense. But there is another candidate with somewhat more impressive credentials: the Patriarch Modestus of Jerusalem, to whom fell the responsibility, shared with the Emperor Heraclius, of restoring the city after the Persians had devastated it in 614. Indeed, the Golden Gate has been credited to him on stylistic grounds,[30] though with no very convincing suggestion of the purpose of such a gate at that time and in that place. That time was in fact a turbulent one for Jerusalem. The Holy Cross long venerated in Constantine's basilica at the site of the crucifixion and burial of Jesus had been carried off by the Persians to their distant capital, and the Jews, who were briefly given charge over the city after its fall to the Persians in 614, apparently received permission to rebuild their Temple on Mount Moriah.

The sixth and seventh centuries are an obscure and troubled period in Jewish history. The Christian Roman Empire had never grown easy with its immovable Jewish recusants, and the Jews for their part were as yet unwilling to accept the inevitability of Roman, and Christian, sovereignty. There were civil and military insurrections down through the fifth century and into the sixth, not only by the Jews but by the Samaritans as well, whose revolts in 484 and 529 raised messianic expectations and increasingly violent Christian repression.[31] Then with the Persian conquest of Syria and Palestine, with which the local Jews openly cooperated, the Jews were briefly given free rein in Jerusalem. A Jewish leader named Nehemiah—the obviously symbolic name carries little conviction in and of itself—ruled the city and, according to one Jewish source, "made sacrifice," obviously at the only place where that was possible, on the Temple mount.[32]

It was a mere interregnum—the Persians reversed themselves and discharged their Jewish seconds as early as 617—but what had occurred was a Jewish reappropriation of the Temple mount, an event whose significance was well understood by contemporaries, and particularly by Modestus, who had lived through it. Heraclius meanwhile struck back deep into the Persian Empire, defeated the shah, and in 628 or 630 returned in triumph to Jerusalem with the remains of the Cross, which were restored to Golgotha.[33]

The Golden Gate, it has been surmised,[34] was built on that occasion in connection with the emperor's triumphal return with the Cross. But only, we may surmise in turn, if something other than debris lay beyond it in that ruined space atop the Temple mount, something that would in the first instance cause Heraclius to enter the Haram area in procession and would then draw the attention of the Muslims to the same place when they entered Jerusalem in turn no more than ten years after Heraclius. What presents itself as an occasion and a motive was the Jewish resacralization of the area in 614. When a similar act of religious defiance to Christianity had occurred on the part of the Samaritans in 484, the imperial reaction was swift and decisive. The Samaritans were driven off their holy place atop Mount Gerizim, and the Emperor Zeno had constructed there a new church of the Virgin, a rather remarkable edifice built in the form of an octagon surrounded by an ambulatory and enshrining a relic of the rock of Golgotha—a building very similar in fact to the Dome of the Rock.[35]

The parallel suggests itself not because of the architectural similarities alone but because the Dome of the Rock is so unusual a monument in the context of its place and time and builders, with no Muslim antecedents at all and very few Christian ones in the near vicinity. It is possible that Heraclius intended to reclaim for Christianity the Temple mount that generations of Christians had ignored but whose status had been profoundly altered by a few brief years of Jewish liturgical occupation.[36] And in the same fashion that Zeno had expropriated the revived Samaritan holy place atop Mount Gerizim, Heraclius had planned or begun to construct a similar octagonal church-shrine around the now consequential rock atop Mount Moriah. The evidence is only circumstantial (the Jewish occupation of the site in 614, a similar building in parallel circumstances in Samaria, and a satisfactory explanation of the apparent anomaly of the Golden Gate), but the hypothesis appears more plausible than to think, as we are now constrained to do, that the remote Muslim Arabs of Mecca rediscovered the significance of the place after a liturgical hiatus of half a millennium and then proceeded to enshrine it with an absolutely unique building.[37]

If we have managed to escape one odd conclusion, we have been thrust into another no less odd: that in 638 the Muslims took from the Christians what was intended as a "new" holy place, new to Christians at any rate, and restored it to another intent that stood far closer to a Jewish veneration of what was long ago, and only recently had been once again, a Jewish holy place. The notion is not an alien one to the Qur'an, however. The appreciation of Jerusalem in the original Muslim revelation was biblical and not Christian, and though the city is not mentioned by name there—nor is Mecca, for that matter—some at least of the references are unmistakable; sura 17:5, for example, speaks of the double destruction of the Temple.[38]

The word used for "Temple" in this latter verse is *masjid,* the same applied to the Ka'ba sanctuary at Mecca, and the two locutions appear together in the famous opening verse of the same sura, the crucial text for the subsequent Muslim appreciation of Jerusalem:

> Praise be to Him who caused His servant to journey by night from the *haram*-shrine [*al-masjid al-haram*] to the farther shrine [*al-masjid al-aqsa*], whose environs we have blessed, to show him some of our [miraculous] signs.

The "*haram*-shrine" of this verse appears to refer to the sanctuary at Mecca and was so consensually understood by the Muslim tradition. What the tradition had less initial agreement on, however, was the location of the "farther shrine." One tendency was to link it with the suggestions of supernatural visions elsewhere in the Qur'an and so understand it as heaven, perhaps the farthest reaches of heaven. We cannot say how early that reading of the text was, but it does seem likely that the interpretation that eventually prevailed—namely, that the "farther shrine" was in Jerusalem—only became current toward the end of the seventh century, precisely when the Umayyads were enshrining the Jerusalem *haram*. And what is most important to our purposes, 'Umar did not seem to know of that identification when he stood on the Temple mount as Jerusalem's conqueror in 638.

If indeed he was there at all. The earliest historical traditions of the Muslim community are neither early nor demonstrably very historic, and analysts of those traditions have been particularly suspicious of Sayf ibn ʿUmar, the mid-eighth-century savant who transmitted the bulk of the information about the conquest of Jerusalem and what happened there after the Muslims arrived.[39] A great deal happened in the next century, to be sure, and it is often those later internal developments within the "Abode of Islam" that are more accurately reflected backward into the preserved accounts of the early days. Such surely was the case with Jerusalem, where the conquest settlement was invoked not merely to defend subsequently argued tax arrangements, as happened in many places,[40] but to regulate, rationalize, and justify relations with the non-Muslim communities and, in the matter of Jerusalem, to give the city a Muslim importance *from the beginning*.

The earliest and barest accounts suggest that the city had no such importance, that it fell quietly and matter-of-factly, and it may be seriously doubted that the Caliph ʿUmar made a special trip to Jerusalem, on demand from the Christian patriarch no less, to accept its surrender and dictate the very special and notably anti-Jewish terms enshrined in that arrangement.[41] We may take it as probable, however, that the surrender was negotiated on the side of the vanquished by the Patriarch Sophronius, as happened elsewhere in the empire with the collapse of Roman civil authority; that tribute was arranged; and that the inhabitants were guaranteed, according to the common pattern, security of their persons, property, and the free exercise of their religion. But what the city's conquerors thought of their prize we cannot tell. They knew from the Qur'an that Jerusalem was a biblical and so necessarily a Muslim holy city, but they must also have quickly learned that the Christian claims there were in the third decade of the seventh century even wider and deeper and more impressively substantial than those of the all but invisible Jews of Jerusalem.

Muslim legend portrays ʿUmar receiving and shrewdly turning aside advice on Jerusalem from both Sophronius and "Rabbi Kaʿb," the latter an early Jewish convert to Islam in whose mouth so many Jewish traditions were placed in those years.[42] These accounts are as openly tendentious as the alleged surrender terms, and the Jewish recollection of those dramatic events of the seventh century is quite different. Some Jews quite close to the event saw the coming of Islam in almost messianic terms:

And a king shall go forth from the land of Yoqtan
And his armies will seize the land. . . .
Gog and Magog will incite one another
And kindle fear in the heart of the Gentiles.
And Israel will be freed of all their sins
And will no more be kept from the house of prayer.
Blessings and consolations will be showered on them,
And they will be engraved in the Book of Life.[43]

Were the Jews actually restored to their "house of prayer" by the Muslim conquerors of Jerusalem? In the eleventh century, after four hundred years of Muslim sovereignty, the Jews of Jerusalem still thought they had been. In their tradition they had pointed out to the first Muslims the actual site of the Temple, and in return for that and other help, they were free to pray on the Temple site and even undertook to keep it clean. According to another Jewish account, the Arabs had handed over to them "the courtyards of the House of God where they prayed for a number of years."[44] The Jewish tradition, then, had no recollection of being banned from Jerusalem by the first generation of Muslims; on the contrary, the Muslim conquest of Jerusalem was remembered by them as a restoration, not merely to the city but to the Temple mount itself.

But the Muslims established themselves there as well, as we have it from a disinterested eyewitness to the site. The Western Christian Arculf, who visited the city in 670 or 680, remarks of the Temple mount that "the Saracens put up a rectangular house of prayer, crudely constructed . . . on some remnants of ruins" and that it was large enough to accommodate 3,000 people[45]—a reference not to the Dome of the Rock, which was a shrine and not a house of prayer, but rather to the first assembly mosque in the city, the ancestor of what came to be known as "al-Aqsa."

The traditional way of approaching the Haram al-Sharif, the "Noble Sanctuary" that the early Muslims laid out atop the Herodian platform on the Temple mount, is through an inspection of the two religious buildings that dominate the *temenos* from at least the last decade of the seventh century: the Dome of the Rock and the Aqsa mosque. But if we turn elsewhere in that same landscape, we may have a somewhat clearer appreciation of the intentions of the early Muslim rulers of the holy city. In 1967 Israeli archeologists began to unearth a large building, and then an entire complex of buildings, adjoining the southern side of the platform of the Haram.[46] The excavations continue, but what has so far come to light is what appears to be a large Umayyad palace with direct access to the Haram at both ground and roof level, and west of it a series of other buildings that extended both westward along the city wall and northward along the Western Wall of the Haram and perhaps as far as Wilson's Arch under the Bab al-Silsila.

This was a very large public works undertaking whose intent and function may not have been fulfilled before the dynasty itself expired in A.D. 750 and the political fortunes of both city and empire were directed from Baghdad. What was the intent? We cannot be certain, but the complex was one of the largest, if not the largest, Muslim building project undertaken in the first century of Islam. Elsewhere the Umayyads chiefly adapted and reused; here in Jerusalem they planned and built, a secular building purely and simply, administrative or residential perhaps, and in the very shadow of the Noble Sanctuary to whose own buildings the complex at its southern end was obviously related in design and concept.

But if we cannot as yet say precisely why, we can certainly speculate who was the mover of this vast secular initiative at the foot of the Temple mount. By the time that Arculf journeyed to Jerusalem in 670 or 680, the city had a new ruler, Mu'awiya ibn Sufyan, an early companion of the Prophet, longtime governor of Syria and, after 661, the caliph of a badly divided Muslim community. This fifth caliph eventually chose to rule the community from Damascus rather than from Mecca or Medina, but that may not have been his original intent. An anonymous and Christian but doubtless early source attests that Mu'awiya was crowned in Jerusalem.[47] It was Mu'awiya, then, who had the emotional investment in Jerusalem and who offers himself as a likely candidate for the sovereign who initiated the grand design embodied not merely in the vast administrative and residential complex at the foot of the Haram but also in the two religious buildings intended to sacralize the space atop it. Mu'awiya, it appears, intended to rule the *Dar al-Islam* from Jerusalem.

There may be some confirmation of this in one of the Jewish apocalypses whose kernel goes back to the time of the conquest. Its version of early Islamic history is more than a little disordered, but in one of its versions it seems to refer directly to Mu'awiya as "a lover of Israel" who "restores the breaches of the Temple," who "hews Mount Moriah and makes it straight and builds a mosque there on the Stone of Foundation," while in the same work the efforts of 'Abd al-Malik and his sons are reduced to "repairing the Temple."[48]

The project, which may have included extending the Herodian platform far to the north, was not finished in Mu'awiya's lifetime, and the Dome of the Rock was signed and dated by the Caliph 'Abd al-Malik in A.D. 692 and the Aqsa mosque attributed to his son al-Walid.[49] Both the latter princes were prodigious builders throughout the East, on a scale comparable to Justinian, Hadrian, and Herod, and though the Aqsa has been rebuilt so often that its original effect is considerably blurred, the Dome of the Rock is a marvelously sophisticated and elegant building set down confidently and harmoniously in the midst of the Haram al-Sharif. But the Aqsa, for all its numerous rebuildings, is an edifice whose function, if not always its form, is perfectly transparent: it was from the beginning and remains a mosque, a *masjid al-jama'a*, or assembly mosque, from the size of it, intended to accommodate the entire population of early Muslim Jerusalem and identified, as its name reveals, with the "Farther Shrine" mentioned in the Qur'an.[50] The Dome of the Rock is something quite different, however, at once more complex and baffling: a shrine.

The Aqsa is located at the southern end of the Haram, convenient to and connected with the Umayyad palace abutting it at the southern wall. The collocation of palace and congregational mosque was common in the earliest urban building projects undertaken by the Muslims, and in this case there may have been the additional inducement of reusable building materials, since the location was identical to the site of Herod's Royal Stoa, one of the more monumental buildings in that king's precinct and one whose still visible remains were probably the *ruinas* referred to by Arculf. The broad and lavishly columned basilical space enclosed within the Aqsa would have used them to advantage, as would the palace built amidst the debris down below. The Dome, on the other hand, rests upon its own platform in the middle of the Haram, directly atop a large exposed area of bedrock outcropping, which the building with its double octagon encloses and obviously enshrines.

The intent and function of the Dome of the Rock has been widely debated. It was once generally agreed, on the basis of statements of authors like Ya'qubi, that 'Abd al-Malik intended to divert the *hajj* from Mecca, where he was faced with civil insurrection, to Jerusalem, and that the Dome, a shrine with an inner ambulatory for the liturgical *tawaf*, or "circling," of a sacred rock, was his substitute for the Ka'ba.[51] It no longer seems so simple, however, and the reasons for doubting if not outright rejecting that explanation are sound and convincing.[52] But something *was* astir in Jerusalem in Umayyad times, and we can read its echoes if not clearly its causes in the debate being conducted under the cover of "traditions" put in the mouth of the Prophet regarding the relative sanctity of Mecca and Medina and the upstart "third mosque" in Jerusalem.[53]

What was disturbing some Muslims may have been revealed in the excavations at the south end of the Haram platform. The size and elaborateness of the palace and its adjoining settlement suggests that someone, perhaps Mu'awiya himself, had *political* plans for Jerusalem. And if they were political, they had also to be religious at that point in Islamic history. If Mu'awiya intended changing the center of the *Dar al-Islam* from the Prophet's home in Medina, there would have to be an ideological as well as a practical basis for the move. And the ideological basis lay close at hand in the obvious, Quranically certified sanctity of Jerusalem. What was required was some symbolic yet public and visible expression of that sanctity *in an Islamic context*. And that expression was the Dome of the Rock, a building perhaps planned and perhaps already begun by Heraclius as a reproach to newly kindled Jewish pretensions on the Temple mount, taken in hand by Mu'awiya and then finally completed and signed by 'Abd al-Malik in 692.[54]

One approach to the question of the Dome of the Rock has been to look at the catena of Quranic texts that its builders chose to display in mosaic around the interior.[55] Viewed from that perspective as well, the Dome is both a royal and a religious *prise de possession* of the holy city, a building whose imperial message and iconography echoes in intention the new Muslim palace to its south and whose religious message seems beamed to the Christian presence atop Golgotha across the Tyropean valley: Islam is at hand; Christianity is transcended.[56]

If the Dome of the Rock is an at least implicit repudiation of the Anastasis' claim for a risen Christ, it is also an acceptance and affirmation of the biblical associations of the place. The Dome, it appears almost certain, was not originally built to commemorate a way station on Muhammad's "Night Journey" but to celebrate the biblical, Abrahamic, and so *muslim* connections of that spot atop Moriah, connections suddenly and unexpectedly alive on the eve of Islam and to which the Muslims now laid claim.[57] It was only with the community's growing confidence in its own independent religious identity, and perhaps for polemical reasons as well, that the Night Journey associations of the rock and its shrine began to gain ground and the opening verse of sura 17 glossed accordingly. The identification was current when Ya'qubi was writing in 874, and at least from that time onward the two associations, the Abrahamic and the "Muhammadan," dwelled together under the Dome, much in the way that both the Cross and the altar of Abraham were connected at the Christians' Golgotha.[58]

By about A.D. 800, then, the main lines of the Jerusalem Haram and its monuments were defined. Though the religious mythology of the place grew more complex with the passage of time and secondary shrines within and without it multiplied through gift and endowment, the dimensions of the Haram have not substantially changed, nor have those of the secondary platform and Dome that stand upon it. What did occur, however, is what might be called a "secondary enshrinement" worked on the primary *sacrum*. The Jewish Temple in Jerusalem had a graduated system of parapets and gates to keep impurity and the unpurified at a safe distance—part of Antiochus IV's defilement of the Temple was breaking down those barriers against the profane—but in the tenth-century Muslim Haram on the same site the 'Abbasids began the erection not of barriers but of an architectural "frame" here and there around the platform of the Dome in the form of graceful arches over the stairways leading up to the shrine building, and the work was continued along the northern side by the Mamluk Sultan al-Nasir Muhammad in 1321 and 1326. A few years earlier that same ruler had begun to extend the "shrine frame" outward to the edge of the Haram itself, and over the course of thirty years (1307–37) constructed a continuous portico along most of the western edge of the sanctuary.[59]

3. THE GREAT CHURCHES

There is little to wonder at in the progression from an Abrahamic to a properly Muslim appropriation of the primary holy place of Jerusalem; the same thing occurred at Mecca where the pre-Islamic holy places associated with the *hajj* were first revealed in the Qur'an (2:125–27) to have had privileged associations with Abraham and Ishmael in patriarchal times, and it was this fact and their association with events in the life of Muhammad that bestowed their sanctity on them in Muslim eyes. Only later and very gradually did the "Muhammadan" connections of Meccan sites begin to work their way into the religious consciousness of the pilgrims there. In Christianity, on the other hand, it was precisely the events of Jesus' life and resurrection that constituted the redemptive "sacrament" for mankind and thus caused their settings to be regarded as the primary holy places of a Christian Jerusalem.

It is impossible now to trace the exact progress of the Christian recognition of and sentiments concerning the places of Jesus' birth, death, and burial, from the time they are mentioned, often with some topographical details, in the Gospels until Constantine began to construct shrines over and around them in the thirties of the fourth century. Constantine's own intent was quite explicit, however, at least according to Eusebius' reading of the emperor's project: the cave of Jesus' tomb was a new "Holy of Holies," the foundation of a "new Jerusalem" that was replacing its famous Jewish prototype.[60] Eusebius' explanation is not an unfair description of the program of Christianity itself perhaps, expressed not now in the theological language of Paul and the Letter to the Hebrews but in the more material and imperial terms of a religious topography. Constantine intended neither to "annex" the Holy Land nor to displace the Jews from it, since neither required much doing in the fourth century, but to make it Christian in the same way the Romans had earlier reparsed Gerasa or Palmyra or Damascus in their own architectural idiom.

But Constantine's royal predecessors, Herod and Hadrian chief among them, had earlier redesigned municipal Jerusalem, so there was already a visible statement of cult or empire in at least some of the places identified by pious recollection and miraculous invention as Christian holy sites, though precisely what those buildings were we cannot say for certain. We do know that when Hadrian visited the city in 129 or 130 he found it still largely in ruins after the destruction of A.D. 70. It was then, we are told, that he "resolved to rebuild the city, but not the Temple" and, according to another account, the emperor named his new municipal foundation Aelia Capitolina "and on the site of the temple of the god he raised a new temple of Jupiter." Was there, then, a Roman temple where Herod's had stood sixty years before? Jerome, as we have seen, saw no temple on Mount Moriah, nor did the Bordeaux pilgrim, though both attest to the presence of statues there.

If we turn from the Temple mount to the Upper City, and more precisely to the sites that interested Constantine, we find something else, however. Eusebius' account of the place is quite circumstantial: Hadrian covered the place around Jesus' tomb with earth, laid down a stone pavement and built a shrine to Aphrodite on the spot.[61] If Eusebius' reference to Hadrian's paving of the area is to the construction of a Roman forum, as seems likely, then the Jerusalem temple of Jupiter Capitolinus that is attested on the coins of the city is better placed there than on the Temple mount.

Eusebius, who was probably reflecting the emperor's own thinking on this point, read Constantine's actions in Jerusalem as a contest or, better, a Christian triumph over both the Jerusalem of the Jews, now reduced in its essentials to an empty space on the eastern mount, and pagan Aelia and its shrines. Of the two rivals, the latter undoubtedly was more important in a city that had been cleared of Jews and all traces of their cultus for over a century and a half and had been remade into a Roman municipality whose shrines and monuments still stood and functioned in Constantine's day. Constantine's shrine-tomb and basilica in honor of the death and resurrection of his Savior stood, then, like the Capitolium they replaced, on the imperial forum at the heart of Hadrian's Roman city.[62]

Jerusalem was holy to the early Christians only by remembrance. The Christian community there had twice to flee from the savage reprisals of an insurrection against Rome, and the Jewish authorities, who now represented the most conservative and separatist type of Jewish sentiment, had become progressively disaffected from the Christians who were once their coreligionists but who were coming to be looked upon more and more as *minim*, "heretics," or worse. And for the growing number of Gentile converts who were now and ever after the main body of the *ekklesia*, Jerusalem was an unknown city and Palestine a remote and foreign land known only from the Gospels. It was the self-appointed task of Constantine to convert that fading memory of the homeland of Jesus into a new reality.

There may have been Christian churches, or at least a church, in Jerusalem before Constantine, from the time when Jesus' followers gathered in the *coenaculum*, or upper room, after his death down to the days of the Bar Kokhba war when the Jewish-Christian community left Jerusalem for good.[63] But those earliest churches were almost certainly private houses used for both assembly and liturgical purposes, while Constantine's constructions were large public buildings whose primary purpose was neither communal nor liturgical; rather, they were intended to memorialize the great redemptive acts of Jesus' life. And their long-term effect was to convert Jerusalem into a Christian holy city and Palestine into a new Christian Holy Land.[64]

Every Christian church and shrine is in some sense liturgical in that the Eucharist is celebrated in it. It was celebrated in Constantine's Palestinian basilicas as well, but only for the benefit of the pilgrims who had come to each of those places for quite another purpose, to visit and venerate the sites associated with Jesus' birth (Bethlehem), death (Golgotha), resurrection (the Holy Sepulcher or Anastasis), and Ascension into heaven (the Imbomon on the Mount of Olives).[65] Their very form betrays the dual functions of the buildings: a primary polygonal martyrium to commemorate the site itself and a large attached basilica to accommodate the visitors. In Bethlehem the object is particularly clear: outside the nave of the attached basilica was a large colonnaded atrium and, outside that, another even larger courtyard, which could serve as an accommodation for the pilgrims and for the tradesmen who serviced them.[66]

The complex shrines that rested functionally within or by the side of Constantine's Palestinian churches were not so much examples of the early Christian martyria tradition as new Christian reflections of the heroic mausolea dedicated to the memories of the Roman emperors. Christianity was now after all a public and official cult, a preferred religion, and the churches of the fourth century already began to reflect that changed status. Christian churches may have begun as private homes or as modest memorial shrines over the graves of revered martyrs, but with Constantine they became part of the official cultus, in part imitations and in part replacements of their imperial prototypes. They owed nothing to the long-established pagan cultus of the empire—the churches in no wise resembled temples—but they were modeled instead upon the palace and tomb architecture of the emperors in their intricate hieratic structure, their splendid domes, vaulted ceilings, majestic propylaea outside and lofty arches within the building, their rich decorations of gold and marble and mosaic.[67]

The Golgotha where Jesus died and near which he was buried about A.D. 30 bore little resemblance to that same place a century later. Jesus' execution and burial took place outside the city walls, as was normal; when Constantine chose to enshrine them, the two locations were part of a commercial and temple complex that was the nucleus of Hadrian's Aelia Capitolina, and Constantine's choice of the place, out of the many possibilities of Christian association in Jerusalem, as well as how and what he built there, must be seen as a response to and a reflection of what had gone before. The Christian emperor took possession of the center of Roman Jerusalem. Adorned with the emperor's churches majestically situated over Christendom's holiest places, Jerusalem was more than another holy city for the Christians; it was the officially designated and publicly celebrated holy city of the Christian Roman Empire, a notion powerful enough to attract pilgrims from all over the Christian world and enduring enough to provoke an irredentist crusade more than seven centuries after Constantine planted the idea.

Temple Jerusalem was a city embracing within the selfsame walls the seat of Jewish sovereignty and the center of Jewish cult, two notions similar but not identical in either site or concept, not even when the Hasmoneans boldly rejoiced in the dual title of high priest and king. The city's pilgrims from abroad came to celebrate its religious festivals and not the royal house enthroned in the Upper City. Their focus was on the Temple and, by an officially encouraged extension, on the city; their taxes and tithes were paid to the Temple and its priests; their messianic expectations were Davidic, not Hasmonean or Herodian.

For the Christian pilgrim Jerusalem was at the same time of more limited and diffused interest. There was no Christian Holy of Holies sacred as no other place could be, no unique site or cult or worship; preserved lists of the liturgical feasts celebrated annually in Jerusalem and its environs in the sixth and even the ninth century name scores of churches, each of which enjoyed its own day or week as the center of liturgical activity.[68] In the course of time the Church of the Anastasis did win a certain pride of place,[69] but for all that, Jerusalem and indeed all of Palestine in a sense remained a Christian *landscape*. Nor did Jerusalem possess any political or national associations for the Christians: their ruler governed from Constantinople; their political past was in Rome; their spiritual *qibla* lay not in Jerusalem but in a messianic East.

Each political possession and repossession of Jerusalem casts a new light on the special qualities of holy city and its primary shrine as well as on the nature of the ideological and geopolitical instruments that can be brought to bear to change its peculiar status in one direction or another. When the Romans dispossessed the Jews in A.D. 70 and 135 they destroyed the central shrine, removed the last traces of Jewish political autonomy, and finally banned any Jewish presence in the city and its surrounding territory. In their place the Romans followed the example of Antiochus Epiphanes four hundred years earlier and substituted the primary political and cultural instrument of Hellenism: an urban ideology, or, to put it in its most flat and banal terms, a city plan. And whatever religious practices the Romans instituted as part of that urban program could displace but never quite replace the fiercely exclusionistic claims of a monotheistic cult. Paganism might be an affront to Judaism, but it was never a substitute for it.

Jews, Christians, and Muslims confront each other with far more competitive weapons than the Greeks or Romans could bring to bear, all forged in the selfsame armory, and, paradoxically, with far greater opportunities for peaceful syncretism. While the imperial Christians of the fourth century had little reason to relax or rescind the earlier Roman ban on Jews, the Muslims acted quite differently when their hour in Jerusalem was at hand. The Muslim takeover of Hebron and the Temple mount in 638 was a claim of possession, to be sure, but it was also in a sense an exaltation of places whose holiness was shared by all three religious communities. And since they did not bring with them to the city a developed political or urban ideology, the Muslims' hand lay lightly on the rest of Jerusalem, which was neither redesigned nor administered in some very new or different fashion.

The motives of the Crusaders who approached Jerusalem in 1099 were lethally mixed. If they were moved to the reconversion of the city to its former status as a Christian holy place, a status it still in fact enjoyed despite the Muslims' political control, that impulse was translated at least in part into a political program on the grand scale. The new rulers were constrained not merely to conquer Jerusalem but to occupy and possess it. A new Western feudal system of sovereignty was introduced, property was redistributed, a different system of laws imposed, a novel life-style introduced, and the very demography of the city altered in a fundamental way[70]—all in a manner that was strikingly different from what normally occurred in the wake of a military victory or even a political occupation in the Near East and that bore little resemblance to the events following upon the Muslim conquest of Jerusalem in A.D. 638.

In what sense was Jerusalem a Muslim city before 1099? Seen through Crusader eyes, the answer to that question was twofold: the Muslims had political control of the city; moreover, they possessed what must at that point have been regarded in some fashion as the symbolic center of Jerusalem, the Temple mount. Though they do not appear to have been the issue, all secondary Islamic shrines and mosques were abandoned in the wake of the slaughter or flight of the Muslim population and the Crusaders' initial prohibition of either Jews' or Muslims' living within the city. The conversion of those same mosques into churches does not seem to have been a major Crusader concern, however, particularly since they were few in number and not in any event threatening to the new Christian population from either an architectural or an ideological point of view.

The Haram was a different matter, of course, as the Umayyad builders intended it to be, and the Crusaders moved immediately to effect the religious transfer of what they pleased to call the "House of the Lord" (*Templum Domini*), namely, the Dome of the Rock, and the "House of Solomon" (*Templum Solomonis*), known to the Muslims as the al-Aqsa mosque. The first, obviously identified as the site of the former Temple, was converted into a church and the rock itself covered with a marble pavement and an altar placed upon it; Augustinian canons were appointed as the church's clergy and installed in monastic lodgings built on the esplanade of the Dome.[71] The Aqsa, which the Crusaders must have thought of, perhaps correctly, as on or near the site of Solomon's earlier palace, was at first intended as the palace of the Latin kings of Jerusalem, a piece of royal bravado that Herod would surely have envied, but then, after the establishment of the Order of Templars in 1118, it was given over to them as a church and residence. They built additional quarters for supplies and arms in the sanctuary to thc west of the converted mosque and used space under the southeast corner of the Herodian platform to stable their horses.[72] The king meanwhile took up more natural quarters in the western citadel compound.

That was one part of the Crusader program; the other was equally predictable: the reconstruction and enlargement of the original Christian holy place, the Anastasis, already much altered from Constantine's original since it had been twice destroyed (by the Persians in 614 and the Fatimid Caliph al-Hakim in 1009) and twice reconstructed (first by the Patriarch Modestus [d. 634] and then by the Byzantine Emperor Constantine IX Monomachus in 1048).[73] The Latin reconstruction proceeded very slowly indeed, and the church was finally reconsecrated only in July 1149, on the fiftieth anniversary of the Crusader conquest of the city. And in another deeply symbolic gesture, the Latin patriarch took over its ecclesiastical administration from the now departed Greek metropolitan.

We have graphic descriptions of the Salah al-Din's reappropriation of the Jerusalem Haram in 1187.[74] When the city fell some of the Muslim troops spontaneously scrambled to the top of the Dome and removed the golden cross that crowned the Crusaders' *Templum Domini*. Then on the sultan's own orders the Aqsa and the Dome were stripped clean of their Christian trappings. The wall that the Templars had constructed across the *mihrab* in the Aqsa was removed, and the prayer niche was expensively relined with marble. Lecterns with precious Qur'ans were set out in the mosque, and new carpets were laid down. Though the city had fallen on a Friday, the first official congregational prayer was postponed for a week, and in the interval a fierce competition developed as to who would be honored by preaching the first Friday sermon in the restored al-Aqsa; the sultan himself chose a Damascus divine to deliver the discourse.

The Dome of the Rock was likewise purged. The Christian reliefs and decor were removed. The marble slabs the Crusaders had extended over the rock were also stripped away, and it became immediately apparent that the priests there had been chipping away parts of the stone and presumably selling the pieces as relics to Christian pilgrims.[75] Finally, there was a debate as to what should be done to the Christians' primary holy place at the Anastasis. Some contended that the Church of the Holy Sepulcher should be destroyed, but the majority, who perhaps better understood the nature of holy places, argued that it would do no good; the Christians would still visit the site. In the end Salah al-Din agreed to let it stand, just as the apocryphal 'Umar was reported to have done when the Muslims had first taken the city.

4. THE MECCAN *HARAM*

When and at whose hands did the Muslim sanctuary originate? The question, already posed by Dozy in a critical sense more than a century ago,[76] is likely a vain one since we are asking in effect when Mecca became holy and why, and there is as little ground for a response to that question at Mecca as there is at other primitive cult sites. Rusafa, as we have seen, *became* holy because of the presence of the bones of a Christian saint, a historically dated Christian saint, at that site. But when and why Baalbek or Palmyra or Mecca acquired its reputation for holiness we cannot say with any degree of confidence. We can conjecture that, as at Palmyra, it was the presence in that otherwise arid place of a water source, the Zamzam, that rendered Mecca a holy place in the first instance.[77]

For later generations of devotees it was not, however, the Zamzam that had the primacy of place in the sanctity of Mecca; it was rather the cubical building, the Ka'ba, the "House of the God," which stood in its midst, that constituted the chief shrine of the city. We need not, of course, accept that as the original reason Mecca was deemed holy—a building after all is a *construction,* a man-made shrine marking or commemorating some other, more fundamental presence—but we must at least attempt to address the origins of the particular cult associated with it.

If we inquire of the extant Muslim sources the origins of the Ka'ba and, more generally, of the cult practices associated with

Mecca in historical times, we are faced with a great many different kinds of information. The second sura of the Qur'an tells us that Abraham and Ishmael built the Ka'ba and established the rituals connected with it—the latter preserved faithfully by Islam—at God's command. Around this central core the later Muslim tradition has erected (1) a cosmological theory connecting the building and the site variously with a celestial prototype and, in the manner of Jerusalem, with different theories about the navel of the earth; (2) a large body of midrash concerning the earlier history of the building between Adam and Abraham; (3) a number of sometimes coherent and sometimes conflicting local traditions that attempt to connect the Biblical history of Mecca—that is, its Abrahamic and Ishmaelite phase—with what was recalled about the settlement from earlier, purely Arab traditions, (how, for example, the city and the shrine eventually came into the hands of the Quraysh); and finally (4) a fairly consecutive narrative, available in both Meccan chroniclers like Azraqi and Islam's more catholic historians like Tabari, on the structural changes undergone by the building and the site after the establishment of Islam.

To begin where the Muslim begins, with the Qur'an, it is God Himself speaking here in the second sura:

> And after God made trial of Abraham with his commands, He said: "Behold, I have appointed you a leader of the people." Abraham said: "And what of my offspring?" God said: "My covenant does not include evil-doers."
>
> And We made the House a place of assembly for the people and a secure place, saying: "Take as your prayer-place the Station of Abraham [*maqam Ibrahim*]." And We placed an obligation upon Abraham and Ishmael: "Purify my House for those who make the *tawaf* around it and those who take thought of it and those who make prostration and bow down in worship."
>
> And when Abraham said: "Lord, make this land secure and give fruits to its people, so many as believe in God and the Last Day," He answered: "As for the unbeliever, I shall leave him in peace for a short while, then I shall force him into the doom of the Fire, a sad end."
>
> And when Abraham, together with Ishmael, was raising the foundations of the House, Abraham prayed: "You indeed are the Heeder, the Knower." (124–27)

This is straighforward, if somewhat obscure, and indeed the exact historical context of some of these verses, which apparently refer to the Meccan *haram* of Muhammad's own day, were soon lost to his followers. The later commentators of the Qur'an, for example, had little idea of what a "place of assembly" (*mathaba*) was or of its connection with the pre-Islamic *haram;* nor did they understand where or what was the "Station of Abraham," since verse 125 appears on the face of it to refer to the entire *haram* area by that name, while a quite specific place of that name continued to be shown *within* in the *haram.*[78]

Neither the cosmological nor the midrashic history of Mecca is germane to our purposes here,[79] but the Meccan local tradition supplies, as has been noted, additional details on both the construction history of the Ka'ba and the political situation at Mecca after Abraham.[80] Thus Ishmael, the putative ancestor of the Arabs, could not control the sanctuary that he and his father had founded. He was constrained by circumstances to marry the daughter of a local Jurhumite—that is, a non-Arab—chieftain. She bore him twelve sons, one of whom, Nabit, succeeded his father as lord of Mecca.[81] But very briefly:

> God multiplied the offspring of Ishmael in Mecca and their uncles from the Jurhum were rulers of the temple and judges in Mecca. The sons of Ishmael did not dispute their authority because of their ties of kindred and their respect for the sanctuary lest there should be quarrelling or fighting therein. When Mecca became too confined for the sons of Ishmael they spread abroad in the land, and whenever they had to fight a people, God gave them the victory through their religion and they subdued them.[82]

It was under the Jurhum and their successors, the Banu Khuza'a, that paganism was introduced into the sanctuary, a displacement of the Abrahamic cult that infected the sons of Ishmael as well, though with a careful distinction:

> They say that the beginning of stone worship among the sons of Ishmael was when Mecca became too small for them and they wanted more room in the country. Everyone who left the town took with him a stone from the sacred area to do honor to it. Wherever they settled they set it up and walked around it as they went round the Ka'ba. This led them to worship what stones they pleased and those which made an impres-

sion on them. Thus as generations passed they forgot their primitive faith and adopted another religion for that of Abraham and Ishmael. They worshipped idols and adopted the same errors as the people before them. Yet they held fast to practices going back to the time of Abraham, such as honoring the temple and going round it, the great and the little pilgrimage, and the standing of Arafat and Muzdalifa, sacrificing the victims, and the pilgrim cry at the great and little pilgrimage, while introducing elements which had no place in the religion of Abraham.[83]

Ibn Ishaq, the biographer of Muhammad, likewise gives us a portrait of pre-Islamic paganism in Mecca and environs:

. . . Quraysh had an idol by a well in the middle of the Ka'ba called Hubal. And they adopted Isaf [or Asaf] and Na'ila by the place of Zamzam sacrificing beside them. They were a man and woman of Jurhum . . . who were guilty of sexual relations in the Ka'ba and so God transformed them into two stones . . . Every household had an idol in their house which they used to worship. When a man was about to set off on a journey, he would rub himself against it as he was about to ride off; indeed, that was the last thing he did before his journey; and when he returned from his journey, the first thing he did was to rub himself against it before he went into his family.

Now along with the Ka'ba the Arabs had adopted *tawaghit*,[84] which were temples which they venerated as they venerated the Ka'ba. They had their guardians and overseers and they used to make offerings to them as they did to the Ka'ba and to circumambulate them and sacrifice at them. Yet they recognized the superiority of the Ka'ba because it was the temple and shrine of Abraham the Friend of God . . . Quraysh and the Banu Kinana had al-'Uzza in Nakhla, its guardians and over seers were the Banu Shayban of Sulaym, allies of the Banu Hashim . . . Their practice when they sacrificed there was to divide the victim among the worshippers present. Ghabghab was (the name of) the slaughter place where the blood was poured out.[85]

All of this—the Ka'ba, the black stone embedded in its side, the circumambulation of the sanctuary, the names of the pagan deities, and even the *ghabghab*, the place of the ritual slaughter, is rich material for the historian of comparative religion. For example, much that went on at Mecca by way of cult is highly redolent of either the Jewish cult tradition or a set of religious and cult perceptions in which the Jews likewise shared. The first assumption, that the cult at Mecca was specifically Jewish, founders somewhat on our inability to explain how or when Jews should have been present in Mecca when no mention is made of that fact in either the Arab or the Jewish sources.[86] There were, on the other hand, Jews at Medina before Islam, as all our Arabic sources testify, and it is not implausible that whatever routes and circumstances brought them there could also have carried them to Mecca.[87] It seems, moreover, increasingly certain that the notion of the Abrahamic origins put forward in the Qur'an was a familiar one to the still pagan Quraysh, as were the biblical stories to which the Qur'an so often *alludes* without actually *telling* them.

The second hypothesis, that we have to do at Mecca with cult notions drawn from the same Semitic matrix from which the Jews derived their own perceptions and practices, has had a long and distinguished line of advocates from the time of Robertson Smith (1894) and Wellhausen (1897). It is surely, misgivings about positing such a thing as a "Semitic religion" aside, easier to defend. But even granted the truth of this hypothesis, we are still left with the specific and explicit connection of Abraham with Mecca and the familiarity of the Qur'an with the literary goods of the biblical Israelites. It is no longer convincing to say, as once was commonly held,[88] that the Abrahamic connection was "invented" by Muhammad as a riposte to his rejection by the Jews of Medina after his emigration there, since the references unmistakably occur well before the Prophet had any connection with Medina or its Jews.[89]

Muhammad was, then by his own account, a prophetic reformer who had been sent to restore rites first established by Abraham and corrupted over the centuries by usurpers at the *haram*. But there was an almost immediate crisis of conscience when Muhammand undertook to include the two pilgrimages called the *hajj* and the *'umra* among the licit rituals; the earliest converts must have understood, as we certainly do, that those same pilgrimages were among the legacy of paganism.

The second sura of the Qur'an addresses that question:

> And behold, al-Safa and al-Marwa are God's tokens, and whosoever makes the *hajj* of the House and makes the *'umra* does not incline

toward evil because he makes the turning (*tawaf*) in them; and whoever complies, it is good. (158)

As is clear from this verse and from the passage in Muhammad's biography already cited, the cult earlier said to have been established by Abraham in connection with the Meccan House, as the Prophet called the Ka'ba, did not remain in its pristine state but had by Muhammad's day lapsed into idolatry and so was understood as a pagan ritual by the Qur'an's somewhat puzzled audience. Thus the question implicit in 2:158 "How can a Muslim perform what are pagan rites at what is a pagan shrine?" The answer has already been supplied: the Ka'ba was not a pagan shrine and the *hajj* and the *'umra* were not pagan rituals since the House had been built by Abraham at God's command and the pilgrimage rites were his promulgation.[90]

While we can make no firm judgment on the Qur'an's version of the remote origins of the Meccan *haram* and the building that stood in its midst on the basis of what the Arab sources tell us, it is possible to track some of the pagan practices that may be inferred from 2:158 in another direction. The *haram* or *hawta*, its rituals, privileges, and taboos, all constituted an important *social* and *economic* institution in the settlements that possessed them. And in the case of pre-Islamic Mecca, it was the dominant institution.[91] This earlier notion of an Arabain *haram* must be kept separate from its later "enshrined" version that Muslims knew at Mecca. The *haram* was not originally an urban institution at all—witness the frequent prohibitions against hunting within its limits—and Mecca had just such a territorial "enclosure." According to the chroniclers, Muhammad redefined this sacred territory, or rather restored Abraham's original boundaries to it, once he had gained political control over Mecca. Thus the limits stood at 1½ hours of journeying outward along the Medina road, 3½ hours outward on the Yemen road, 5½ hours on the Ta'if road, 3½ and 5 hours out along the Iraq and Jedda routes respectively.[92] This constituted the sacred territory of Mecca, and it was these places at which the pilgrim donned his ritual attire and beyond which, at a somewhat later date, the non-Muslim was forbidden to advance toward the Holy City.

We do not know how this circumscription first occurred at

Mecca, but at Medina we can watch the actual creation of a *haram*. The city known originally as Yathrib was still in mid-synoikism at the time of Muhammad's arrival there in 622. Indeed, we can observe its final stage in the document known as the Constitution of Medina and preserved in the Prophet's *Life*,[93] as well as in the later traditions wherein Muhammad does not negotiate but creates the Medina *haram* by his own Prophetic authority.[94] The Meccan *haram*, on the other hand, had been in existence, in both the wider and the narrower sense, long enough to have become fully institutionalized by Muhammad's day, and the recollection of his community was soon colored by rapid architectural conversion of the "*haram* shrine," the *masjid al-haram* immediately around the Ka'ba, into a formal urban sanctuary.

If we restrict our attention to the *haram* and the Ka'ba as urban phenomena, we may at least make some pertinent historical observations on the basis of the traditions about pre-Islamic Mecca and its shrine. If, for example, it is true that the rise of Mecca to whatever prominence it enjoyed before Muhammad was the result of the integration of commercial, political, and religious factors, then it is likewise true that the progress of urbanization that followed upon this success effected substantial changes upon the *haram*, while the Ka'ba, on the other hand, became the focus of a considerably more successful resistance to those same urban pressures.

Whatever first made Mecca holy, it is clear that the *definition* of its sanctity, the *haram* that was Mecca's *temenos*, embraced at the time of Muhammad, and had for some time before him, a variety of holy objects and holy sites. In addition to the building called the Ka'ba, there was the black stone embedded in its side; the Zamzam well; the *hijr*, a low semicircular wall that stood off one of the faces of the Ka'ba; the "Station of Abraham," now described as another stone, now as a particular site, and even on occasion equated with the entire *haram;* the pillar of the Ka'ba and the cave of the Ka'ba; and a great many idols thought to have been of more recent origin and removed by Muhammad.[95] There was no certitude about many of these features in the decades after the Prophet, and it took more than a few generations to get this potpourri of Meccan sanctity sorted out.

Some of what was found in the *haram* may have been the result of a deliberate synoikism—the name 'Amr ibn Lu'ayy occurs rather often in the sources as a promoter of this ingathering of sacred objects—and some doubtless stood in the midst of the Meccan *haram* for as long as there was such. But to the extent that Mecca took commercial profit from this pilgrimage-integrated collection of sacred sites and objects, to that same extent did the *haram* contract in upon itself. The pre-Islamic *haram* known to Muhammad at Mecca was not an imposing place; it was little more than a clearing really, with the Ka'ba in its midst, and marked off only by the exterior walls of the houses of the Meccan merchants that huddled closely around it and entered by the alleyways between them. It was not until the early Muslim rulers of Mecca, particularly 'Umar (A.D. 634–44) and 'Uthman (A.D. 644–56) forced back this encroachment by buying out the private owners who held land immediately around the Ka'ba and began the construction of a proper enclosure that the pressure was retarded, if not entirely dissipated.[96]

Once established, this frame around the *haram* became in effect its face, to be enlarged, enhanced, and bedizened with the wealth of empire. 'Abd al-Malik began the construction of the roofed galleries separating the *haram* from the growing city around it, and his son al-Walid took in hand their mosaic decoration; the same two rulers were responsible for the completion of the primary constructions on the Jerusalem *haram*.

In contrast to this increasing monumentalization of the facade-frame of the *haram*, a process that continues to the present day, the Ka'ba within it underwent remarkably little change, perhaps because the issue of whether it was to be glorified as a monument or preserved as a relic arose and was resolved early in Islamic history. The first historical building project concerning the Ka'ba occurred in Muhammad's own lifetime, and he helped with the work. Azraqi dates it to A.D. 605, when a flood had destroyed the building. At the same time, we are told, an Egyptian ship was wrecked on the nearest shore of the Red Sea, and it was out of the timbers of this wreck that the new Ka'ba was in fact constructed. More, among the survivors was a Coptic craftsman named Pachomius who directed the construction of the timber roof—like David's and Solomon's Israelites, the Meccans would have had little experience of building anything as urban as a timber roof[97]—and, somewhat more startlingly, decorated the interior with images, including one of Abraham and another of the Madonna and Child.[98]

If this might appear an innovation—though perhaps only in the light of somewhat later Islamic attitudes toward figurative art—there was no trifling with the Abrahamic foundations themselves: when the Quraysh attempted to dig these up there was a blinding light and all Mecca shook. The Quraysh wisely desisted in the light of this divine warning that God wished to dwell where Abraham had first built a house for Him.

If this event of 605 guaranted the permanence of the site, the form of the building arose as an issue—and was settled—some three quarters of a century later in the circumstances surrounding the insurrection of ʿAbdullah Ibn al-Zubayr.[99] This scion of one of the old companions of the Prophet rose up against the new dynasty of the Umayyads in 682 and declared his own sovereignty in Mecca. The Umayyad Caliph Yazid sent out a punitive force against him from Syria, and in the course of the siege of the Holy City that followed the Kaʿba took fire from incendiary missiles and was almost entirely consumed in flame.

The siege, begun in 683, broke off after two months at the news of the death of Yazid, and Ibn al-Zubayr resolved to use the respite to rebuild the Kaʿba. There was some opposition to this project, particularly to Ibn al-Zubayr's declared intention of returning the Kaʿba to its original Abrahamic condition, which, we now learn, the Quraysh had altered. A Prophetic tradition was adduced in evidence, to wit, that Muhammad had told his wife A'isha that he himself had contemplated the destruction of the preserved building and its reconstruction along Abrahamic lines, joining it to the *hijr* behind and opening two doors into it, both at ground level. So Ibn al-Zubayr prevailed, and he apparently rebuilt the Kaʿba in just that manner. The two doors were installed at ground level—the present Kaʿba has one at about the height of a man—but it would be interesting to know just how the Kaʿba was joined to the semi-circular *hijr*, which hovers at one wall like a disconnected apse; rejoined, the two would have indeed seemed like a small basilical church.[100]

The Umayyads eventually returned to the matter of Ibn al-Zubayr. He was chased from Mecca, and when the Syrian commander reported what had been done to the Ka'ba to the new Caliph 'Abd al-Malik (A.D. 685–705), the latter ordered that the innovative structure be torn down and the *Bayt Allah* be rebuilt as it had been when Muhammad—and the Quraysh—had worshiped there.

This was the end of the struggle for architectural orthodoxy at Mecca. The sense prevailed that the building reared by the Quraysh in 605 was—the alleged Prophetic tradition notwithstanding—authentically Abrahamic and so should remain. And so it has. A long succession of Muslim rulers of very different sectarian persuasions have had the opportunity of enlarging, monumentalizing, or even entirely redesigning the Ka'ba, but none has availed himself of the opportunity. The Ka'ba as it stands in Mecca today is still essentially the building that 'Abd al-Malik had restored to its Quraysh prototype.

This profoundly antiquarian attitude toward the Ka'ba stands in sharp contrast to what was being done to the surrounding *haram* by those same rulers. 'Umar and 'Uthman had begun its enlargement, as we have seen, and 'Abd al-Malik adorned it somewhat in the same manner as he had the Dome of the Rock in Jerusalem. This process of enlargement and adornment of the *haram* continued under the next dynasty until the 'Abbasid Caliph al-Mahdi extended its area in 777 and again in 781, at which point the *haram* nearly reached its nineteenth-century dimensions.[101] The *haram* was now surrounded by a high wall into which were let twenty-three gates; within were arched and columned porticos inscribed with appropriate verses from the Qur'an, the Prophetic traditions, and, of course, references to the royal builder.

This project was, like all such enlargements and adornments at Mecca, an expensive one. Not only had skilled labor to be imported, but the building materials themselves were brought in from abroad. If a ruler intended to use something other than the local stone, for example, marble or limestone had to be shipped in from Egypt or Syria, usually by boat to the port of Jedda, then dragged inland to Mecca.[102]

The extension of the *haram* at the expense of earlier private properties that were already crowding in upon it in pre-Islamic days was met with another wave of pressure from without the perimeter. The conversion of the *haram* and the Ka'ba to Muslim shrines made Mecca a prime object for investment for a new aristocracy of Muslims. Properties around the *haram* may not have realized large monetary profits—merely keeping them in repair would have entailed a considerable expense—but they reaped, in the manner of holy places, an incalculable reward in visibility and prestige.

The first to have fully understood this may have been the Caliph Mu'awiya (A.D. 661–80), the son of a Meccan merchant prince and the founder of the Umayyad dynasty. We have already seen his work and that of his dynastic successors at Jerusalem. Jerusalem was in a sense *their* city, a new Muslim enterprise where the Umayyads had no competitors and no rivals. In Mecca the situation was quite different, as we have aleady seen in the insurrection of Ibn al-Zubayr. But the Umayyads were also scions of that city, descendants of the Quraysh's commercial aristocracy. And if they cultivated the shrine, as 'Abd al-Malik certainly did, they were likewise aware of Mecca's other past as a city. Mu'awiya, in addition to buying up a great number of houses and other commercial properties in the city, invested heavily in agricultural development in the hinterland, perhaps the first and last to have done so.[103] A later member of the house, Sulayman, was among the first to address himself to the problem of the city's water supply.[104]

It was doubtless the infusion of investment capital, in addition to the Umayyads' somewhat worldly attitudes toward life and empire, that gave the Mecca of those days the somewhat unlikely (though not without parallel in other holy cities) reputation as a place where a life of ease and pleasure might be pursued by the young, the idle, or the wealthy. True, much of this reputation derives from Umayyad court poets, who may have been somewhat given to exaggeration on the score of wine, women, and song,[105] but the more sober chroniclers report that the Umayyad governor had finally to restore at least a semblance of propriety to the shrine by segregating the sexes when they performed their devotions in the *haram*.[106]

With the next turn of political fortunes in Islam the ʿAbbasids replaced the Umayyads. They could not hope to outdo their predecessors in Jerusalem, which they largely ignored, but Mecca, with its aura of legitimacy, which resonated nicely with the ʿAbbasids' own ʿAlid and legitimist pretensions, was more to their liking. The early ʿAbbasid caliphs from Mansur to Harun al-Rashid beat a continuous path of pilgrimage from Iraq to Mecca—Mansur made the *hajj* on seven different occasions, Harun on nine—and invested heavily and often in the shrine's beautification. More, they established their own sumptuous domiciles around the *haram*.

Up to the time of Harun visiting caliphs stayed at the Quraysh's old assembly hall of the *Dar al-Nadwa*, which Muʿawiya had bought for a large sum from its private owner. Harun built his own residence, with annexes for the crown princes, on the northern side of the *haram*. His wife Zubayda had her own palace on the western side, and the queen mother Khayzuran, another generous benefactor of Mecca's holy places, also lived in the vicinity. The caliph's chief vizieral family, the Barmacids, likewise established residences in the city.[107]

These palatial dwellings were not easy to maintain. Princes and courtiers came and went, and even in the most stable of times the houses were not permanently occupied. The material fabric of the buildings deteriorated quickly and badly in the face of fires, floods, and local encroachment. Meccan magnates and officials, the heirs to privileged function connected with the *haram* and the *hajj*, jostled for position in the same space. To overlook the Kaʿba itself was obviously the most favored position in all of Islam, and the wealthy and the powerful succeeded year after year to these coveted sites.

Enthusiasm for a second residence in Mecca must have diminished somewhat in the tenth century with the accession of the Ismaʿili Fatimids in Egypt and the spread across the steppe of the more fanatical Ismaʿili Qarmatians from Bahrayn. The latter invaded Mecca in 929, slaughtered pilgrims and inhabitants alike, plundered the city and carried off the black stone of the Kaʿba to their own redoubt. The stone was returned twenty-two years later when even the Qarmatians understood that no profit would come of such a hostage.[108] The restoration brought no relief, however; for decades thereafter Mecca, its inhabitants, and pilgrims were in a state of almost perpetual siege.

In the twelfth century all the lands from Iran to Egypt returned to Sunni sovereignty, and the new Sunni pietists who now controlled the destiny of the *Dar al-Islam* began to construct around the *haram* not palaces but new, institutional buildings, law schools and Sufi hospices, that effectively ended the private ownership of this precious real estate. We shall see more of this type of institutional investment in both Mecca and Jerusalem, but in neither place did the founders solve the problem of maintenance or assuage the desire of others to possess property of their own on the margin of the *haram*.

Between the twelfth and the sixteenth centuries the bulk of investment in Mecca went into these educational and religious institutions, but the advent of a new dynasty to leadership of the Muslim community, the Ottoman Turks, brought a new draught of investment to Mecca. New dynasties, like recent converts, required a public display of their piety toward the legitimate tradition, and the Ottomans took the fastest and shortest, though not necessarily the least expensive, road to it: they poured money into Mecca, not now into law schools and convents but into the *haram* itself, and particularly the *temenos* structure that surrounded and enclosed the sacred space. Between 1572 and 1577 Selim II took in hand a major and thorough reconstruction of the surrounding wall, gates, arches, and porticos, all in a quite lavish style,[109] and this structure remained in effect the face of the Meccan *haram* until the Saudis began their own investment in the Holy City.[110]

The primary shrines of both Muslim Mecca and Muslim Jerusalem were defined early on in the career of Islam: at Jerusalem the platform reached its present dimensions at least by the time of ‘Abd al-Malik at the end of the seventh century, and in Mecca the space around the Ka‘ba was effectively canonized by the reign of al-Mahdi. In neither Mecca nor Jerusalem was there any attempt or even inclination on the part of the Muslims to extend the holy of holies onto new terrain, and subsequent benefactors of the two holy cities contented themselves, as we shall see, with the enshrinement and adornment of secondary locations, the overwhelming number of them within the sanctuary itself or along its immediate edges. The Christians, on the other hand, had no such self-imposed restrictions in their holy city: they were free to roam Jerusalem, and indeed all of Palestine, in search of new shrines. Constantine, as it turned out, was merely the initiator of the Christian sacralization of Jerusalem that went on, in fits and starts, down to the sixteenth century and beyond.[111]

NOTES

1. Josephus, *Ant.* XV, 380–425; *BJ* I, 401–02.
2. 1 Kings 8 (the transfer of the Ark and the dedication services); 1 Kings 7:1–12 (the palace complex).
3. Ezra 4–5.
4. Hag. 2:3
5. Josephus, *BJ* I, 400, and for a contemporary assessment of his motives: Netzer et al. in Levine 1981: 48–80.
6. Levine 1981: 64 and n. 3
7. Though not perhaps Herod's own palace. Here Herod chose to follow the example of the Hasmoneans rather than Solomon: he built his palace at a safe distance from the Temple, up on the Hellenized western hill, where its impressive remains are still visible beneath a corner of the Citadel and the nearby garden of the Armenian Patriarchate: Tushingham 1968.
8. Josephus, *Ant.* XV, 400; M. Middoth 2:1; on the dimensions of the present Haram: Golvin 1971: 25.
9. The chief modern proponent of a reduced Herodian platform is Father Bellarmino Bagatti of the Franciscan Biblical Institute in Jerusalem; see Bagatti 1965, 1979 and Vogt 1974. The critical issue here is of course the presence of traces of the Herodian platform corners at the northern end of the present Haram, and the evidence for that seems to be doubtful at best.
10. On the cosmology: Schürer 1973: 292 n. 12.
11. Hollis 1934; Vincent 1954.
12. Some of the rabbinical traditions are collected in Vilnay 1973: 78 ff., and cf. Schürer 1973: 308 n. 71.
13. The meager evidence for the survival of the Jewish Temple cult is reviewed by Clark 1960 and Guttann 1967. For the Christian recollection of Herod's Temple, crossed here too with biblical nostalgia for Solomon's building, see Ferber 1976.
14. Epiphanius, *On Weights and Measures* 54C; Dio, *Roman History* LXIX, 12.
15. On the portrait of Hadrian's Jerusalem temple on coins, Price and Trell 1977: figs. 311–12.
16. *Ep.* 58, 3; cf. Wilkinson 1981: 165 and 324 ad loc. For the archeological evidence that Jerome was correct and that Hadrian's temple to Jupiter Capitolinus is better located on the forum in the Upper City, Corbo 1982: 1, 33–38.
17. Text in Wilkinson 1981: 151 and n. 4 and 321 ad loc.
18. Mark 13:2; Matt. 27:2.
19. Text in Wilkinson 1981: 156–57. When the Piacenza pilgrim visited the city about 570, the "stone rejected by the builders" was shown to him on Mount Sion; Wilkinson

1981: 83, 22.

20. On the indirect evidence for this, Schürer 1973: 535–36.

21. Sozomen, *HE* V, 22; Theodoret, *HR* III, 20. On this entire complex episode: Avi-Yonah 1976: 191–204. The rock, noted by the Bordeaux pilgrim in 333, could not have been first discovered on this latter occasion, of course, but it may very well have been further cleared.

22. M. Yoma 5:2.

23. Even if we put aside or solve the problem of the dimensions of the Herodian platform (see n. 9 above), the placement of the presently situated rock under the Ark and so the Holy of Holies would present serious site problems, at least as far as the Temple of Herod is concerned, by pushing the entire structure too far to the east of the platform. It is somewhat easier, again on purely architectural grounds, to imagine the present rock at or under the great altar in the Court of the Priests; see Avi-Yonah in Yadin 1976: 13.

24. The legends, which come to a kind of canonical form in the mystical Spanish *Zohar,* are assembled in Vilnay 1973: 1–16, and in the following pages are seamlessly associated with the Muslim legends around the *sakhra*.

25. Pesiqta Rabbati 47 Braude 1968: 2, 804.

26. Much of this section of chapter 4 has appeared as "Who Built the Dome of the Rock?" *Graeco–Arabica* 2 (1983), 119–38. On the problem of the "rock," see, for example, Schmidt 1933, Vogt 1974, and Donner 1977 among a great many others.

27. Wilkinson 1977: 83, 18.

28. Wilkinson 1977: 83, 17.

29. Corbett 1952: 7–8; on the possible transformation of "Beautiful" to "Golden," see Finegan 1969: 130.

30. Creswell 1969: I/2, 465.

31. On this period: Avi-Yonah 1976: 232–65.

32. Ibid.: 265–70.

33. On the date: Frolow 1953, and cf. Conybeare 1910 and Baynes 1912. When Arculf visited the East ca. 670, what appear to have been the main sections of the Cross were not in Jerusalem but in Constantinople: Wilkinson 1977: 113–14.

34. Creswell 1969: I/2, 465. There are, moreover, detailed descriptions of the emperor's triumphal entry into Constantinople, a ceremony that took as its traditional point of departure the "Golden Gate" of that city: Stratos 1968: 240–245, and on the Constantinopolitan Golden Gate, ibid.: 398.

35. Procopius, *On Buildings* V, 7, 5–7; on the church, Krautheimer 1965: 116 with plan.

36. Something similar had certainly taken place at Golgotha sometime after 614 when the Christians began to connect the cave beneath Golgotha, already noted by Arculf (Wilkinson 1977: 97, 2) as some kind of memorial chapel, with the tomb of Adam; cf. Bagatti and Testa 1978: 62.

37. I owe a good deal of this intriguing hypothesis, though none of its deficiencies of expression or argument, which are completely my own, to Mr. Meir Ben-Dov of the Israel Department of Antiquities. For his own views in his own words, see Ben-Dov 1982.

38. For this and the subsequent career of the Jerusalem Temple in Muslim religious art and literature, Soucek 1976.

39. On Sayf, Wellhausen 1899: 6–7; Hill 1971: 26–27; Noth 1973: 19–23.

40. This becomes apparent when the differing accounts are displayed side by side, as they are in Hill 1971.

41. On the unlikeliness of 'Umar's visit: Noth 1973: 161–62; and for the terms: Fattal 1958: 45–47. One of the later "descendents" of what Sayf maintained was a written and

sworn document is the so-called Covenant of 'Umar, which has even less claim to authenticity: ibid.: 60–69.

42. The various versions are collected in Le Strange 1890: 134–44.

43. Lewis 1974: 199. This and another apocalyptic Jewish text presented in Lewis 1950 (see n. 49 below) are interpreted in a far more radical fashion in Crone and Cook 1977: 4–9.

44. Mann 1920–22: 1, 44–47.

45. Wilkinson 1977: 95, 14; cf. Creswell 1969: I/1, 32–34.

46. The earliest results are reported by Ben-Dov in Mazar 1969 and 1971 and most recently in Ben-Dov 1982: 293–322.

47. Guidi 1903–07: 77.

48. Lewis 1950: 324–25, and for the identification of the first reference as Mu'awiya, ibid.: 328. Lewis thinks the time referred to was not Mu'awiya's caliphate but his governorship of Jerusalem.

49. Muslim travelers' descriptions in Le Strange 1890: 57–137 and modern analysis in Creswell 1969: I/1, 65–131 (the Dome), and Hamilton 1949 (the Aqsa).

50. For its place in the evolutionary history of this type of building, Sauvaget 1947: 93–121.

51. Text of Ya'qubi II, 311 in Le Strange 1890: 116 and Marmadji 1951: 210, and its canonical reception in Goldziher 1969–1971: 2, 44–45.

52. Goitein 1966: 135–38; Grabar 1973: 49–50.

53. Kister 1969.

54. The connection of Mu'awiya with the Dome of the Rock is entirely circumstantial: the possibility that as early as 628 or 630 Heraclius had already intended some such building as part of a Temple mount complex that also included the renewal of the Golden and the Huldah Gates; the length of time that it would have taken to restore or rebuild the Haram complex to bring it to its present Muslim state (cf. Goitein 1980: 324–25), particularly if the Herodian platform was smaller than is generally supposed (see n. 9 above); and the prevalence of traditions, none of them normative, to be sure, linking that ruler to the city in some intimate fashion. Cf. Crone and Cook 1977: 11–12.

55. For what follows, though not necessarily the conclusions drawn from it, Grabar 1973: 52–67.

56. Though the message of the Dome seems to be directed toward the Anastasis, the Muslim building gives no sign of having been modeled on the Christian one across the Tyropean Valley. Constantine's rotunda over the Sepulcher was clearly *oriented,* that is, the face of the building, which was embellished with a large columned porch (see the model in Wilkinson 1978: fig. 133), gives entrance to the front of the tomb within. Further, the top of the Anastasis dome was pierced with a prominent *oculus* opening to the sky. The *Qubbat al-Sakhra,* on the other hand, is a perfectly symmetrical, unoriented building with a closed dome, to say nothing of the fact that it is not a tomb at all.

57. Grabar has pointed out (1973: 50–52) the oddness of having a *qubba* commemorating Muhammad's ascension next to the Dome of the Rock if that latter building was supposed to commemorate the same event . And on the same score, it is equally odd that the mosque nearby and not the Dome should be called al-Aqsa. On Abraham as the first *muslim*: Qur'an 2: 130–135, 3:67. And on the Dome of the Ascension: Le Strange 1890: 170.

58. The parallel should not be pushed too far. The Christian was not limited to merely associating the two; he could even synthesize them by the current typological reading of Scripture whereby Adam foreshadowed Jesus and was his "type." The Muslims connected the cult through site and not exegesis. Thus the standard exegesis of sura 17:1, which is

on full display in Zamakhshari, for example (Gätje 1976: 74–77), usually does not invoke Abraham.

59. Burgoyne 1976: nos. 4–6 (the 'Abbasid *qanatir*); 55, 56, (the northern *qanatir*) and 48 (the western *riwaq*); cf. Drory 1981: 198–99, and for a complete survey of the Haram area, Golvin 1971: 23–31.

60. *Life of Constantine* III, 28 and 33. It may have been Eusebius' idea, put forward for his own somewhat political motives, to explore the Abrahamic connection, not in Jerusalem but in Hebron, by suggesting that it was not an angel but Jesus who manifested himself to Abraham at the oak of Mamre: *Life:* III, 51, and see Rubin 1982: 88–89. It did not at any rate become the standard exegesis of Gen. 18–19.

61. *Life of Constantine* III, 26. In Jerome's version, written sixty-odd years after Eusebius' time, there was a Hadrianic shrine to Jupiter over the place of the tomb and a sanctuary of Venus at the place of the crucifixion (*Letter* 58; *To Paulina* 3), a description that squares with the admittedly difficult archeological evidence reported by Corbo 1982: 1, 33–38.

62. For the forum, Eusebius, *Life* III, 35. The late evidence of the *Paschal Chronicle* 613 puts a *trikameron* in Hadrian's Jerusalem, possibly a triple-vaulted Capitolium, as well as a *kodra*, or square (*quadra*), which may refer to the empty Temple platform, though the author of the report locates neither building; cf. Vincent and Abel 1914–26: 6–18, and the reconstruction of the building complex on the forum offered in Wilkinson 1978: figs. 125–32.

63. Eusebius, *HE* IV, 5. Eusebius had heard that there was in Jerusalem a "great church built by the Jews" that survived until Hadrian's war in A.D. 135: *Demonstratio Evangelica* III, 5.

64. So Eusebius in his *Life of Constantine* III, 25–43, but Epiphanius, *Panarion* 30, 4–12 adds another motive: the dissemination of Christianity, particularly in the still deeply Jewish Galilee; cf. Avi-Yonah 1976: 165–74.

65. Ovadiah 1970: nos. 22a, 65a (Golgotha-Anastasis), and 74a–b (Imbomon).

66. Krauheimer 1965: 38.

67. Ibid.: 18–20.

68. A number of such liturgical calendars are collated and their sites defined in Milik 1960.

69. Thus the two principal Christian festivals celebrated in pre-Islamic Jerusalem were Easter and the Encaenia, the latter the day that marked the anniversary of the dedication of the Anastasis on September 13, 335 and connected as well with Helena's *inventio* of the True Cross; cf. Beck 1959: 261, 262; Black 1954; and Wilkinson 1981: 79–80.

70. Prawer 1972: 34 ff. and 1980; Holmes 1977.

71. Vincent and Abel 1914–26: 969–73; cf. Le Strange 1890: 134.

72. Le Strange 1890: 108–09, 166.

73. Harvey 1935; Coüasnon 1974; Corbo 1982; and for al-Hakim's firing of the Anastasis, Canard 1965.

74. Gabrieli 1969: 144–46 (Ibn al-Athir), 164–75 (Imad al-Din).

75. We have no confirmation of this from the Christian side, but there is little reason to doubt it. Witness this scene described by one of the participants, Daniel, the Russian monk who was visiting the Holy Sepulcher in 1106–07:

> I prostrated myself before the tomb and covered with tears and kisses the place where the pure body of Our Lord Jesus Christ had lain. Then I measured the length and width and height of the tomb as it is presently, an act no one can do when there are people about. I honored the Guardian as much as was in my power and offered, as my means permitted, my small and poor gift. When he saw my devotion to the Holy Sepulcher, the Guardian pushed back the stone that covered the tomb at the place where the

head would have been, broke off a piece of the sacred stone and gave it to me as a blessing, adjuring me not to mention it to anyone in Jerusalem. (Khitrowo 1889: 81–82)

76. Dozy 1864: 15.

77. So already Snouck Hurgronje 1886: 5.

78. On the classical exegesis of this passage, Gätje 1976: 100–02 and Hawting 1982: 30.

79. For a sampling of this material, see Gaudefroy-Demombynes 1923: 30–31.

80. Azraqi 1858: 307 ff.; Qutb al-Din 1857: 23–72, chiefly from Azraqi.

81. Tabari I: 1131.

82. Ibn Ishaq 1955: 45–46.

83. Ibn Ishaq 1955: 35–36.

84. See Fahd 1968: 240.

85. Ibid.: 37–38.

86. Dozy, who was the first to make this case, summed up his own thesis as follows:

1. The Meccan holy place was founded at the time of David, and by the tribe of Simeon. These Simeonites were the so-called Ishmaelites, and were also known to the Arabs as the "first Jurhum." 2. The Meccan rituals were established by these same people. The civil enmity that followed can be clarified from Israelite history; and so too many terms by which these rites were described have a Hebraic origin. 3. In the Babylonian Jews came to Mecca after their release from exile . . . These are the people called by the Arabs the "second Jurhum." (Dozy 1864: 15–16)

87. The present state of our knowledge on the pre-Islamic Jews of Medina is resumed in Gil 1984.

88. Beginning with Snouck Hurgronje's *Het Mekkaansche Feest,* published in 1880; cf. Hawting 1982: 27.

89. The evidence is convincingly collected in Rahman 1976.

90. Cf. Qur'an 2:27 and 3:97.

91. Wolf 1951: 337–39; Serjeant 1962: 55.

92. Wuestenfeld 1861: 113.

93. Ibn Ishaq 1955: 231–33; cf. Serjeant 1962: 48–50.

94. *Mishkat al-Masabih* XI (The *Hajj*), 16.

95. Kister 1971 has studied the traditions concerning the "Station of Abraham" and Hawting 1982 a number of the other religious presences in the *haram.*

96. Wuestenfeld 1861: 121–22.

97. The Umayyads used Christian craftsmen for much the same reason on their constructions in Jerusalem, and when 'Abd al-Malik, the same caliph who completed the Dome of the Rock in Jerusalem, wished to make repairs on the *haram,* he despatched a Christian architect to Mecca to supervise the work; Wuestenfeld 1861: 147.

98. Azraqi 1858: 105–09. According to the same source, when later Muhammad took Mecca from the pagan Quraysh, he ordered all the graven images, including Abraham's, destroyed, but he allowed that of Mary and the Christ Child to remain within the Ka'ba, which it did until the building was destroyed in the siege of 683.

99. Azraqi 1858: 140–43

100. A possibility that has prompted one scholar (Lueling 1977) to speculate that the original form and function of the Ka'ba was a Christian church.

101. Wuestenfeld 1861: 162–64; Snouck Hurgronje 1888: 12. There were minor extensions under Mu'tadid in 894 and Muqtadir in 918.

102. Wuestenfeld 1861: 162, 164, and, for the supply of timber from Lebanon or even India, ibid.: 265. The enormous expense this entailed may be seen from the fact that the order for the Ikhmimic marble, which al-Mahdi planned to use in his reconstruction of 781, was replaced, at the caliph's death, by local stone covered with plaster; ibid.: 163.

103. Kister 1972: 84–90, who lists them in detail from the sources.

104. Wuestenfeld 1861: 152.

105. So, for example, *Kitab al-Aghani* XXI: 97, and cf. Mas'udi, *Muruj* IV: 254–55.

106. Wuestenfeld 1861: 148. There are reports of similar goings on at the dome in Jerusalem; see Peters 1985: 496–98. Another infusion of capital in connection with al-Mahdi's rebuilding project in 771 led to similar results, and in 778 or 779 the caliph had to address an open letter to the Meccans accusing them of permitting the city to become notorious for singers, gambling, high prices, and unfair weights and measures. Text in Wuestenfeld 1861: 164–70.

107. Wuestenfeld 1861: 175, 180–81.

108. Wuestenfeld 1861: 212–13.

109. Qutb al-Din 1857: 283–90; cf. Wuestenfeld 1861: 316–21.

110. Snouck Hurgronje, who lived in Mecca in 1884–85, looked upon Selim's still impressive porticos around the primitive Ka'ba and was moved to reflect what mordant irony upon the two so different buildings: "So entstand allmählich um die rohe Ka'ba, welche Muhammad noch als genügend für Allah und seine aus dem armsten Lande der Welt zusammenströmenden Gäste betrachtete, ein Tempel für den civilisierten Gott des späteren Islams." (Snouck Hurgronje 1888: 16).

111. The newest of Jerusalem's Christian holy places, the so called Garden Tomb in the northern outskirts of the Old City, has little claim to authenticity as the site of Jesus' burial, but it does respond far more directly than the present dark and incense-filled Church of the Holy Sepulcher to what some Christian sensibilities would prefer the tomb to look like. "Discovered" in 1883 by the imaginative General Gordon, the Garden Tomb has survived and flourished to the present, and the Israeli authorities, who may be as troubled by the Chruch of the Holy Sepulcher as some Baptists and Presbyterians, though on quite different grounds, have plans to improve the area by removing a nearby bus depot. The early history of the Garden Tomb is traced in Silberman 1982: 152–53.

CHAPTER V

Secondary Shrines

The holiness of the central place, the chief shrine, inevitably extends itself over the city. This extended sacralization, taken in conjunction with the pragmatic reality that the pilgrim will spend some time in the city, leads to a multiplication of secondary shrines *in the city and its environs.*

Some cities are merely that, urban centers where men and women work and pray and recreate and reside; others are ideas as well. "O Roma Nobilis" rolls like an anthem across the centuries of Christian Europe, and the content within and the echoes without the name "Athens" embrace far more than the layout of streets, the mass of buildings or even the few people who lived in that place in the fifth century B.C. Jerusalem is another such name and place, a city and an idea

When the physical city called Jerusalem had its absolute beginnings is obscure and of little importance to our present purpose. But the idea that grew up around it, and eventually possessed the city, we can observe slowly taking shape in the Bible. The biblical praise of Jerusalem begins with the national hero David—for a time the city even appears to have borne his name, "City of David"—and not the builder Solomon, and so there is from the start of the Jewish tradition about Jerusalem a palpable political emphasis that both transcends and overshadows the holy place that Solomon and Zerubbabel and Herod each enhanced in turn. Jerusalem and Judah and Israel, land and people, were all bound together in an indissoluble union: the glory of one was the glory of all; the fall of one was the woe of all.

This is no more than patriotism of place perhaps, pride in the nation focussed on the political and religious capital of the people. But that was by no means the end of it, that national enshrinement on the order of a Paris or a Moscow; the prophets of

Israel would go even further. In Jeremiah, for example, it is not the Ark or the Temple but the city itself that is the seat and throne of God, and the theme is repeated and expanded throughout the post-Exilic literature of Jews. Then, with the destruction of the Temple, the holy city takes wing into another dimension. The apotheosis of Jerusalem is spread across the pages of the apocrypha, such as 2 Baruch and 4 Ezra; it is repeated in the benedictions of the synagogue prayers; it is meditated by the rabbis: Jerusalem is a heavenly city, a spiritual and eternal prototype of this earthly place.[1]

It was perhaps this translation of Jerusalem onto a spiritual and conceptual plane that enabled the Jews to survive the total destruction of the nation's capital and cult center in A.D. 70; it must explain as well our own hesitation between asserting that Jewish Jerusalem has only one holy place or that for the Jews all of Jerusalem was holy. Both are likely true. For the seven hundred years between Josiah, the king of Israel, and Titus, its Roman conqueror, sacrifice to the God of Israel could be offered only on the Temple mount in Jerusalem, no matter where the worshipper lived; and by the end of that period many of the laws of purity, and so of holiness, had been extended over the entire city and even beyond, to the whole Land of Israel.[2]

Both Muslim and Christian Jerusalem stand in sharp contrast to this Jewish regard born of both nationalism and an almost physical fear of ritual defilement. Islamic Jerusalem had in fact only one holy place because the early Muslims had no political or historical associations with the city in their reading of the pre-Islamic past: for all its biblical resonances, the Muslim connection with Jerusalem began with Muhammad, or perhaps more realistically, when the city fell to them in A.D. 638. With far less passion David had once taken Jebusite Jerusalem, but unlike the Israelites, the occupying Muslims had no David or Solomon to move both crown and altar into their new possession. For the Christians, on the other hand, all of Jerusalem was holy, not in the Jewish transcendental or ritual sense, however, but simply because the primary associations of the life and death of Jesus, miracle and memory, were scattered wholesale across the city.

Whether or not this more generalized analysis is correct, there is no evidence for secondary religious shrines in Second Temple Jerusalem. There were tombs, some quite costly and impressive, round about the city's limits, but they appear to reflect no more than the normal desire of the rich and the powerful, some of them priests, to leave behind a prestigious monument to themselves. They were not, at any rate, the centers of any kind of discernible cult either then or later, even though there is other, more literary evidence that some kind of a tomb cultus did exist among the Jews.[3] And if there were synagogues in the city, as there seem to have been, they too appear to be normal manifestations of the type of prayer and assembly hall that was becoming common among the Jews at the turn into the Christian era and were to be found indifferently in Palestine and the Diaspora.

There is another, somewhat indirect piece of evidence for the lack of secondary shrine development in Jewish Jerusalem. After the destruction of the Temple Jewish ritual did not shift, even in some minor liturgical key, to other, secondary sites. The Temple was mourned at the Temple, first atop the mount itself, it appears, and then eventually at the western foundations of the Herodian platform, where the practice has continued into modern times. Otherwise the Jews of the post–A.D.70 era worshipped at home or, their faces turned toward Jerusalem as their *qibla,* as Muhammad himself had once done, in community synagogues, wherever they chanced to be.

There is one interesting exception to the conversion of Jewish Temple liturgy into synagogue rituals that could, like the Christians' own version of the Temple sacrifice, be celebrated anywhere. As we have seen, Jews continued to journey to Jerusalem after the destruction of the Temple for occasional visits—to mourn on the Ninth of Ab, for example, whenever political conditions permitted. Those conditions took a decided turn for the better at the Muslim conquest of the city, and thereafter there was a permanent and important Jewish congregation in the city and numbers of Diaspora Jews who came to visit it

One can imagine many grounds for such visits, pious remembrance, legal affairs—after 638 the gaon, the chief legal authority of the "western" Jewish Diaspora, resided in Jerusalem—and even business, but only one was connected with a ritual unique to the city. In a practice that seems to have begun after the Muslim occupation, the Jews of Jerusalem—and pilgrims to the city—assembled on the seventh day of Succoth, or the Feast of Tabernacles, the day called Hoshana Rabba, and in public procession performed a sevenfold "turning" round about the gates of the Haram and then ascended singing to the top of the Mount of Olives to view the site of the Temple and to hold what became the annual legal and legislative assembly of the Jewish congregation in Palestine.[4]

Though copies of the Torah may be enshrined within them, synagogues themselves are not normally regarded as shrines, and in fact there was some opposition to the degree of Torah enshrinement that went on *within* some synagogues.[5] But history and politics can create their own holy places in a religious society. Thus the medieval synagogues of Jerusalem, the oldest extant example of which dates from the time of the French scholar Nachmanides who came to Jerusalem in 1267, have become in effect Jewish secondary shrines since the Israeli occupation of the Old City in 1967. The remains of those buildings were, so to speak, architectural confessors and martyrs in something approaching the Christian understanding of those terms: confessors in their attestation of a continuous Jewish presence in the city during a long Muslim interregnum; martyrs by the fact of their wholesale destruction, from what were perceived to be religious motives, in the years between 1948 and 1967. And like their earlier Christian analogues, the Ramban synagogue, the Ashkenazi Hurva next to it, and the nearby Sephardic complex named after Yohanan ben Zakkai are all presently the objects of a new enshrinement as secondary Jewish holy places within the Old City.[6]

There is no one to protest the relatively modest enshrinement of Jerusalem's medieval synagogues, but just to the east of them stands another "hallowed place" that better illustrates the spread of holiness, its collision with other, different claims to the sacred and its very modern competition with a new rival, secular nationalism. The remains of Herod's Temple platform have been the displaced locus of Jewish cult in Jerusalem since the first Christian century and services have been held at one or another place in its vicinity throughout the past and down into modern times. Indeed, there is some evidence to suggest that in the tenth century, though for how long before or after we cannot say, there was a synagogue in a cave or chamber high *within* the western wall of Herod's Temple platform.[7] But even if this suggestion is correct, none of the brief and scattered references to the site make any mention of what is today, and has been in a verifiable fashion from the sixteenth century onward, the chief site of Jewish public cultus in the Holy City in that same vicinity, the celebrated "Western Wall." This latter is a stretch of massive Herodian stonework on the same western side of his Temple platform, which ran, until 1967, for about ninety feet southward from the Gate of the Chain Street to the Maghrebi Gate entry to the Haram, and was connected by a later generation of Jews with a far older tradition that God's presence, in Hebrew his *Shekina*, would never leave the Western Wall.

The tradition occurs in its earliest form in those collections of biblical exegesis known as the "Midrash Rabbah," in that on the Song of Songs, for example, from the seventh or eighth century, where it is said, in reflection on the verse (2:9) "There he stands outside our wall": "Behold, He (God) stands behind our wall, that is, behind the western wall of the Temple, which the Holy One, blessed be He, swore would never be destroyed . . ." Or again in "Exodus Rabbah" of the tenth century, where a certain Rabbi Aha is reported to have said: "The Presence of God never leaves the Western Wall."

Two of the exegetical works that make up the "Midrash Rabbah"—that on Lamentations, from about the fifth century, and that on Ecclesiastes, from perhaps the seventh—give extended, identical, and obviously legendary accounts of why the wall in question was not destroyed:

> When he [Vespasian] conquered Jerusalem, he divided its four walls among four commanders, and it was Pengar who got the western gate [*pyle*] . . . and from heaven they decreed that it should not be destroyed. Why? Because the Presence of God is in the west . . . They [that is, the other three commanders] destroyed the sections that had been assigned to them, but he [Pengar] did not destroy his. Vespasian sent for him and said to him: "Why did you not destroy your section?"

He answered: "By your life! I did it for the glory of the empire, because had I destroyed it, nobody would ever have known what you destroyed. Now, people will see and say, 'Look at Vespasian's power! What a strong city he has destroyed!'" . . .

The story is a transparent retelling of an incident related by Josephus (*BJ* VII, 1, 1–2) whereby Titus did in fact exempt from destruction part of the western side of the city, the three Herodian towers that made up the citadel, to impress future generations with his power. What this seventh century retelling cannot mean, of course, is that the emperor or one of his commanders left one of the Temple walls standing, which they did not, or that they destroyed three sides of the Herodian platform and spared the fourth; the platform base they left completely intact, as far as we can tell. The tradents of Midrash Rabbah knew this perfectly well, and so we can only assume that God's continued presence was a spiritual one and was not precisely localized by them or by anyone else of those generations immediately preceding and following the rise of Islam. The assumption appears to be confirmed by most of the evidence we have at hand until the sixteenth century. When the Jews made public prayer in Muslim Jerusalem, they generally made it atop or around the Mount of Olives, or at the eastern gate of the Haram which was called by them and by the Muslims the Gate of Mercy and by the Christians the Golden Gate.

With the Ottoman occupation of Jerusalem something must have changed, though we are not sure what or why. Two stories were told by a later generation, one about 1730 by Moses Hagiz concerning Selim, the Ottoman conqueror of the city, and the other by Eliezer Nahman Poa of Suleiman, the sultan who built its still-standing walls. In both cases it was the Turkish ruler who was said to have cleared the filth and refuse from around the present site of the Western Wall and, at least by implication, first permitted the Jews to pray there. Whatever the case, Jewish visitors from the early sixteenth century on describe what is unmistakably the western wall of Herod's Temple platform and connect it with the earlier tradition of the "Presence of God." Thus in 1658 the Karaite Moses Yerushalmi could write:

Now, everybody knows that one wall and one wall only is left from the Temple, and that we must weep and keen for the destruction of the Temple [there]; this wall is called the Western Wall . . . Near the Western Wall the Arabs built a house of prayer and surrounded it with a wall, and the Western Wall is also within the [same] wall so that nobody [presumably Christians] may enter. But the Jews are allowed to go there, and they pay a tax of 10 *paras*. The Jews of Jerusalem pay the tax for the whole year and may go there as often as they wish. But you must approach from the outside and not from the inside [that is, from the Haram] for great sanctity rests on the Western Wall, the original sanctity which attached to it then and forever more.[8]

The most complete medieval description of both the site and the wall comes, however, from the gifted observer Gedaliah in the opening years of the eighteenth century:

The Western Wall which remains from the Temple is very long and high. For most of its height it is very ancient and the stones are very large. Some stones are five or six cubits wide and the same is true of their height. But I do not know how thick they are; if I could see them at the end of the Wall I could tell, but a courtyard has been built actually against one [that is, the southern] end of the [exposed section of the] Wall and at the other [northern end] stands the house of an Ishmaelite judge . . . The Ishmaelites have added to the height of this ancient Wall with new building until it has become very high; in these new walls are also gates to go in and out through them. Only Ishmaelites are permitted to enter the site of the Temple, but not Jews and other peoples unless, God forbid, they convert to Islam. Because they [the Muslims] say that no other religion is worthy enough to enter this holy site. Although God had originally chosen the Jews, because they sinned He deserted them and chose the Ishmaelites. Thus they speak continuously.

We go to the wall to pray, we are actually standing "behind our wall" [Cant. 2:9], close by it. On the eve of the New Moon and on the 9th of Ab and other fasts [the Jews] go there to pray and, though the women weep bitterly, nobody objects. Even though the Ishmaelite judge lives close by and hears the weeping, he does not object or rebuke them at all. Occasionally a young Arab comes to annoy the Jews but they give him a small coin and he goes off. If a dignified Ishmaelite or Arab witnesses such impudence, he severely reprimands the child.

The Temple site is far from the streets the Jews live in, and we have to go through markets and other streets to get to the Western Wall. Prayer is generally more desirable by the Wall.[9]

The focus of such services at the base of the western wall of the Temple platform is thus two or three centuries old, and in Ottoman times had become so traditional that it was construed as a privilege, with the usual safeguards and the just as usual limitations that such religious privileges carry with them. By the end of the nineteenth century it had become a fairly serious source of contention among the Muslims and Jews of Jerusalem and the rulers of them both, first the Ottomans and then the British.[10]

Since 1967 the Western Wall has been in Jewish hands and this transfer of sovereignty was accompanied by a dynamic extension of the holiness of the site in a number of new directions: outward toward the west, once a Muslim residential quarter and now bulldozed into a spacious plaza, part of which has been reserved as the liturgical "space" for the Wall and appropriately marked as a *haram;* and southward along the precinct wall, under a Muslim *madrasa* and the Haram gate known as the Bab al-Silsila, around and past a series of ancient constructions that have been well known, if little understood, since their rediscovery in the nineteenth century by the British engineer Charles Wilson. "Wilson's Arch" and its associated tunnels far below the Haram gate are an important piece of archeological and so "secular" evidence for the Jewish city during Second Temple and perhaps even earlier times, and, one might guess, for the Umayyad reworking of the Herodian platform.

Holiness spreads more quickly than science, it appears, and shortly after its expropriation in 1967, the "Wilson's Arch" complex was converted into a synagogue, an act that effectively forestalled the "secular" archeologists of the Israeli Department of Antiquities but gave what seemed like a free hand to the equally interested excavators of holy places in the Ministry of Religious Affairs. More, it initiated the downward passage of quite another, Muslim form of holiness from the religious buildings overhead. Today only the sound of prayer emerges from under "Wilson's Arch," however, since rabbinical digging proved in the end to be equally intolerable to both the Israeli government and the Muslim guardians of the Haram.[11] But the point has nonetheless been made: the site, which once had no religious significance whatsoever, has been sacralized by occupation and use.

Constantine had acted little differently in his day, and the pagan inhabitants of fourth century Jerusalem were probably astonished to discover that something surpassingly holy lay under their forum in the Upper City, and perhaps only somewhat less so when the emperor tore down the temple of Jupiter Capitolinus there and put up a mausoleum and basilica in its stead. There were Christians in the city who remembered those and other evangelical sites, of courses, and their connection with their Risen Savior; both before and after the emperor's work Christian piety was making its own identifications and establishing its own cults.[12] Many of these other sites were connected with other events of Jesus' own life, whether recorded in the Gospels or simply remembered by the local tradition, or with the life of his mother or John the Baptist; others were connected to the earliest generation of Christians and were occasionally accompanied by an *inventio*, the miraculous discovery of the saint's physical remains, which then constituted the church eventually built over them a true martyrium

One of the most celebrated of these discoveries took place in A.D. 415, when the remains of the Christian protomartyr Stephen (Acts 6:8–7:58) were uncovered at Kafr Gamla outside the walls of Jerusalem. The *inventio* came about through the only somewhat unlikely agency of Gamaliel, the temperate rabbi of Acts 5:34–39, who appeared in a dream to the parish priest Lucian and revealed to him not only the site of his own burial but those of Nicodemus and Stephen as well. The story spread quickly over the whole Christian world in ecumenical Greek, Latin, and Syriac versions, and by 451 the Empress Eudocia had built a basilica over the place of the saint's martyrdom.[13]

Eudocia's role in the story is altogether typical. Though many of the churches in and around Jerusalem were constructed from benefactions of wealthy laymen and a surprising number of the clergy, the largest and best known of the ecclesiastical buildings were imperially inspired and financed.[14] Constantine, Theodosius, Eudocia (who lived in retirement in Jerusalem between 443 and 460 and also endowed her new home with the practical gift of a wall), Zeno, and Justinian all invested heavily in the holy city, inevitably inspired by motives situated in that well-known but not easily defined neighborhood where piety and politics pray together in holy cities. But with objectives different from those of the first of the imperial benefactors. Constantine's Jerusalem was a Jesus-centered though still a Roman city: a Christian basilica stood precisely where the Capitolium had, on the edge of the forum in the heart of Hadrian's Roman Aelia. By the sixth century, however, Jerusalem was a Church-oriented city that had in some degree moved back to its ecclesiastical origins on Mount Sion.

Sion, as the Christians quite mistakenly came to call Jerusalem's southwestern hill—the original Sion, like the City of David that grew up by it, was on the eastern spur projecting south of the Temple mount—was within the walls of Herod's city and it was there, the Christian tradition recalled, that Jesus had celebrated the Last Supper with his disciples. And it was there too that the followers of the crucified Messiah had gathered to await the descent of the Holy Spirit, the Pentecostal event that marked the birthday of the Christian Church. The tradition is early: Eusebius knew of it; Cyril preaching in Jerusalem about 348 makes reference to an "Upper Church of the Apostles" on Mount Sion; and Egeria in 370 received instruction on the entire range of traditions connected with the place.[15] Our earliest pilgrim source, the pious visitor from Bordeaux who was in the Holy City in 333, supplies an additional interesting detail: there were once on Sion, the new Christian "Sion," seven synagogues, of which only one remained.[16] The seven synagogues reappear in the account of Epiphanius, who connects them with Titus' destruction of the city in 70:

> He [Hadrian] went to Palestine, which is called Judea, forty-seven years after its destruction, and came to the famous and illustrious city of Jerusalem which Titus, the son of Vespasian, had overthrown in the second year of his reign. And he found the whole city levelled to the ground and the Temple of the God utterly destroyed. All that survived were a few houses and the church of the God which was small and which had been set up in the place to which the disciples had returned after the Savior had been taken up from the Mount of Olives and where

they had gone up into the Upper Room. It had been built there, that is, in the part of Sion that had escaped the destruction [of the city], the section of the residential quarter in the vicinity of Sion and the seven synagogues which alone remained standing on Sion, like solitary huts, one of which survived until the time of Maximus the bishop [A.D. 331–49] and the Emperor Constantine, "like a booth in a vineyard," as it says in Scripture.[17]

What may have occurred, then, was that parts of the Jewish quarter of Mount Sion, together with its synagogues, survived the debacle of A.D. 70. Among them too was a house-church of the Christians. It received no particular attention, none from Constantine certainly since neither the Bordeaux pilgrim nor Eusebius, both of whom knew of the Christian traditions of Sion, make any mention of a church on the hill. But ten years after Eusebius wrote there was a church on Sion, Cyril's "Upper Church of the Apostles," and by the time Egeria arrived the church on Sion had been integrated into the Holy Week liturgy.[18] By then Mount Sion no longer stood within the city, however. Titus had razed the earlier wall, and when Hadrian reconstructed the city in the second century, he built its southern wall along the line of the present Turkish wall, and Sion stood southward outside it.[19]

But it did not remain there. In the mid-fifth century Eudocia rebuilt the older, more encompassing southern wall and Mount Sion and its ecclesiastical dependencies once again stood within Jerusalem. The gesture was not so much intended to promote development as to acknowledge it: on the basis of pilgrims' reports and the somewhat later Madaba map, Mount Sion had by then all the appearances of an important Christian complex, with a large church, monastic establishments and a number of sites identified not only with Jesus' last days in Jerusalem but with his mother and James, the "brother of the Lord" and the first head of the Christian community in Jerusalem.[20]

Though ignored by Constantine, the later growth of the establishments on Sion and the presence there of a large basilica—on the Madaba map it is portrayed on the same scale as the Nea of Justinian and larger than the Holy Sepulcher—gives reason to think that investment, imperial investment, was being made in that southern suburb of Jerusalem, and the motives may have had more to do with ecclesiastical politics than with the belated discovery of holy places. The fifth century was a period of both contest and controversy for Jerusalem. The contest was for Church primacy with Caesarea Maritima, which since Herod's day had been the political and administrative capital of Palestine, and though visible in the fourth century, at Nicea, for example, and possibly in Eusebius as well, the contest was not finally resolved in Jerusalem's favor until the accession of the energetic and ambitious Patriarch Juvenal.[21]

Jerusalem had a strong claim to hegemony in its splendid churches, its vigorous monastic life and the antiquity of its liturgy.[22] And in that liturgy in the fifth century appeared what may have been the most persuasive claim of all: there was in Jerusalem the congregation that could boast of being "the mother of all the churches," and it was to be found not at the Anastasis but on the summit of Mount Sion, whose remarkable fifth-century development can hardly be unconnected with Juvenal's aggressive promotion of his See.[23]

The climax of the Byzantine shift of emphasis toward Mount Sion and the southern quarter of the city was the construction of the most monumental of all of Jerusalem's churches, the Theotokos or the New Church of the Mother of God which was dedicated by Justinian in 543 and whose construction was described in awed terms by the emperor's architectural biographer Procopius.[24] On the Madaba map it sits massively upon the southern end of the main Byzantine north-south avenue, just inside Hadrian's old and now otiose city gate and before the ascent to Sion and the shrines there.[25] Today it is no more than an immense buried corpse: the church, Jerusalem's largest, and paradoxically unconnected with any holy place, was destroyed by an earthquake, possibly in A.D. 746, and never rebuilt.[26]

Why was the *Nea*, or "New Church," built in the first place? The original idea was not that of Justinian but of Elias, an earlier patriarch of Jerusalem, and when Elias went into exile and was unable to complete it, the monk Sabas came up from Jerusalem to Constantinople and prevailed upon the emperor to interest himself in the project.[27] None of that information comes from

Procopius, who is otherwise so generous in detail but in this connection makes only a passing reference to the emperor's "pious faith" as the motive for the construction of the Theotokos. But the name itself may provide some clue. Theotokos, "Mother of God," was a theological slogan through most of the fifth and sixth centuries, a defiant statement thrown in the teeth of Nestorians who emphasized the human nature of Jesus and so could not accept the bald paradox represented by the title "Mother of God."[28]

Justinian passed his entire reign (527–65) caught up in that controversy, and he had no more faithful allies than the monks of Palestine, the same who brought the project to the emperor's.[29] In 533 Justinian had published his own formal profession of faith addressed precisely to Jerusalem. In it he affirmed his belief in a Jesus Christ who "became incarnate from the Holy Spirit and Mary, the holy glorious Ever-Virgin and Theotokos . . . ," and ten years later he reaffirmed it in the Nea.[30] The emperor's enormous cathedral, which commemorated no known holy place, was more likely a shrine to a theological idea, a thesis in stone that passed away far more quickly than the shrine-tomb of a rural saint.

Justinian was, with the possible though not very certain exception of Heraclius, the last great Christian builder in Jerusalem until the Crusades. The Persian invasion and occupation of 614 devastated its Christian holy places, and whatever construction went on under Christian auspices in Jerusalem in the thirties of the seventh century could not have been much more than an attempt to pick up and reassemble the fragments of a glorious past. And yet, if we look to Arculf, who visited the city in the last quarter of the seventh century, after four decades of Muslim occupation, we have no sense of a city in either ruin or oblivion.[31] The Christian holy places of an earlier day were still being venerated in an open manner, though neither we nor Arculf can say how closely the churches and shrines he visited resembled their fourth- to sixth-century prototypes.

Nor are the earliest Muslim reporters on Jerusalem of much assistance in measuring the impact of either the Persian or indeed the Arab occupation of the Christians' holy city. Beginning with one of the earliest of their number, al-Mas'udi (ca. 943), the Church of the Holy Sepulcher receives consistent notice, though almost always with the snide play of *al-Qumamah*, "Dung," for *al-Qiyamah*, "Resurrection," which no medieval Muslim author seemed able to resist, and there are occasional brief asides on the buildings on Olivet or Sion, both of which places eventually became objects of Muslim veneration as well, Sion as the site of the tomb of David and the Mount of Olives for exactly the same reason the Christians prayed there, as the site of Jesus' ascension into heaven.

Muslims too believed that Jesus had been taken up into heaven, one day to return, so they had on the Mount of Olives none of the theological difficulties posed to them by what the Christians alleged as the burial place of the "Prophet Jesus," whom the Qur'an (4: 157–58) quite clearly asserted had not suffered death on the cross. As for Sion, a pre-Christian Jewish tradition located the tomb of David in Jerusalem,[32] but the Christians would apparently not have it so and at first the burial place of the Messianic progenitor was shown to pilgrims in various places near Bethlehem, Jesus' own birthplace. This was still being done in Islamic times, by Arculf in 670, for example. But since the Christians also identified their "Sion" with the historical city of David, the additional connection had also to be made, if not at first by the Jews, then certainly by the Christians, at least by the tenth or eleventh century when the site on Sion is mentioned in an anonymous "Life of Constantine," and Muqaddasi writing in 985 notes it as a tradition of the "People of the Book" that the Tomb of David is on Sion."[33] The Crusaders certainly thought so when they took the city.

It is from the time of the Crusades that our first circumstantial account of the tomb comes, from the pen of Benjamin of Tudela, a Jewish traveler who was in Jerusalem about 1170.

On Mount Sion are the sepulchers of the House of David, and the sepulchers of the kings who ruled after him. The exact place cannot be identified, inasmuch as fifteen years ago a wall of the church of Mount Sion fell in. The Patriarch commanded the overseer to take the stones of the old walls and restore therewith the church . . . [Two workmen discover a cave and in it is the golden crown and scepter of David and

Solomon and other kings.] . . . So the men rushed forth in terror and they came unto the Patriarch and related these things to him. Thereupon the Patriarch sent for Rabbi Abraham el-Constantini, the pious recluse, who was one of *mourners of Jerusalem*, and to him he related all these things according to the report of the two men who had come forth. Then Rabbi Abraham replied, "These are the sepulchers of the House of David; they belong to the kings of Judah, and on the morrow let us enter, you and I and these men, and find out what is there." And on the morrow they sent for the two men and found each of them lying on his bed in terror, and the men said, "We will not enter there, for the Lord doth not desire to show it to any man." Then the Patriarch gave orders that the place be closed up and hidden from the sight of man unto this day. These things were told to me by the said Rabbi Abraham.[34]

The Crusaders paid no particular attention to the site of David's tomb on Sion and Christian visitors from abroad do not mention it among the holy places on Sion. But once back in Muslim hands after 1187, the Davidic affiliations probably revived, and by the fifteenth century the tomb was already the object of the controversy vaguely foreshadowed in Benjamin's text, but now embracing the Muslims as well. In 1429 the Jews of Jerusalem purchased from the sultan of Egypt "una certa capella situata nel Monte Sion e posseduta e officiata dai nostri frati [i.e., the Franciscans] ove sta il sepolcro del profeta David et d'altri Regi . . .", an act never quite forgotten or forgiven by the Western Christians, and thereafter the tomb site on Sion changed hands a number of times until 1452 when the Muslims took it as their own.[35]

With the Muslims now in full possession of their own holy place on Sion, commemorated by a mosque, the new question could be raised whether the Christian ritual in the church above constituted a defilement of the place. This time the question went as far as Jerusalem's new ruler, the Ottoman sultan in Istanbul, and he ruled against the Christians. In 1524 the Franciscans were expelled from the Cenacle and twenty-five years later were forced to give up all their minor shrines on Sion.[36]

Beyond these sites there is not much other comment on the numerous Christian holy places by the Muslim visitors to the city,[37] though the ones they do mention are treated, the drearily predictable *al-Qumamah* aside, with respectful reserve or at least with dispassion. As we might expect from visitors to what was to them a vividly exotic and often a palpably hostile environment, Christian visitors from the West, who seem to have been undeterred by the disastrous outcome of the Crusades,[38] have left far more lively and colorful impressions of the Holy Land. From their memoires Muslim Jerusalem of the late Middle Ages appears filled with places of Christian veneration, more, certainly, than we were aware of in the sixth or even the eleventh century. The Crusaders themselves had a great deal to do with this obvious proliferation of secondary shrines since they invested heavily in church construction during their brief occupation of the city.[39]

But those were major sites. The astonishing growth of minor shrines may in fact have had more to do with the Latin Church's practice, already mentioned, of attaching specific indulgences to visits to specific sites in the Holy Land. The precision of the indulgences may have been due to the punctilious lawyers and accountants of the Roman Curia, but the exact topographical situation of the events, real or legendary, associated in Jerusalem with the life of Jesus, his family and his disciples, certainly reflects the Crusaders' residence in and familiarity with the Holy City.

By the thirteenth century most of those sites were already fixed.[40] They were found all over Palestine, of course, as had been true from the beginning, but the heart of the pilgrimage lay in Jerusalem, where the tradition of the Via Dolorosa and its chapels was established and the sites and liturgical binding that later came to be known as the "Stations of the Cross" were coming together as a ritual, though with distinct liturgical limitations. Muslim sensibilities and tradition did not permit very public display of their religious practices to the "People of the Book." For the Jerusalem Jews that inhibition had mostly to do with getting permits, often at great expense, for the construction or repair of synagogues in the Jewish quarter,[41] but for the Christians, who had potential holy places scattered all over the face of the city, and were considerably more aggressive, the Muslims' distaste of others' liturgical displays put a brake on what had been developing in Byzantine times as a devotional or liturgical circuit of the places connected with the last hours of Jesus in Jerusalem. After the Crusades some of the sites associated with this devotion were simply inaccessible to the Christians, and attempts at holding public processions on the streets between those that were often provoked acts of hostility and occasionally violence on the part of the local Muslim population.[42]

Some site identifications tended to waver and change,[43] but the climax of the entire *Christian* pilgrimage experience was and remained at the central holy place of the Holy Sepulcher, where the sites connected with the final events of Jesus' life were now enshrined within a single complex building. And if the late-blooming Jewish veneration of the "Western Wall" site is understood as selfcompensation for displacement from the Temple proper, the same is doubtless true of the multiplication of Christian shrines within the Church of the Holy Sepulcher.

The division of the Christian community into competing sects went back to the fifth century but that competition escalated sharply from the time of the Crusades when the Latins replaced the Greeks at the major sites in Jerusalem and then were replaced in turn at the Muslim reconquest of the city. Often enough the principal sites went to the highest bidder to the Muslim authorities, with the losers demoted to lesser shrines within the building. The Gospels, and particularly the apocrypha, were a rich source of incidents from the last hours of Jesus, and these events were promptly identified with places about the church and parcelled out, often foot by foot, within the sectarian subdivisions around Golgotha and Jesus' sepulcher. If the Greeks had a firm hold on the tomb itself, the Coptic, Syrian, Latin, and Armenian pilgrims could be shown another venerated, if somewhat less important, site that had the great advantage of being within the sect's own property and control within the church.[44]

In Mecca sectarian rivalry took a somewhat different form. Here the contest was not so much among sects as the four legal "schools" which among themselves divided the ritual allegiance of Sunni Muslims. The rulers of the Muslim community belonged now to this legal rite and now to another, and the accession of each new dynasty in Cairo or Istanbul was accompanied by a predictable reconstruction or enlargement of the kiosk with in the *haram* that marked the "station" where the prayer-leader of each rite led the prayers for his group.[45] And just as the latter-day Greek dominance within the Church of the Holy Sepulcher was signaled by their possession of the tomb of Jesus, so the rise to a paramount position in later Islam by the Shafi'ite school was demonstrated at Mecca by the fact that their "station" was in fact the "Station of Abraham."[46]

As for the Jerusalem Muslims, they did not venerate a great many shrines outside the *haram* area proper of the city. The "Noble Sanctuary," or *Haram al-Sharif*, dominated the religious attention of Muslim Jerusalem almost as completely as the Temple had the Jewish city, not in the same liturgical sense, however, since the Aqsa was simply a mosque, albeit a particularly holy one, and the Dome of the Rock had no liturgical function at all.[47] The Haram served rather as a magnet that drew within itself all the biblical and historical associations that the city had for Muslims. King David's prayer-niche, for example, was shown in the tower named for him near the Citadel, but it was also reputed to be located within the Haram itself.[48] Medieval Muslim authors—Christian and Jewish visitors were only rarely permitted within the precinct—give a full inventory of the secondary shrines on the Haram platform, some of them connected with the Prophet, mostly in the context of his Night Journey and Ascension, some with the life of Jesus; while others reflected the eschatological expectations that the Muslims nourished in connection with the Temple-Haram area.[49]

The Crusades made the Muslims newly aware of Jerualem as a city holy to themselves as well as to the Christians. In the era after the reconquest there appears for the first time on a large scale literary works whose sole purpose was to praise the "merits" of Jerusalem,[50] and the city's newly restored Muslim rulers invested heavily, as we shall see, in various public facilities with a distinct pious or ideological cast. There were new secondary shrines as well, particularly outside the city, though here the motive may have been as much strategic as it was devotional.

Sites associated with early or legendary prophets, which have always abounded in Palestine, have the advantage of being both highly mobile and subject to multiplication. In the era after the Crusades there newly appeared in villages just outside of Jerusalem what can only be called "shrine-settlements" dedicated to Moses and the Qur'anic prophet Salih. Their purpose was one now familiar from more contemporary exemplars at Hebron and the West Bank, security, in this case the security of the Muslim residents of Jerusalem in the face of large numbers of Christian pilgrims who still descended on the Holy City, and it seems not entirely coincidental that the feasts of the Muslim saints they celebrated fell close upon the great Christian holy days celebrated in Jerusalem.[51]

Mecca shows a very similar multiplication of secondary shrines within its sanctuary,[52] though in this instance the term *secondary* must be used with caution since a number of the sites in the immediate vicinity of the Ka'ba may also be pre-Islamic in origin and in no way derivative from the Ka'ba cultus. The Zamzam spring is one such, and the same may be true of the so-called "Station of Abraham" with its own sacred stone, and the odd fragment of wall called *al-Hijr* and associated with Ishmael.[53] Immediately outside the *haram* is still another relic of the pre-Islamic ritual pilgrimage, the *via sacra* between Safa and Marwa where the pilgrim had to run his "course."[54] And further abroad are the rites performed at Arafat and Mina, also "secondary" only in the sense that the Abrahamic associations later current among Muslims had probably been laid upon older pilgrimage traditions that remain nonetheless visible not too far beneath their Muslim veneer.[55]

What is more pertinent to our present purposes, however, is the multiplication of post-Islamic shrines in and about Mecca that have nothing to do with the original *hajj* liturgies but commemorate the Prophet himself, his family and associates, and so became for the visitor to the holy city "stations" of pious pilgrimage (*ziyara*), if not of the *hajj* proper. One of the most important was the house of the Prophet's wife Khadija, which in fact was Muhammad's own after their marriage and where his daughter Fatima and her two children Hasan and Husayn were born.[56] It was bought from a private owner by Khayzuran, the mother of the Caliph Harun al-Rashid, and she had an oratory built there.[57] The pilgrim might also visit Muhammad's own birthplace,[58] which likewise had an oratory through the beneficence of the same queen mother. The homes of the early caliphs and heroes Abu Bakr, 'Umar, 'Ali, 'Abbas or the house where Muhammad's beloved Aisha was born were also shown.[59] And around the city and in the hills nearby were other shrines to be visited, including the *qubbas* erected over the graves of Muslim saints in the Ma'la cemetery.[60]

Most if not all the *qubbas* and tombs have long since disappeared from Mecca and environs under the Wahhabis' stern disapproval of such "innovations," and many of the pan-Abrahamic shrines shared or contested by Jew, Christian and Muslim in Palestine and meticulously cataloged by Tewfiq Canaan at the beginning of this century have fallen into neglect and disrepair. But the enshrinement impulse itself is far from exhausted. Many of the early Islamic shrine-tombs built to the first heroic generation of Muslims celebrated not martyrs who had died for their faith, as their earliest Christian counterparts had, but heroes who had fought for it and had had their almost immediate triumph in the victorious spread of Islam. They were *political* saints, so to speak, and the allure of such figures, and what they represent, is always ripe for revival in new political contexts. The cultus of political sainthood has always been vital at such holy cities as Karbala and Najaf, as we have seen, and is showing increased vigor in Jerusalem and environs, where even the long disused art of hagiological divining known as the *inventio* has had a sudden revival in the search for the bones of political saints who perished in the national-religious wars against Rome, and which are then "translated," as Saint Stephen's were of old, to appropriate new shrines for the veneration of the faithful.

NOTES

1. The course of Jerusalem's transcendence is charted through the literary sources by Davies 1982: 81–91, but it has also left its mark on visual representations of the city and its Temple: Metzger 1969–71 and Rosenau 1979. In the sixteenth century the trend began to reverse itself. As Jewish immigration to Palestine increased, Eretz Israel, and with it the holy city of Jerusalem, slowly floated back to earth and into the concrete and historical present: Ben Sasson 1975.

2. See M. Kelim 1:6–8.

3. Simon 1973: 102–04 and Jeremias 1958. The line between holiness and nationalism is a thin one, and a number of Second Temple era tombs have been included, for example, in Ben Abraham Halivi's *A Modern Guide to the Jewish Holy Places* (Jerusalem, 1982), though without any particular emphasis on their sanctity.

4. Mann 1920–22: 1, 44, 63 n. 1; Goitein 1971: 201, 284–85. The circumambulation of the Haram was certainly a *tawaf* in the manner of what went on around the Ka'ba in Mecca, but it is hardly a borrowing from Islam, since circumambulation was already prescribed for that day in M. Sukka 4:5, though around the great altar of the Temple. But the Jerusalem Jews certainly saw the resemblance with the Muslim ritual, and one Jewish pilgrim expressed regret that because of illness he could not make the *hajj* to Olivet that year (Goitein 1971: 588 n. 3), while another contemporary document calls the pilgrims taking part in the rituals "hajjis" (Goitein 1974: 529).

5. Goitein 1971: 155–56.

6. Their history and plans for their restoration are sketched briefly by Netzer, Cassuto, and Tannai in Yadin 1976: 118–26. Shimon Ben-Eliezer, the late author of the popular work entitled *Destruction and Renewal: The Synagogues of the Jewish Quarter* (2nd ed.; Jerusalem, 1975), was not oblivious to the possible theological difficulty in their enshrinement and he preferred the expression "hallowed" places to the more troublesome "holy."

7. The arguments for the identification of the "cave" synagogue of the sources with the chamber in the western platform wall behind "Barclay's Gate" have been made by Gil 1982: 270–72; for the Muslim traditions connected with the place, see Matthews 1932.

8. Translated by Mordechai Naor in Ben Dov et al. 1983: 69.

9. Translated by Mordechai Naor in Ben Dov et al. 1983: 69–70.

10. Grievances over the cultus as the Wall finally came before a British Royal Commission in 1931, and its ruling shows the precise spelling out of rights that characterizes most judicial dispositions on holy places: Massignon 1951/1963: 215–18.

11. The story is told in detail in Benvenisti 1976: 277–322.

12. There is a complete listing of these secondary shrines in Vincent and Abel 1914–26. Those identifiable on the Madaba map and related documents are studied in Milik 1961, and those with extant remains are noted in Ovadiah 1970: 75–98.

13. Peeters 1950: 53–58; on the basilica. Vincent and Abel 1914–26: 766–804.

14. On the distribution of dedications in the surviving churches of Palestine, Ovadiah 1970: table 8.

15. Eusebius, *Demonstratio Evangelica* I, 14, and Cyril, *Catechesis* 16, 4, (Baldi 1955: nos. 728, 729).

16. Wilkinson 1981: 156–57.

17. Epiphanius, *On Weights and Measures* 14 (Baldi 1955: no. 733), cf. Optatus (A.D. 370), Baldi 1955: no. 731.

18. Egeria: Wilkinson 1981: 136 and 141, where she describes the building as having been "altered into a church"; cf. ibid.: 39.

19. Tsafrir 1977: 154–57.

20. For the archeological and literary evidence: Baldi 1955, nos. 736–44; Wilkinson 1977: 171–72 (Gazetteer); Milik 1961: 142–44; Tsafrir 1975; Pinkerfeld 1960; Pixner 1976; Mackowski 1980: 139–45.

21. Beck 1959: 97–98; Honigmann 1950; cf. Rubin 1982.

22. Beck 1959: 197.

23. On the "mother of all the churches" in the fifth-century liturgy of St. James, Baldi 1955: no. 738.

24. Procopius, *On Buildings* V, 6, 1–26 (Wilkinson 1977: 75); Avigad 1977.

25. Milik 1961: 145–50. Arculf's account of the churches on Sion, written about a century after the making of the Madaba map, is reproduced in Wilkinson 1977: 100.

26. For the very recent discovery and excavation of the Nea, Avigad 1983: 229–46.

27. Schwartz 1939: 175.

28. There is a brief survey of the history of the expression in Frend 1972: 1–18.

29. For the involvement of Sabas and the Palestinian monastic community in the theological disputes of the sixth century: Frend 1972: 151–52, 189–90; cf. Bacht 1953–62.

30. Justinian's profession of faith was published in *CJ* 6, 1, 1; cf. Frend 1972: 267–68.

31. Wilkinson 1977: 95–102.

32. Josephus, *BJ* I, 2, 5.

33. Wilkinson 1977: 204.

34. Benjamin of Tudela 1907: 24–25.

35. Baldi 1955: 514–520. The Franciscan Francesco Suriano saw the place in ruins in 1485 and commented bitterly:

> E la cason de questa tanta ruina forano li cani Iudei, perchè dissero alli Saraceni che sotto quella capella staeva la sepoltura de David profeta. La qual cossa intesa dal Signor Soldana, commandò che questa sepoltura e loco fosse tolto da li fratri e dedicato al culto loro, a così fo facto. (Baldi 1955: no. 780)

36. On the medieval history of the Christians on Mount Sion, Hoade 1981: 308–313.

37. The Muslim accounts of the Holy Sepulcher and other Christian holy places in Jerusalem are collected in Le Strange 1890: 202–12; cf. Harawi 1957: 66–67, and compare the Christian evidence for the churches of the Muslim city before the Crusades in Milik 1960.

38. Savage 1977: 66–67. The gross decline in Christian pilgrimage to Palestine did not occur until the Ottoman occupation of the land, and meanwhile accounts of the Holy Land continued to flow back to Europe from the travelers and pilgrims who did go there. The narratives were surveyed earlier by Tobler 1869 and Röhricht 1890 and most recently by Schur 1980.

39. Enlart 1925–28 for a complete survey of the Crusader constructions; cf. Vincent and Abel 1914–26: 945–73 for their secondary churches.

40. There is a full list in the anonymous "Pilgrims' Guide" written in 1280 and published in Michelant an Raynaud 1882: 229–36.

41. See, for example, Peters 1985: 531–33.

42. See Peters 1985a. The "Way of the Cross" did find an eventual place in Christian devotion, but it was principally in Catholic Europe where Christians were free to lay out a scheme of those same Jerusalem "stations"—sometimes in scale out of doors, more often in a highly stylized form inside churches—and perform their processions there. The indulgences connected with visiting those sites in Jerusalem were in the end transferred to their European counterparts.

43. Cf. the fourteenth-century list in Savage 1977: 55–57.

44. On the ecclesiastical geography within the church in the eighteenth century, see Peters 1985: 507–08. Some groups were too late in arriving to find *any* place. The Abyssinians had to be content with the roof of the building, whence they could *look* inside, and Protestants still take their chief form of self-compensation outside the city, at the so-called Garden Tomb; see chapter 5, n. 113.

45. Snouck Hurgronje 1888: 13.

46. Ibid.: 11.

47. Not that some did not attempt to give it one. Perlmann 1973 has published (translated by Sandra Levy in Peters 1985: 496–98) an early Ottoman complaint about the

growth of innovative liturgical practices on the Haram, and it is not the only one of its kind.

48. Harawi 1957: 66–67; Le Strange 1890: 168, 213.

49. Le Strange 1890: 151–71; cf. Matthews 1949: 18–22.

50. Sivan 1971.

51. Canaan 1927: 299–300.

52. Gaudefroy-Demombynes 1923: 71–112; Hawting 1982.

53. Gaudefroy-Demombynes 1923: 102–09; Kister 1971 (*Maqam*); Hawting 1982: 34–35 (*Hijr*).

54. Gaudefroy-Demombynes 1923: 225–34.

55. As was already apparent to the first modern investigators of the subject: Smith 1894; Wellhausen 1897.

56. Ibn Jubayr 1949–51: 114, 163 Ar./134, 189 tr.; cf. Burckhardt 1829: 171–72. Khadija's tomb was also venerated in the cemetery of the Ma'la quarter: ibid.: 172, and Harawi 1957: 204.

57. Wuestenfeld 1861: 180.

58. Ibn Jubayr 1949–51: 162–63 Ar./188–89 tr.; cf. Burckhardt 1829: 171.

59. Cf. Harawi 1957: 198–99.

60. Ibn Jubayr 1949–51: 116–17 Ar./136–37 tr.; Harawi 1957: 200–04; Burckhardt 1829: 172–76.

CHAPTER VI

Servants of the Shrine

Shrines require acolytes, from priests to offer sacrifices to sweepers to clean out the sanctuary, and these members of the primary service industries *constitute an urban group or class that has an important role in both the economic and political life of the holy city.*

The Christian priesthood descended directly from its Jewish prototype, and the author of the New Testament Letter to the Hebrews took some pains to explain both the connections and the differences between the two institutions. His argument was theological, but the similarities and the differences spill over onto the less sacred terrain of function as well. Both were the sole authorized ministers of sacrificial offerings on behalf of their communities. The Jewish priests performed this primary function only in the Jerusalem Temple; the Christians had no temple, however, or rather, they had many temples and so the Eucharistic sacrifice was offered in settings that ranged from private homes to Constantine's monumental basilicas. Again, the Jewish priesthoods were hereditary; the Christian ones, appointed. And their incomes derived from different sources, as we shall see.

It is the differences rather than the similarities between the two priestly institutions and classes that set apart Jewish and Christian Jerusalem as holy cities. From a functional point of view, the Temple was the priesthood and the priesthood the Temple. Conceptually the Temple, or at least the Holy of Holies, was a type of *Bayt Allah*, but the complex was *used* as the site, and, after Josiah, the only site, where sacrifices were offered by the priests on behalf of the Jewish people. The sacrifices were provided by the people as a matter of religious obligation and, once given, belonged to the Temple priests who served there.

The Jewish priesthoods were a class approaching a caste.

Membership was by blood descent, and the purity of the priestly families was carefully supervised in genealogical records and by a close regulation of all priestly marriages.[1] At the side of the priests stood the Levites, another hereditary class that assisted the priests and shared in the Temple management. Priests and Levites were both organized into courses or "families," and though all did not actually serve in the Temple, they were as a group dedicated to and defined by that service and had a right to share in the sacrificial offerings, tithes, taxes and gifts that constituted the Temple's income. The number of priests and Levites is not easily calculated,[2] and the actual income from tithes and dues is even more uncertain.[3] What is known is that there was in Palestine in Second Temple times a closed body of people who served the Jerusalem sanctuary in a variety of liturgical functions and who derived a substantial amount of *their* income from *its* income.[4]

This is only the surface. The Temple was not merely a building or even a sanctuary; it was a type of temple-state,[5] and as such its priestly "citizens" enjoyed all the prestige and status of an elite society. More, the upper echelons of the priesthood, the high priests and their families, were both wealthy and politically powerful members of a polity that was now a kingdom and now a theocracy.[6] There was both economic and political power in the Jerusalem Temple and it was exercised by the priesthoods necessarily and uniquely associated with it.

As we shall see, the Jerusalem Temple and its operation generated a considerable secondary commercial activity, but it also had its own nonpriestly employees who were engaged in the service and supply side of the cultus there. Many thousands of workers were engaged in the Herodian Temple's long and complex construction, and for the ordinary daily functioning of its liturgy there were required numbers of bakers, barbers, cleaners, weavers, clerical and maintenance personnel, all paid out of the Temple's own funds.[7] And finally there were the many beggars who assembled in Jerusalem, as they did in every holy city, to collect their share of the alms prescribed to every Jew.[8]

With the destruction of the Temple in A.D. 70 this elaborate economic network collapsed and disappeared. There was neither a cult center nor sacrifices to generate income and no privileged class of ministers to derive either their living or their wealth from it. After A.D. 135 the Jewish priesthoods and indeed the Jewish holy city of Jerusalem had no existence other than in the rabbinical discussions about Temple dues and sacrifices in the yeshivas of Galilee and distant Iraq. In their place was a new Christian Jerusalem and Christian priesthoods offering sacrifices in churches scattered all over the city and indeed all across the new Christian diaspora.

But in Jerusalem at least it was neither offering nor sacrifice that was the primary reason for the Christian pilgrims' attendance at those newly consecrated sites; it was the holy places themselves that were being celebrated, an act that required neither offering nor minister. Jerusalem's priests were exactly what they were in Alexandria or Milan, servants of a liturgy that was common to all Christians everywhere, exceptional in Jerusalem in no way save in the special sanctity of the shrines in which they served. Even the bishop of the city had in the fourth century to struggle to maintain his limited jurisdiction in the face of the more powerful bishop of nearby Caesarea Maritima which in that century as in the first overshadowed its less wordly upland sister.[9]

Once the Christian Church became established in the Roman Empire and began to enjoy first the protection and then the overt and professed favor of the emperor and the law, the clergy of Jerusalem, as elsewhere in the empire, were paid out of the income of their churches, and in this instance fairly well paid since the Jerusalem churches appear to have been substantially endowed. Unfortunately we have no figures, neither on the numbers of the clergy nor on the churches' revenues, but on the analogy of other places of equal importance, those revenues were already considerable in the time of Constantine and escalated sharply in the sixth century.[10]

The bishop, in the case of Jerusalem, the Patriarch, was the chief officer of the Christian congregation in a city, and in the sixth century he was paid a stipend the equivalent of a provincial governor's, while the other clergy were also well taken care of. There were other, nonclerical officials on the staff, as there had been in the Temple, readers, singers, doorkeepers, and the staffs of charitable institutions, of which Christian Jerusalem had many, all of them salaried out of the churches' revenues and offerings.[11] On one calculation, more than half of all the churches' substantial revenue went to paying the stipends of bishops and clerics.[12]

Just as there were in Jerusalem more large churches than either its own size, wealth or political importance would have dictated, so the clerical establishment in the holy city was probably somewhat more numerous and perhaps better paid than in a comparably sized city in the empire. But there is little to suggest that the Christian clerics of Jerusalem ever rivaled in either wealth or power the Jewish priesthoods, which enjoyed the actual supervision of the Temple and had a religiously prescribed share in offerings that were likewise the subject of a religious obligation. No one of its visitors ever remarked that Christian Jerusalem was either a clerical state or even a remarkably wealthy city.

When the Muslims arrived in Jerusalem in 638 it was assuredly not wealthy: in 614 the Persians had burned many of the Christian churches in the city, confiscated their treasuries and slaughtered large numbers of the inhabitants.[13] But as for being a clerical state at that point, that may not have been far from the mark. Jerusalem's surrender negotiations with the Muslim armies were conducted not by a secular or civil Roman authority like the governor, but by the chief priest of the city, the Christian Patriarch Sophronius, while the terms of the capitulation were ratified on the Muslim side by no less than the Caliph 'Umar himself.[14]

The Christian pilgrim Arculf visited Jerusalem about thirty years after the Muslim takeover, as we have seen, and there is nothing in his account to suggest that the event had greatly disrupted the Christian life of the city. Nor is there any trace in his narrative of the Persian depredations of some sixty years earlier, though he could not have known what the city was like before the destruction. And what of the priesthoods, the various servants of the shrines? Here we are on better ground, specifically the *Commemoratorium*, which is a kind of memorandum on the churches of Jerusalem and their staffs and possibly prepared on behalf of Charlemagne who was engaged at the beginning of the ninth century in negotiations with the Caliph Harun al-Rashid on the subject of the Holy Land.[15]

The document is not complete, but some of the information in the memorandum is extremely detailed. The Holy Sepulcher, we are told for example, had a staff of 150 and required an annual outlay of 630 gold pieces for the upkeep of the clergy, 540 for the servants of the shrine and another 300 for physical maintenance. The church itself had nine priests, fourteen deacons and six subdeacons, plus twenty-three canons, thirteen churchwardens, and forty-one monks. The patriarch was assisted by an executive secretary who was his second in command, an administrative staff of six, and seventeen servants. The staffs of other churches were considerably smaller: Sion had seventeen in all; and Mary's Tomb near Gethsemane, thirteen priests, six monks, and fifteen nuns. The anonymous author is aware of the growing ethnic mix in the city. The monks and nuns in and around Saint Mary's, for example, celebrated the liturgy in Greek, Latin, Syriac, Georgian, Armenian, and Arabic. One final interesting and revealing note: among the patriarch's annual expenses is one entered as "580 gold pieces paid to the Saracens."[16]

The political importance of Jerusalem's patriarch may have been due in the first instance to the failure of the Roman civil authority which by Sophronius' day was already incapable of protecting or even governing many of the empire's Near Eastern cities. But on a later occasion an effort was made to convert Jerusalem to formal ecclesiastical rule. Godfrey of Bouillon, the first Crusader ruler of the occupied city did not enjoy the title of "king"; he had to make do instead with the humbler "Advocate of the Holy Sepulcher," and indeed promises appeared to have been made to the pope that once their rule became more extended, Jerusalem would be turned over to papal sovereignty in the person of the Latin patriarch.[17] This did not occur—Baldwin was formally crowned king in Jerusalem no more than a year after the pledge had been made to the pope—but a compromise of sorts was worked out. The Latin Christian quarter of the city, roughly the northwest quadrant around the Church of the Holy Sepulcher, was to be the autonomous preserve of the patriarch. It was not entirely an innovation. According to William of Tyre,

Christians had been autonomous within that same quarter since 1063 when a treaty had been negotiated between the Fatimid Mustansir and the Byzantine Emperor Constantine X Monomachus. As William describes it:

Up to that time [A.D. 1063] the Saracens and Christians had dwelt together [in Jerusalem] indifferently. Thenceforward, by the order of the prince, the Saracens were forced to remove to other parts of Jerusalem, leaving the quarter named to the faithful without dispute. By this change, the condition of the servants of Christ was materially improved . . . From that day, then, and in the manner just described, this quarter of the city had had no other judge or lord than the Patriarch, and the church therefore [after the Crusader conquest] laid claim to that quarter as its own in perpetuity.[18]

But for the rest, Crusader Jerusalem, whatever the impulses that brought it into political being and whatever rights and privileges were given to the *properties* of the Church, remained in the matter of sovereignty as secular as the Jewish, Roman and Muslim city had been before it. But its priesthoods were assuredly different. The sixth century churches of Jerusalem were staffed with regular members of the clergy under the jurisdiction of the patriarch. There were monks and nuns there too, many of them living in nearby Judean monasteries, but others had taken up residence, as the *Commemoratorium* makes clear, as both permanent associates and transient guests in the city's churches and convents. The monastic population of Jerusalem was fractious at times during the great theological controversies that shook Palestine and the rest of the East in the fifth and sixth centuries,[19] but it was sectarian theology that excited the monasteries in that era and not yet wealth and properties.

The Crusades changed that picture in fundamental ways. When the Latin Christians occupied Jerusalem in force in 1099, they brought with them a new monastic institution, the religious order on a Western model, associations of clerics who lived under a common rule, with headquarters in Rome and dependent communities and properties all over Christian Europe. Augustinian canons controlled the *Templum Domini* atop the Haram and they likewise administered, under the patriarch's sometimes uneasy eye, the Church of the Holy Sepulcher. Benedictine monasteries dotted the countryside and eventually, long after the Crusaders departed Jerusalem, the Franciscans continued to maintain a presence there as "Custodians of the Holy Land," with their first headquarters on Mount Sion. Felix Fabri, once a lodger there, describes how the friars came into its possession:

> The Convent of the Minorite Brethren stands in a most pleasant, beauteous and lofty place [on Mount Sion]. Before they came to Jerusalem there was there a convent of Canons Regular, but after the loss of the Holy Land, [Rupert] King of Sicily bought this place on Mount Sion from the Sultan, and also the Chapel of the Blessed Virgin in the Valley of Jehoshaphat and the church at Bethlehem, with the monastery there, and gave for them in gold, paid on the spot, thirty-two thousand ducats of approved weight. He also brought the Minorite Friars to Mount Sion, and entrusted to them the ownership and management of the aforesaid places: wherefore the Pope himself is wont to constitute the Guardian of Mount Sion as the Superior of the whole eastern church in these parts.[20]

The few Christian clerics who were permitted to live in Jerusalem in the years after the fall of Acre and the final disappointment of Crusader hopes for the recovery of the Holy Land eked out a piteous existence as wardens and guides in their enclave on Mount Sion. Gifts and alms came from the Christian princes of Europe, but they appear to have been barely adequate to support the community and pay the taxes and fees imposed by a generally unsympathetic Muslim administration.[21]

Nor were the other Christian communities very helpful. Once again it is Felix Fabri who supplies the details: "And all of these they need, for they gather in no alms from the Easterners, neither from the infidels nor from the Christians, but get all their means of living from the Westerners." When Christian pilgrims arrived in the Holy Land they were exhorted in their initial instruction to be generous with the Friars: "The pilgrims must show respect to the poor convent of the brethren of Mount Sion in Jerusalem, by whose help pilgrims are conducted into and out of the Holy Land, and must by their alms cherish this convent and help the brethren thereof, who dwell there among the infidels for the comfort of the pilgrims."[22]

But it had not always been thus. When the Crusaders possessed Jerusalem the Church of the Holy Sepulcher and the other shrines in the city rejoiced in a full complement of canonical and regular clergy to celebrate the holy offices. And there was likely little problem in supporting them since the patriarchate in particular owned domestic and public properties not merely in its own quarter but all over the city and, indeed, all over the Kingdom, and enjoyed, as we shall see, both rents and duties in the city, income that was rivaled by that of other religious groups that stood outside the patriarch's immediate jurisdiction, the new military religious orders.

The coherence, discipline and extra-jurisdictional prerogatives and loyalties of the monastic orders of the Latin Kingdom of Jerusalem gave them an importance never enjoyed by the pre-Crusade Christian monks and clerics of that city. And if that was true of the monastic orders of the Latin West, it was certainly so of the so-called military orders that stood midway between Christian priesthoods and the secular feudal aristocracy of Jerusalem and were in a sense more powerful than either by reason of their international character, their wealth and properties and particularly the military might that made them the last and essential prop of the Latin Kingdom of Jerusalem.[23] And though their power eventually extended in space and time far beyond the Holy Land and the Crusades, the military orders were born, shaped, and nurtured in the Latin Kingdom of Jerusalem, a condition inexplicable in any context other than the densely mixed political and spiritual atmosphere of the holy city.

As we have seen, among the first of the Crusaders' acts in newly occupied Jerusalem was the replacement of the patriarch and the clergy administering the Church of the Holy Sepulcher with a Latin bishop and the Canons of Saint Augustine, a gesture that had nothing to do with Islam. The Crusaders were in fact confronted with a double appropriation of a city that was in the tenth century a Muslim and, in a very real sense, a Christian city, as Muqaddasi complained and as Christian shrines, property, clergy and pilgrims loudly proclaimed. The Muslim displacement was a relatively simple matter in both form and ideology since it was the professed object of the Crusade and could be effected by political means. The other conversion of Jerusalem from an Eastern to a Western Christian holy city was at once more complex and more painful.

It is likely that neither side, Latin or Eastern Christians, fully anticipated or understood the consequences of the course upon which the Latins had embarked. The antagonism between Eastern and Western church, which had been feeding for centuries on cultural, theological and economic differences, was an open matter, but like all such disputes in principle, it was far easier to conduct with the long-range weapons of excommunicatory bulls and expunged diptychs than in the house-to-house and shrine-to-shrine fighting that now loomed in Jerusalem. This was, moreover, a theological matter and so it fell not to the new king and his nobles but to the Latin Church, its head in Rome and his delegates in Jerusalem, to dislodge all those heretical and schismatic Greeks, Armenians, Jacobites, Copts, and untidy others from their long possession of the Christian shrines of Jerusalem. It was done, not to all groups or in all places, but it was done, with great and persistent ill-feeling as its wage.[24]

The issue of the Latin and the Eastern Churches, summarized in its most succinct and painful form in the transfer of the Jerusalem patriarchate from a Greek to a Latin prelate, illustrates another peculiarity of the Christian holy city. Both the authority and the sacral quality of the Christian tradition was vested from the beginning in *offices* and in a unique fashion in the episcopate. The Christian bishop was the spiritual successor of the Apostles and so both the bearer, in his own person, of the deposit of faith as well as the prime minister of the *barakat* transmitted within the Church's sacramental system. The holiness of Christian Jerusalem certainly resided in places, as becomes transparent once the quantitative *barakat* measure of indulgences begins to be attached to acts performed in those places, but the bishop was in some sense the executor and agent of that *sacrum*, just as he was of the *sacramentum*. Thus the transfer of the Jerusalem patriarchate was as highly significant in the parochial Christian contest for Jerusalem as was the transfer of buildings on the Haram in the confrontation between Christians and Muslims.

We have seen too how the Muslims own intentions toward

Jerusalem were somewhat uncertain at first, and how eventually they put their hand to expropriating that sacred city for Islam, in the first instance by constructing on the Temple mount the complex that came to be known as the Haram al-Sharif. At least by the time of ‘Abd al-Malik and his son al-Walid toward the end of the seventh century a body of workers had been assembled from Syria and Egypt, some of them common laborers and others stone and mosaic craftsmen, and possibly lodged, together with the Haram servants, in the new buildings also being put up at the southern end of the precinct.[25] Those other sanctuary servants, who eventually numbered some three hundred, were slaves given out of the caliph's own possessions, his "fifth" of the conquest booty, and they were subsesquently supported out of endowment funds from the public treasury, the Bayt al-Mal.[26] In addition there were families of Jews and Christians who performed various services for the sanctuary as a hereditary right, sweeping and cleaning and return they were exempted from the poll tax required in Islam of all non-Muslims.[27]

The construction workers eventually disappeared but the Haram slaves remained a permanent feature of the Jerusalem sanctuary and are noted by many later visitors to the city.[28] Their tasks were not liturgical, of course, but had to do with cleaning, maintaining and policing the precinct and its buildings. The religious functionaries must have been soon added, however, the various imams, muezzins and preachers who lived in the Muslim quarters of the city,[29] served the sanctuary, received a regular subsidy from the state and finally were exempt from the normal taxes.[30] When Evliye Chelebi visited Jerusalem in 1648–50 the Aqsa mosque alone had 800 salaried functionaries paid from the sultan's Privy Purse.[31] The large number was due in part to the fact that here, as in Mecca, liturgical functions had perforce to be shared by the four legal "schools" of Sunni Islam. Thus there was an imam and preacher for each, the latter group divided in "courses," somewhat like the Jewish priesthoods, so that each preacher had a week of service. The rest of the number was made up of muezzins, "choristers" who orchestrated the prayer ritual, particularly when there were large numbers involved, a variety of Qur'anic reciters, and a kind of sanctuary police.[32]

This was only part of the clerical establishment in Muslim Jerusalem. Though we cannot calculate the exact numbers until the surviving endowment documents have been published, similar liturgical officers were attached to the city's many convents and law schools, and the latter had additional academic personnel and the former an apparatus devoted to the care, feeding and spiritual instruction of pilgrims to the city. Where they differed from the Haram organization is that their endowment was of the private and individual type known as *waqf*, while the Haram was a formal government responsibility—and prerogative—and was underwritten as such.

It is perhaps worth underlining once again in this new context the well-worn truth that Islam had no priesthoods. The "learned," or *ulama*, who lived in Jerusalem and taught in its *madrasa*s were more exactly rabbis, legal savants who enjoyed in Islam exactly what their counterparts did in Judaism: the privileges and prerogatives of a learned class and the status that came from their connection with the religious law of the society. The calling, and its attendant power, tended to run in families, and the *ulama* were certainly arranged in a hierarchy imposed either from without, by a government like the Ottomans', for example, which successfully coopted their number, or from within. There was a government-appointed chief qadi of immense power in Ayyubid as well as in Mamluk and Ottoman Jerusalem, and the heads of the prestigious Shafi'ite *madrasa*s, the "official" school of all of those regimes, were, like the bishops of important sees and the geonim of important yeshivas, somewhat more equal than others.

But the position of the Jeruslem *ulama* was, for all that, one of status rather than of office. The Jewish High Priest and the Christian bishop, here in particular the patriarch of Jerusalem, could claim a power that was different in kind and even superior to that of the secular ruler. The distinction was not so neat in Islam on either side, and the *ulama* had simply to make do, to test their prestige and status against a sultan or his deputy who could claim a *charge* over Jerusalem that few Christian princes after Constantine would have dared put forward. There was probably little inclination on the part of the *ulama* to propose such a test.

Everywhere in Islam the *ulama* found their chief means of support in *waqf* endowments. The principal donors might be any man of means, government officials, fief holders, or one of the great merchants, for example. There were not many such in post-Crusader Jerusalem. The city had limited sources of commercial or agricultural wealth and so it depended more heavily than any comparable city on royal investment and subsidy to support the large numbers of clerics who lived there and who, like their brethren in Mecca, were sustained in part by an imperial subsidy and in part by endowment funds.

As was true of the Temple and Jerusalem's endowed churches before them, a substantial part of the income of the *waqf* and state-supported Muslim institutions of Jerusalem and Mecca went to the support of their staffs, which in the case of these two holy cities were quite large. The extent of these subventions and the effect they must have had on the economic life of the Islamic city is suggested by a some remarks of Ibn Battuta à propos of Damascus and likely even truer of the holy cities.

> Every man who comes to the end of his resources in any district of Damascus finds without exception some means of livelihood open to him, either as imam in a mosque, or as a reciter in a *madrasa* or by occupying a cell in a mosque, where his daily requirements are supplied to him, or by recitation of the Qur'an or employment as a keeper of one of the sacred shrines, or else he may be included in the company of Sufis who live in a *khanaqa*, in receipt of a regular allowance for upkeep money and clothing . . . And anyone who wishes to pursue a life of studies or devote himself to the religious life receives every aid to the execution of his purpose.[33]

The salaries were not immense in any event: religious functionaries were from the eleventh century onward paid much the same scale as a skilled laborer, though *madrasa* faculty generally exceeded that.[34] As time passed, however, they steadily lost ground to their competitors in the market place. In the fourteenth and fifteenth centuries their salaries actually declined, both in absolute and relative terms, the result likely of the general impoverishment of the Mamluk economy in that era and an oversupply of clerics turned out by the large numbers of *madrasa*s. Indeed, there is evidence that staff members of *waqf*-

supported institutions held posts but shared the fixed salary allotted to it.[35]

As has already been suggested, Muslim Jerusalem's substantially subsidized religious institutions like law schools and convents,[36] where the endowment invariably included a resident staff or associated members, gave the city a stable, if not always permanent, religious class as part of its population. We have no way of even guessing what percentage of the total population of Jerusalem these "religious" may have represented in premodern times, but it was certainly not negligible, and in terms of income, education or prestige, they surely constituted the only real Muslim aristocracy in a city that was not particularly notable for either its commercial ventures or its political importance and had moreover a considerable Christian population during most of its history under Islam.

After the Muslims took political control of Jerusalem in 638, the Jews too once again had a clerical establishment in the city. Since the second century the central organ of Jewish self-government, the Yeshiva, and its head, the gaon, were located not in Judea but in the somewhat more comfortable climate of Tiberias in Galilee. But soon after 638 gaon and academy returned to Jerusalem where they remained, with temporary interruptions, until the Seljuq conquest in 1071, when the new seat was Tyre and, after 1127, Fustat or Old Cairo.[37] The restored Jewish rabbinate of Jerusalem were no longer servants of a shrine, of course, as had been their priestly predecessors in the city, but like the contemporary *ulama* of Jerusalem, servants of the Law, which in both instances had become the dominant institution of the community.

The Yeshiva was not simply a school, as the term later came to be used, but part curia, part tribunal, school, and legislative body, and its head had acknowledged jurisdiction over all the Jews of the "Western" Diaspora, while his counterparts in Iraq were the chief legal authorities for the Jews of the Muslim "East." Thanks to the documents preserved in the Geniza, or storehouse, of the old synagogue in Cairo, we have a fairly detailed picture of the structure of both the Palestinian Yeshiva in Jerusalem and of the community it served.[38] At its head was the gaon who, together with the president of the Court and board of five "international" notables, constituted the Council of the Yeshiva. Though its judicial sessions often took place at Ramle, the administrative capital of the country under the Muslims, the Yeshiva itself was located in Jerusalem, and its administrative and educational activities took place there, the liturgy in the community synagogue, study in the *Bet ha-midrash*, and a good deal else in the house of the gaon or the president of the Court.[39]

The members, or perhaps "fellows," of the Jerusalem Yeshiva—the *havers* or scholars, community judges, preachers, and cantors—constituted, exactly like their Muslim counterparts—the qadis, *'alim*s, imams, and muezzins—the legal aristocracy of every Jewish community where they were found, and no place more than in Jerusalem certainly, where the Yeshiva head and council dominated what could never be regarded as just another Jewish community. The Geniza documents on the Jerusalem Yeshiva and the community there in the eleventh century do not, however, encourage us to think that either was very large, for all their prestige, though there is abundant evidence that they were poor. Not from oppression, however, but because the Jerusalem Jews, compared, let us say to their contemporaries in Cairo, had a very limited commercial income—they lived largely through begging in the Diaspora—and quite unusual expenses connected directly to the fact that they had to play both host and benefactor to Jewish pilgrims to the city, some of them rich but others indigent indeed.

These medieval Jewish servants of the Law in Jerusalem were a far cry from the former Temple priesthoods. They were narrowly community-bound. They possessed no political leverage in the city as the Christians did by reason of their numbers, their properties, their customary privileges, which the Ottomans eventually converted in legal rights, and the ever more real possibility of appealing to Christian allies outside the *Dar al-Islam*. The Jewish clerical eminences of Jerusalem, whatever status they enjoyed in the eyes of their coreligionists, were shrineless and unpropertied and so were tied directly and vulnerably to the political good will of their Muslim rulers and the charitable benevolence of their own Jewish Diaspora where, in fact, in the early twelfth century they themselves chose to live. And when Jews began to trickle back into Jerusalem in the sixteenth century, they came as individuals; pious immigrants perhaps, not yet the vanguard of a restoration.

The departure of the Jerusalem Yeshiva for the true seat of Muslim power in Cairo and the exclusion of the Jewish population of the holy city by the Crusaders destroyed much of the community organization that the Jews had patiently built up in Jerusalem since the seventh century. Jews slowly returned to the city in the wake of the Muslim reconquest in the twelfth century but the descriptions of Jewish travellers there over the next couple of centuries are very uneven in their appraisal. A French visitor in 1334 found the city filled with European Jewish immigrants leading rich and prosperous lives as merchants, scholars in the profane sciences and adepts of Torah and Kabbala, the latter supported out of community funds.[40] A century later Rabbi Meshullam of Volterra found the city in a ruinous condition, though the Jewish clerical hierarchy was still intact, a mélange of Europeans and Easterners, Ashkenazis and Sephardis.[41] And yet no more than six or seven years later Obadiah da Bertinoro, another and very circumstantial reporter from Europe, paints a portrait of the community on the brink of extinction.

According to Obadiah, there were in Jerusalem only 70 Jewish families of the poorest class, a disproportionately large number of widows from Germany, Spain and Portugal, and a hierarchy just emerging from a self-inflicted sectarian pogrom within the community. Many of the Jewish facilities lay in ruins or had been sold off and in the recent past the community elders had made the situation worse by extorting money from their coreligionists by alleging shortages in funds to pay the Muslim poll tax. Obadiah is discreet and striving with great energy to be objective, but what emerges from between his lines is a fiercely explosive struggle between Ashkenazi and Sephardic factions of the Jerusalem community. The Arabs are blameless in the matter, he writes home to his brother; the problem is an internal one.[42]

Mecca had far more Muslim pilgrims than Jerusalem had Jewish ones, and the Meccans contrived to thrive on those visitors. But though the chief avocation of most Meccans was some form of pilgrim-connected commerce, the largest professional group in the city was that associated in one way or another with the *haram*. They were not very much different from what we have already seen in Jerusalem, imams, preachers, muezzins and below them, the various servants who cleaned and maintained the precinct, all of them salaried by the mosque and paid out of its endowment.[43] There were some differences, however. In Mecca there was what appears to be an extraordinary number of teaching *ulama* attached to the shrine itself. That there should be such was not in itself unusual since the Meccan *haram* was after all a mosque and so instruction would normally be given there. What may have been unusual was their number. The *madrasa*s of Mecca were extremely fragile institutions, as we shall see, and it would seem plausible that many of the *ulama* originally attached to a law school there would have contrived to get themselves seconded in one way or another to the firmer endowment of the *haram* when their own *waqf* began to disintegrate.

What is even more peculiar to the sanctuary at Mecca was the possession of hereditary rights over the Zamzam spring and the Ka'ba itself by certain groups whose history goes back to before the beginnings of Islam. In the days before Muhammad Mecca was run—"governed" may not be quite the apposite word here[44]—by a tribal group called the Quraysh who simultaneously held in their hands the economic control of the city, that is, its trade, and the guardianship of the shrine and its functions. They were in not in any formal sense clergy, though the prominent families bore theophoric names[45]; rather, they were concessionaires who held exclusive rights like access to the Ka'ba and the privilege of selling water to the pilgrims to the shrine.[46] Further, they had the right to collect taxes, one from their fellow Quraysh to support and subsidize pilgrimage, and the other a duty tax on the commerce generated by that pilgrimage.[47]

It was an ingenious system, and on one common interpretation of the beginnings of Islam, the Quraysh opposed Muhammad because they thought he would destroy the pilgrimage and so undermine their valuable franchises. If so, they were much mistaken. Muhammad left the Quraysh their profitable pilgrimage franchises and destroyed the commerce instead. It mattered little in the sequel. Some Quraysh abandoned Mecca and followed the path of politics and power to Syria and the Caliphate itself; others lapsed into pensioned indolence in the holy cities of the Hejaz; and some finally, like the Banu Shayba, continued to exercise their traditional prerogatives—and collect their dues—around the Ka'ba, figures of some prestige there perhaps, but no longer the aristocrats of Mecca.

The franchise to sell water was obviously an important and lucrative one in parched Mecca.[48] The water came from the sacred source of the Zamzam within the *haram*, and the rites connected with it were integrated into the chain of Abrahamic traditions that was woven around the holy places in and about Mecca in very early Islamic times. There was apparently an early contest for the control of the spring, or better, for the profitable privilege of the *siqaya*, supplying water to the pilgrims, a contest eventually won by al-'Abbas and his descendants.[49] Under the caliphs who descended from his family, the Zamzam and the nearby booth where 'Abbas had reportedly supervised the distribution of the water began to undergo an *enshrinement*, which was essentially complete when Ibn Jubayr described it in 1184.[50]

How long the privilege remained in the hands of 'Abbas' direct descendants cannot be determined, but at some point the rulers of Mecca began to farm out control of the Zamzam as a franchise to the highest bidder. It was well worth the price since down to the beginning of the nineteenth-century Meccan pilgrims were taxed for the privilege of access to the spring and its miraculous waters and the fees went directly into the hands of the enfranchised director of the Zamzam and his assistant *zemazim*.[51]

The Banu Shayba were longer-lived in their traditional charge over the Ka'ba, its covering and its contents. The latter was in effect the temple treasury of Mecca, which was at times substantial and at times empty since it was enriched by frequent pious donations and impoverished by equally frequent despoliations by those assigned to guard it. The Caliph 'Umar was the first we know of to have sent the spoils of conquest to Mecca, booty from the capture of the Persian capital of Ctesiphon, which was hung within the Ka'ba, much as Herod did his war trophies in the Jerusalem *haram*.[52] Under the 'Abbasids, however, spoils of another sort began to arrive in Mecca. During the reign of Ma'mun the Shah of Kabul embraced Islam and his throne was sent to Mecca as a symbol of his new allegiance. Shortly thereafter the ruler of Tibet was converted. In this instance he sent to the holy city his favorite idol seated on a throne and wearing a golden crown. This tableau was displayed for three days on the streets of Mecca—with both written and oral instructions on what it meant—and then the crown was hung up in the Ka'ba and the throne put into the *haram* treasury, which is to say, the house of the Banu Shayba.[53]

The Banu Shayba tradition appears to be very ancient; they were perhaps the authentic pre-Islamic guardians of the shrine and they were still exercising their charge in the late twelfth century, when Ibn Jubayr was in the city, and indeed even in the nineteenth when Snouck Hurgronje noted them there.[54] And as with the Zamzam, there was something more than prestige involved: the Banu Shayba exacted a charge for visiting the interior of the Ka'ba, a concession they manipulated to great profit. For long periods, for example, they apparently opened and closed the Ka'ba at their own pleasure, and on the payment of large sums of money. This led on occasion to demonstrations, and sometimes to violence, in the *haram*. In 1222 caliph and concessionaires came to terms: against the payment of a fixed and guaranteed sum the Banu Shayba would keep the Ka'ba door open night and day during the pilgrimage season.[55] The proprietors found other compensations, however: they sold pieces of the cloth covering of the shrine and even souvenir whisks made from the brooms used to sweep out the *Bayt Allah*.

Both the 'Abbasids' hold on the Zamzam and the Banu Shayba's on the Ka'ba were manifestations of what might be called the "old politics" of the Meccan sanctuary where in pre-Islamic times sovereignty and religion were welded into a fixed union at the *haram*. Control of the shrine represented both political and economic power and that power was sorted out among the aristocracy of the city.[56] The "new politics" makes its appearance with the presence of secular officials appointed by distant powers that claimed sovereignty over the holy city. Mecca had caliphally appointed governors from the beginning, but with the rise of the local dynasty of the sharifs they were effectively displaced, and sovereignty over Mecca was merely *signaled*, normally by the mention of the ruler's name in the Friday prayers. In 1269, when the Mamluk Sultan Baybars came on pilgrimage, that condition changed and thereafter the rulers of Egypt attempted to rule Mecca directly. How successsful they were we cannot say since the sharifs appear to enjoy considerable authority after that date. When the control became obviously more effective was in 1438 when the Sultan Jaqmaq appointed a permanent official to oversee the holy cities of the Hejaz with the title of "Inspector of the Haramayn."[57] By 1453 that office had grown to three, prefects in Mecca and Jedda and an inspector of the Holy Places with extended powers over the finances of the shrines of both Mecca and Medina.[58] This oversight system continued under the Ottomans, who moreover kept a permanent garrison in Medina and appointed their own chief qadi to dispense justice in Mecca.

There were temple slaves in Mecca, just as there had been in Jewish Jerusalem,[59] and from a very early date. They performed menial tasks and were apparently not worth much notice from visitors to the *haram*. In Ottoman times, however, their place was gradually usurped by black eunuchs, the *Tashwiyya*, expensively outfitted in livery and sent out from Cairo or Istanbul as gifts to the sanctuary. Though they occasionally swept out the *haram* in some vaguely recollected reflex of the past, the *Tashwiyya* were anything but menials. They were the shrine police and enjoyed a comfortable income from both the mosque's endowment and the special funds sent out from Istanbul for their support, to say nothing of the gifts given them by pilgrims, particularly African pilgrims, to court their favor and occasionally supercilious esteem.[60]

Ibn Battuta's observant eye caught another Meccan phenomenon, the holy man drawn by the sanctity of the shrine to take up at least temporary residence in or near its precinct. The type was formalized in Islam, "sojourners" in holy places, or as the same author describes them in the Great Mosque of Damascus, where "there are a great many 'sojourners' who never leave it, occupying themselves unremittingly in prayer and recitations of the Qur'an and liturgies . . . The townspeople supply their needs for food and clothing, although the 'sojourners' never beg for anything of any kind from them."[61]

At Mecca those unspecified "liturgies" were of course connected with the Ka'ba in whose shadow the "sojourners" lived. Ibn Battuta describes a number of them and was particularly struck by their custom of performing the *'umra* or Lesser Pilgrimage, once or even twice daily and their obsessive repetition of the *tawaf*, the sevenfold circumambulation of the Ka'ba, sometimes to the extent of performing it seventy times in the course of a single day, sleeping only rarely and circling the Holy House even through the night.[62] The type is familiar perhaps, the earlier ascetic of fourth- and fifth-century Christian Syria like Symeon Stylites now transferred to an urban and an Islamic milieu and with his compulsion displaced from the merely difficult to the liturgically implausible.

There is little wonder at finding such men in Mecca. If holy cities are capable of drawing great numbers of believers to worship there, they also have the power of exercising an even greater attraction on the spiritually sensitive adept for whom the holy place is an inexhaustible source of blessings. What is perhaps unusual about those Meccan "sojourners" is their fascination with the liturgy; the holy man is more often found venerating the charismatic, at the tombs and shrines of saints, for example, or feeding on the richer stuff of mystical contemplation.

In Judaism the charismatic calling of which the biblical prophets and their "bands" are such apparent examples had all but disappeared in Second Temple times under and into the institutionalized and juridically defined purity/holiness of the priesthood, and thereafter it had to struggle against the overwhelmingly propagated ideal of the scholar which, if it did not condemn the charismatic, did not much encourage that way of life nor indeed public speculation on the mystical themes so attractive to "spirituals." Nor was radical asceticism, of the type practiced by Christians, for example, and which generally drew the Christian holy man away from cities, even one as holy as Jerusalem, and into the wilderness, ever a particularly strong or attractive element in Judaism. But buried at the heart of the Jewish liturgy was the notion of atonement and mourning, and certain ascetical practices like fasting followed naturally in their wake.

As we have seen, the custom of mourning the destruction of the Temple on the Ninth of Ab was an old one among Jews and was connected, when possible, directly with the Temple site. By the ninth century this practice, which in Jerome's day still had all the appearances of a popular manifestation, had become formalized in Jerusalem. That at least seems to be the conclusion to be drawn from the presence in the city of a group of ascetics and mystics known as the "Mourners for Zion." They first appear in the collection of homilies known as the *Pesiqta Rabbati*, possibly the work of a ninth-century Jerusalem immigrant from Europe who was one of their number,[63] and are described as those who "rise up every morning to beseech mercy . . . who yearn for deliverance every morning, evening and noon." There is not much substance to this, particularly in the Messianic and apocalyptic context in which it appears in the *Pesiqta Rabbati*, but there can be no doubt that we are in the presence of some kind of institutionalized practice in Jerusalem when we read in a contemporary chronicle of donations being made "to the mourners of His majestic House" and "mourners of His everlasting House" in Jerusalem.[64] This sounds like a community, and one well enough organized possibly to solicit and certainly to receive donations from abroad for its upkeep.

Sufism was a widespread phenomenon in post-Crusader Islam, increasingly institutionalized and progressively accepted by the body of the *ulama* that had constituted itself and was accepted by the political authorities as the tribunal of Sunni orthodoxy.[65] The main bodies of Sufis were shaykh-oriented, however, and though they eddied in great numbers along the roads of the *Dar al-Islam*, a Sufi "settlement" in village or city was invariably concentrated around the *zawiya* of some living master or the shrine-tomb of a dead Sufi saint. There were nonetheless Sufis in Jerusalem from fairly early on the Islamic period,[66] and in Mamluk times they found lodging on either a permanent basis in the *zawiya*s and *khanaqa*s of the city,[67] or as "sojourners" in mosque, shrine, or *khanaqa*.

There were "sojourners" in Mecca, as we have seen, and they

appear to be a somewhat eccentric lot with a distinct ascetical bent. At Jerusalem, on the other hand, neither a strongly pronounced asceticism nor indeed a marked shaykh-orientation appears to be the mode. Jerusalem's principal Islamic shrine of the Haram was neither parochial nor particularist nor political; its unique Muslim association was with the Night Journey and the Ascension of Muhammad, both of them, singly or in conjunction, primary *topoi* of Sufi mystical meditation, like Ezekiel's vision of the heavenly coursing "chariot" for the Jew or the divinely lit scene on Mount Tabor for the Christian. Jerusalem's Sufis were collected there for contemplation, not for political action or charismatic direction or tomb veneration and ritual; quietism was the Sufi style in the holy city.

The holy man in the holy city, whether Jewish "mourner," Christian monk, or Muslim "sojourner," was not so much a servant of the shrine as served by it: from it he drew blesssing, indulgence and inspiration. But he was, nonetheless, an important part of the social and economic fabric of the holy city. In Byzantine and Muslim Jerusalem, the monastic and Sufi population was large and important enough to induce government investment in their lodging and upkeep, and those same institutions designed and endowed for the benefit of monk and Sufi became, as we shall see, primary channels for various social services for the population at large: visitors were housed in them; pilgrims were fed in them, most at state expense or endowment.

NOTES

1. Schürer 1979: 238–44:Jeremias 1969: 213–21.
2. Jeremias 1969: 198–207 puts the figure at 7,200 priests and 9,600 Levites.
3. On the various categories of goods and moneys owed the Temple and the priests: Schürer 1979: 257–74 and Jeremias 1969: 105–08.
4. The lesser priestly families were by no means rich, and many of them had other occupations: Jeremias 1969: 206–07.
5. The profile of the classical temple-state is given by Strabo XII, 2 in connection with Comana in Cappadocia, and Mantel (1975: 264–66) has found that it matches the Jerusalem situation in many respects.
6. On the position of the Jerusalem high priests: Mantel 1975 and Jeremias 1969: 96–99 and 147–60.
7. Jeremias 1969: 21–27.
8. Ibid.: 117–18. For begging as an "industry" in Mecca, Burckardt 1829: 210–11.

9. Jones 1964: 882. He was more successful in the fifth century when the Jerusalem Patriarch Juvenal ruled over all three of the provinces that constituted late Roman Palestine: ibid.: 893 and cf. Honigmann 1950.

10. Jones 1964: 903–04.

11. Ibid.: 911–12.

12. Ibid.: 934.

13. For the Christian reaction: Chitty 1966: 155–58.

14. The varying Muslim accounts are resumed in Hill 1971: 59–60; on Sophronius, see von Schönborn 1972 1972: 54–85, and for the presence of ʿUmar on the scene, p. 169 above.

15. Wilkinson 1977: 12. Charlemagne is mentioned in the document and so too is the earthquake (A.D. 746?) that leveled the Nea.

16. Text in Wilkinson 1977: 137–38.

17. William of Tyre IX, 16.

18. William of Tyre IX, 18. On the conflicting claims upon this quarter in Crusader times: Prawer 1980: 297 ff.

19. Cf. Chitty 1966: 101–22.

20. Felix Fabri 1893: 1, 339–40. The pope involved in the original negotiations, Nicholas IV, was himself a Franciscan, as Felix later explains (2, 378–79). When Felix Fabri was writing toward the end of the fifteenth century, there were only twenty-four friars attached to the Mount Sion complex in Jerusalem, but as the European states grew stronger in the succeeding centuries, so too did their interest in the Holy Land, and the Franciscans of Mount Sion lay readily at hand as instruments of both secular and papal policy; cf. Wardi 1975.

21. Felix Fabri 1893: 2, 382.

22. Ibid.: 1, 254.

23. Prawer 1972: 252–79.

24. Ibid.: 214–32, and for the longer-range consequences: Wardi 1975. Such transfers of rite had occurred before in Jerusalem, for the first time in the years after A.D. 135, when a Jewish-Christian hierarchy was replaced, through default, by Gentile-Christian bishops (Eusebius, *HE* IV, 5–6), and often in the sixth century during the theological wars between Monophysites and the Imperial Melkites: Frend 1972: 221–95.

25. Mazar 1969: Ben Dov in Mazar 1971: 43–44; cf. Creswell 1969: I/1 231, 240.

26. Le Strange 1890: 148, 165.

27. Ibid.: 149. The poll tax was was an extremely heavy burden on the non-Muslim community, and so exemption was a considerable privilege; see Goitein 1971: 380–93 for the most concrete details we have on the poll tax.

28. Le Strange 1890: 161, 163.

29. Cohen and Lewis 1978: 89 for the Ottoman tax registers noting the residences of various classes of clerics.

30. On the Jerusalem tax exemptions, ibid.: 15.

31. Chelebi 1980: 72–73. Chelebi passes over the fact that substantial Haram income derived directly from properties in Jerusalem itself; see pp. 321–23 below.

32. Stephan, commenting on Chelebi's text in 1935 (Chelebi 1980: loc. cit.), notes that by his day the numbers were much reduced, that most of the posts had become hereditary in certain prominent families and were supported out of *waqf* funds.

33. Ibn Battuta 1958–62: 149–50. On the early Ottoman subsidies to the Jerusalem clergy, Chelebi 1980: 63.

34. Ashtor 1966: 345; ibid.: 336–37 on the *madrasa* staff.

35. Ashtor 1966: 335.

36. For some of the major orders with convents in Jerusalem, Trimingham 1971: 40, 44, 48, 49 and 60; and for the convents there at the beginning of this century, Canaan 1927: 300–02.

37. Goitein 1971: 201.

38. See, for example, Mann 1920–22: 1, 251–80 and Goitein 1971: 40–90, 211–27.

39. Adler 1966: 133 (Joseph ben Jospeh ibn Chelo).

40. Ibid.: 196.

41. Ibid.: 234–35, 242.

42. Ibid.: 235 (Jerusalem), 245 (Jewish-Arab relations in Safed).

43. Burckhardt 1829: 156.

44. Lammens 1924: 64–65.

45. Wellhausen 1897: 1–10.

46. The first, called the *hijaba*, and the second, called *siqaya*, are described, together with the other related offices of pre-Islamic Mecca, by Azraqi 1858: 66 ff. and discussed by Hamidullah 1938: 262.

47. On the first, the *rifada*, Azraqi 1858: 66; Ibn Ishaq 1955: 55–56; Wuestenfeld 1861: 31–32. On the customs duties, Azraqi 1858: 107; Lammens 1924: 44.

48. On the high price of water there, Azraqi 1858: 51, 444; Burckhardt 1829: 142–43.

49. Gaudefroy-Demombynes 1923: 73–76.

50. Ibn Jubayr 1949–51: 88–89 Ar./103–04 tr. There was one significant addition. In 1611 a grill was placed over the well mouth to discourage pilgrims from throwing themselves down into the spring as an offering to God: Gaudefroy-Demombynes 1923: 85.

51. Ibid.: 87; Burckhardt 1829: 143–48 and Snouck Hurgronje 1931: 21–22.

52. Wuestenfeld 1861: 121; on Herod, Josephus, *Ant.* XV, 11, 4.

53. Wuestenfeld 1861: 190.

54. Ibn Jubayr 1949–51: 93, 164–66 Ar./11, 189 93 tr.; Snouck Hurgronje 1931: 21.

55. Wuestenfeld 1861: 236.

56. On the elements of the system in pre-Islamic Mecca, Wolf 1951 and Serjeant 1962: 53.

57. Wuestenfeld 1861: 286.

58. Ibid.: 288.

59. Jermias 1969: 341, but cf. Levine 1963. On the possibility that there were also eunuchs attached to the Jerusalem Haram in Ottoman times, Cohen and Lewis 1978: 15–16.

60. Burckhardt 1829: 158–59.

61. Ibn Battuta 1958–62: 129 and n. 223.

62. Ibid.: 176, 221, where one of the adepts is divorced by his wife because of his preference for *tawaf* over her.

63. *Pesikta Rabbati*, ch. 34 (Braude 1968: 2, 662–68). For the identification of the author: Mann 1920–22: 1, 47–49. Braude (2, 663 n. 3) thinks to have traced the origins of the group back to the first century.

64. Mann 1920–22: 48–49.

65. The integration can be traced fairly closely in Mamluk Cairo with the introduction of legal teaching, not one of its original functions, into the *khanaqa*: Fernandes 1980: 85–90.

66. For the earliest Muslim mystics attracted to Jerusalem, Goitein 1968: 142–46.

67. The more institutionalized Sufi communities in Jerusalem in Mamluk times are surveyed in Drory 1981: 203–05.

CHAPTER VII

Endowment and Investment

The construction and continued financing of both the primary and secondary shrines, as well as of a number of other public facilities in the holy city, takes the characteristic form of transferred income or endowment, *usually perpetual in intention, and whose inalienable and untaxable nature is protected by law.*

Under both Christians and Muslims, the shrines and public facilities of Jerusalem were supported by endowments, gifts of the income or profits accruing from an inalienable and generally untaxable principal, commercial properties, for example, or agricultural lands. But as far as we can tell, the post-Exilic Jewish Temple that preceded both church and mosque in that city lived entirely off its own direct income from gifts, tithes and taxes, levied or given annually. That income seems enormous to us, but whatever its extent, it must have been large enough to guarantee both the continuous support of the Temple priesthoods and staff as well as the upkeep of the Temple itself, for which the half-shekel tax was specifically designated.

The rabbis represented in the Mishna were well aware of that income and took some steps to regulate it, in the disposition of the Temple tax, for example.[1] Such intentions were religiously motivated, of course, since Temple money was to some extent sacral money,[2] and there are no signs that the more secular intentions of Herod and the later Hasmoneans ever led to similar interventions in Temple affairs, and therein may lie part of the explanation for the absence of an endowment mechanism in Temple Judaism. The pious man of means may certainly *intend* endowment, but the intention could never become institutionalized unless the state guaranteed its special status, its protection from taxes and alienation, for example, as the Jewish kings never did, despite their own occasional generosity toward the Temple.[3]

Two other elements in the Temple's finances should be noted here, the absence of any evidence that the Jewish Temple, contrary to the general practice of temple-states in the ancient world, possessed any land or was used a depository for the valuables of certain rich citizens.[4] For another institution the ownership of land and the disposal of large sums for interest would be a source of considerable endowment; in Judaism the first did not exist and deposited funds and valuables were not apparently used for the Temple's own profit.

From the beginning, Christian churches functioned differently. They were supported, like the Temple, from gifts and offerings, though these were never in the form of a church tax or tithe.[5] Then in the late third and early fourth century churches began to acquire property and land, possessions that became substantial once Constantine set the paradigm of the generous Christian ruler. The emperor not only underwrote, out of both the privy purse and the state treasury, the construction and adornment of church buildings like the Anastasis in Jerusalem;[6] he donated income bearing lands and buildings to churches and by his legislation encouraged others to do likewise. Subsequent legislation made such church-owned properties inalienable and partially reduced their tax liabilities.[7]

New church buildings and their maintenance imposed a burden on the common funds on the mother church from which the new foundations depended for both their clergy and their financing. Imperial legislation in the sixth century addressed itself to this growing problem by insisting that new churches should not be put up unless they were previously endowed with adequate lands and properties.[8] This was likely not a problem in Rome where the *Liber Pontificalis* has recorded the rich endowments given by Constantine to the churches there,[9] and we may assume the same for Jerusalem, even though there are no such detailed records for the city, since imperial investment was the rule there from the fourth to the sixth century.[10] And not merely for churches. Other public institutions that were run by the Church—hostels and hospitals, for example—were similarly endowed, and in one instance we have the actual endowment income: Justinian founded a hundred-bed hospital in the city and settled upon it properties yielding 1850 gold *solidi* annually.[11] The funds had administrators (*oikonomoi, dioiketes*) who were responsible for properties and income alike, with both the patriarch and the imperial authorities in Constantinople paying close and continuous attention.[12]

When the Christian Crusaders regained political control of Jerusalem in 1099, an endowment system was reestablished in the city, though on a basis different from the earlier Byzantine one. There was no longer any Christian Roman Empire from whose immense domains certain agricultural and commercial properties could be deeded to the holy places of Jerusalem; now there was only the tiny Kingdom of Jerusalem itself to provide continuous sustenance. What precisely that sustenance was is revealed in a document from 1114 setting out the allocation of the income of the Church of the Holy Sepulcher.[13] It is in the nature of a negotiated contract between the Latin patriarch and the clergy attached to the church, and in it the patriarch stipulates that the canons will receive a fixed share of the various offerings made to the church. In addition, he grants them the tithes from the entire city, reserving for himself the income from the markets (*funda*) that belong to the patriarchate. These latter must have been some form of *waqf*, commercial properties whose income accrued to a church, and some of the arches of the central market street of Crusader times, the "Street of Foul Smells" (*Malquisinat*), still bear inscriptions attesting that they, or rather the shops beneath them, were the property of the Church of Saint Anne.[14]

A half century earlier the Jews of Jerusalem were supporting their social and charitable enterprises in somewhat the same fashion, though without the benefit of imperial endowment and support. The Jewish community there was not self-sufficient, as we have seen, and many of its expenses were paid from cash contributions collected on an annual basis in more affluent Jewish communities like Cairo and Qayrawan. But there was also some endowment, and in much the same form it manifested itself in Islam.[15] It is possible to trace over two centuries the fortunes of blocks of buildings in Old Cairo whose income had been designated in trust for "the poor of Jerusalem,"[16] and there likewise appear to have been Jewish-owned shops in Ramle whose income had been settled on the Jerusalem community, much like those in the bazaar of the Crusader city.[17]

Islam too had a formal and religiously sanctioned instrument for the permanent endowment of pious causes, the famous institution of *waqf*. Anyone who had valid ownership of land or property could designate the income from that property to be applied to some religious end in perpetuity. The property so designated became inalienable and untaxable, as did its income. The arrangement was drawn up and witnessed in the form of a contract: the property was carefully defined, an executor appointed, beneficiaries precisely stipulated.

Though its origins may be earlier, from the twelfth century down to the beginning of the modern era, *waqf* has been the single most important and pervasive economic institution of Islamic society, with profound effects on the tax structure of the state, the redistribution of wealth in society, the urban fabric of Islamic cities and the support, whether by salaries or simple subsidy, of large numbers of Muslims throughout the Middle Ages. Some of those broader effects will be noted in passing, and though *waqf* endowments subsidized an enormous number of projects across the Abode of Islam, our chief interest here will be in what may have been its single most focused use, the support of the holy cities, and particularly of Mecca and Jerusalem.[18]

Both cities were in fact heavily subsidized, in part by gifts, in part by royal grants, and in large part by the income from properties scattered all over the Muslim world. Or so we guess since there is at present no way of controlling the documentation on those properties, though in Jerusalem itself we do know fairly precisely what was designated as *waqf* for the Haram since it was spelled out in the Ottoman tax registers beginning in the sixteenth century.[19] Some of that income came from what appear to be urban *waqf* properties of a familiar type, income from four of the five baths in the city, for example, and from khans and a dye works. Other elements of Haram income came directly from commercial transactions, like the sale and storage of grain and Jerusalem's chief export product, soap. There was in addition a special tax for the Haram on all the olive trees within the city limits of Jerusalem. Some of the very large items are particularly interesting. There was an enormous tax on the revenues of the Church of the Anastasis, a poll tax on all Christians and Jews living in the city, and a special tax on Christian pilgrims from abroad, all designated for the treasury of the Haram al-Sharif.[20]

We can only speculate about the growth stages of *waqf* endowment in Jerusalem since there is so little evidence of publicly supported institutions in the city in pre-Ayyubid times. With the repossession of the city by Salah al-Din the ground grows somewhat firmer, however. What was perhaps most remarkable about the new regime in Jerusalem was its *supervision* of endowments. According to Mujir al-Din, Salah al-Din himself appointed a lawyer as director of the Haram and gave him specific oversight of its *waqf* administration.[21] Another lawyer supervised the Bayt al-Mal, or public treasury, and regulated the finances of the sultan's own major investment in the city, the Salahiyya Madrasa, formerly the Crusaders' Church of Saint Anne.[22]

The Jerusalem endowments continue down through Ayyubid and Mamluk times, though certainly not on a very lavish scale when we compare the parallel documentation for the same period from Damascus, Aleppo, and Cairo,[23] cities of far greater political and commercial importance to the regime that ruled them. Then, with the turn into the period of Ottoman sovereignty, the preserved tax registers begin to show among the government-controlled revenues a substantial portion devoted to the Haram. This is not so surprising as the absence from those same lists of endowment properties for the other religious institutions in the city. Half of the revenues of the *hammam* built by the Amir Tankiz al-Nasiri went to the support of the *madrasa* he had also founded, and the income from another large bathhouse near the Bab al-Asbat went to the support of Salah al-Din's *madrasa*. Beyond that nothing else is noted, despite the fact that by the sixteenth century there were already in Jerusalem a great many institutions presumably built and supported by religious endowments.

The face of Muslim Jerusalem was quite different from its

Christian counterpart, not that one replaced the other, as was the case with political control, but that Christians and Muslims carved out separate spheres, "quarters," to speak solely in urban terms, and there was a significant difference in the type and function and intent of the public facilities constructed in each. The first Muslims in the city had appropriated, as a reflex of their reading of the biblical past, the Temple mount as their primary sanctuary, and Muslim associations with Jerusalem, soon enriched with traditions connected with the Night Journey and Ascension of the Prophet, continued to center on the Haram al-Sharif. The chief Christian holy place, the Anastasis, stood on the western hill opposite, and the secondary Christian shrines, though diffused somewhat by the geography of Jesus' ministry in Jerusalem, were likewise on the west, either within the orbit of the Anastasis and the Patriarchal palace or on Mount Sion in the southwest, or clustered at the foot and summit of the Mount of Olives eastward outside the city. It is not unnatural, then, that most of the Muslims' subsequent public buildings in Jerusalem should be built in the eastern half of the city where the Muslim population lived and prayed, against the northern and western periphery of the Haram and westward along the lines of the flow of pedestrian traffic on the transverse streets leading from the chief western gates of the Haram.[24]

The earliest Muslim rulers of Jerusalem had asserted their presence in the city with a monumental shrine, a mosque and a palace built near the Haram: a biblical presence, an Islamic presence, and an imperial one. The gesture was both adequate and appropriate in the seventh and eighth centuries, and in view of the limited repertoire of such architectural symbols available to the early Muslims, complete as well. The palace soon disappeared, along with whatever political expectations the Umayyads might have harbored for Jerusalem, but the late Umayyad versions of the shrine of the Dome and the Aqsa mosque survived and flourished, forever without Muslim rivals in that city, though certainly with Christian ones.

The Crusaders breathed new life into both the Christian institutions and their architectural expressions in Jerusalem. Churches, shrines, hospices, and convents staffed by regular and monastic clerics were newly built or newly endowed. For the first time since the Herods, Jerusalem was once again a royal capital, home of king and court, purchased at the price of Christian blood shed in the name of a holy war. It is certain that both events, the Christians' holy war ideology and their reappropriation, reconstruction and readornment of Jerusalem, had an effect on the Muslims' own religious sensibilities in general and in particular on the ideology and fervor of the two great Muslim champions of the Counter-Crusade, Nur al-Din Zengi and Salah al-Din Ayyubi. The change can be read in the new literature that began to appear in Arabic on Jerusalem as a holy city,[25] and equally clearly in the intentions of those same two Muslim princes as they are reflected in their urban investment programs and policies.[26] What they and their immediate successors accomplished was nothing less than the Muslim urbanization of Jerusalem.

Both intentions and programs are visible in Jerusalem, but they can be traced even more distinctly in those two rulers' primary capitals where their political and financial will had free rein over a long period of time, Nur al-Din's in Damascus (1146–74) and Salah al-Din's in Cairo (1169–93).[27] In Cairo in particular Salah al-Din's program of building and endowment shows that what was being fought in the Near East in the eleventh and twelfth centuries was not simply a war for the repossession of Jerusalem from the Frankish usurpers but an even larger and more ominous struggle between Shi'ite and Sunni Islam. The Crusaders were fought with arms, but the Cairo-based Isma'ili Shi'ite threat to traditional Sunnism required other, more ideological weapons, the recently evolved law school or *madrasa* from which orthodox Sunnism was propagated by a new state-connected intelligentsia of lawyers and the state supported and staffed convents that housed Sunni communities of Sufi ascetics.

Both these institutions, the law school and the Sufi convent-residence, were late arrivals in the Islamic world.[28] First the Ayyubids and then the Mamluks associated themselves closely with these Sunni innovations and the bulk of their public buildings in Egypt, Palestine, and Syria were precisely *madrasas* and convents and not the mosques, palaces, and commercial buildings that other Muslim rulers chose to build, earlier and later, in the cities under their control.

There are persuasive ideological reasons for that choice on the part of the Ayyubids and Mamluks,[29] but the choice in the case of Jerusalem was determined, or perhaps reinforced, by other, very local considerations. If, as has been argued, both dynasties generally eschewed palaces and congregational mosques, the first as inappropriate to their claims to political legitimacy as "loyal servants of the 'Abbasid Caliph" and the second as both too imperial and too ecumenical for their particular needs,[30] neither building was very appropriate in a city that had little political importance to either dynasty—in Mamluk times Jerusalem was the province of a province: it received its orders and officials not directly from Cairo but from the governor of Damascus[31]—and already possessed in the Aqsa a state-run congregational mosque of such sanctity and prestige that it effectively inhibited the construction of any but the most modest mosques in Jerusalem, and even those show little of the remarkable verticality of their companion pieces in Cairo and Damascus.[32] And finally, there was nothing in the commercial prospects of Jerusalem to encourage investment in buildings geared to the long distance trade that later enriched the cities of Syria.

Thus, when it came to investing the state's resources in urban public institutions and buildings, the Ayyubids, and following them the Mamluks, who between them built most of the Islamic public buildings in Jerusalem,[33] proceeded exactly as they had earlier in Cairo and Damascus: they built by overwhelming preference *madrasa*s and convents, the *khanaqa*s, *ribat*s, and *zawiya*s of the sources. All of them were Muslim buildings, to be sure, but more specifically Sunni Muslim buildings, and it is the presence of the qualifier that effectively disassociates their intent from the Crusades and places them instead in the mainstream of what has been called the "Sunni renaissance." Salah al-Din was well aware that he was fighting a war against Christian revanchists, but it is notable that once he had retaken Jerusalem and restored the Dome of the Rock and the Aqsa to their original Muslim functions, he converted the Crusaders' two chief buildings in the city, the patriarchal residence and the Church of Saint Anne, not into mosques but the first into a *khanaqa* and the second into a *madrasa*.[34]

From first to last the *madrasa* was the most common and most important public facility built in Jerusalem. Our best evidence begins in the middle of the thirteenth century after the Mamluks had stabilized the political conditions within their domains. By the beginning of the fourteenth century the city had its own resident *Na'ib*, or governor, while the sanctuaries on the Temple mount were under the direct supervision of a special official, the *Nazir al-Haramayn*, and Jerusalem began to number among its residents, in the manner of holy cities, exiled Mamluk barons from Egypt whose wealth and prestige stiffened the economic and social fabric of the city.[35] And that new stability began to be reflected in public buildings. From 1267 to the end of Mamluk sovereignty at the beginning of the sixteenth century there were built in Jerusalem twenty-six documented *madrasa*s and sixteen *ribat*s, *zawiya*s, and *khanaqa*s.[36] Writing in 1495, the city's chronicler Mujir al-Din al-Ulaymi notes thirty-nine *madrasa*s and twenty-two hostels and convents, a great many of them along the periphery of the Haram and almost all of them *waqf*-endowed by Mamluk rulers and notables.[37]

In pre-Islamic times the Ka'ba at Mecca was narrowly hemmed in by the private dwellings, first tents and then houses, of the commercial aristocracy of the city, with a single building, the *Dar al-Nadwa*, serving as the city's public council chamber. As the Meccan *haram* was enlarged in the first Muslim centuries, those private residences were slowly pushed backward and away from the sanctuary. And though they changed hands through purchase and expropriation, they did not entirely lose their character as domestic quarters. In the eighth century Zubayda had a residence on one side of the *haram* and her husband Harun on the other, and even the *Dar al-Nadwa* was bought by Mu'awiya and used by him and subsequent Caliphs into the ninth century as their residence in the holy city.[38]

It was at some later point, perhaps in the twelfth but more likely in the thirteenth century, when the same institutions were gaining currency in Jerusalem, that properties around the Meccan *haram* began to be converted into genuine public facilities, *ribat*s and *madrasa*s, some of the latter with libraries, and supported, as in Jerusalem, by imperial, that is, Mamluk endowments.[39] The most famous and splendid of them was the *madrasa* built in 1476 by the Mamluk Sultan Qa'it Bay of Cairo, the same ruler responsible for two of Jerusalem's most beautiful buildings, the Ashrafiyya *madrasa* on the north side of the Haram and the domed fountain (*sabil*) standing just before it,[40] and endowed it from some commercial properties in Mecca and agricultural lands in Egypt. His Meccan *madrasa* had a large lecture hall, seventy-two rooms for faculty and students, a library for each of the canonical law schools of Sunni Islam and was crowned, in typical Mamluk fashion, with a remarkable minaret.[41]

As in Jerusalem, the public building programs in the holy cities of the Hejaz were supported by *waqf*, the land and enterprises across the face of Islam whose income, operating and administrative expenses aside, went to some pious cause, in this case the upkeep and adornment of Mecca. Just as with the outright gifts, it is impossible to sort out or even number such *waqfs* for the *Haramayn*. Each had a charter, many of them detailed indeed, and a designated administrator, but they were essentially local affairs. We do know that there was an attempt to transmit that income to its destination through the same kind of unofficial network of merchants and travelers revealed in the documents of the Cairo Geniza, but how successfully or how regularly or in what sums we cannot even guess. In the Ottoman Empire, however, the state played a role in both the accounting and the income transmission of the larger public *waqf*s, and so there at least we are on somewhat firmer ground.

The Ottoman sultans regarded themselves as "Servants of the Holy Places," as we have seen, and many of them appear to have taken the responsibility seriously. The supervision of the "Holy Cities Endowment Administration" (*Harameynvakiflari*) was in the hands of the third-highest ranking official of the state, and the funds were kept in a special treasury with its inspectors.[42] In Egypt, where the records are most complete, the Ottomans apparently tried to rationalize the system.[43] Holy city *waqf*s going back to Mamluk times were combined and reorganized and then added to by successive Ottoman sultans and various amirs down to the end of the eighteenth century. Much of the *waqf* income in

Egypt was generated from agricultural land; hence, not only did it generate a substantial amount of grain for Mecca, perhaps half a bushel for each resident, it also required a special delivery mechanism, in this case a grain flotilla on the Red Sea.[44] But here as elsewhere the Ottomans were better accountants than they were managers. The public records show how much grain and cash *should* have been delivered to Mecca, the income minus administrative costs, but they also indicate that the payments in both cash and kind were frequently and almost systematically in arrears in the eighteenth century,[45] and for much the same reason that plagued the gift and grant administration: the funds were being diverted elsewhere.

Despite the graft and mismanagement at the point of dispatch, moneys and grain did arrive in Mecca, though we cannot say how much. And when they are added to the gifts and gratuities given by the pilgrims themselves and to the enormous commercial opportunities offered by the *hajj*, no one, neither sharif nor ordinary Meccan, was in straitened circumstances in the city. On the contrary, there must have been many wealthy Meccans, but there are few signs that any of their considerable income was invested in the holy city or its public facilities.[46]

The sources note a great number of *madrasa*s and hospices built in Mecca from the thirteenth to the fifteenth century, but it should be noted that almost without exception they were constructed in the same narrow zone around the *haram*, that is, one was built after another on the very same site. Fire, flood, mismanagement, and the collapse of endowment all took their toll on the buildings and the properties.[47] Even Qa'it Bay's splendid *madrasa* had seriously deteriorated after seventy years, and the building ended its days as a privately owned hostel for Egyptian pilgrims.[48]

Though such public facilities were still being built in the city in the sixteenth century and beyond, they fared little better. The Istanbul-appointed chief justice of the city rented out to Turkish *hajji*s the famous Sulaymaniyya *madrasa* not far from his Hall of Justice,[49] and Snouck Hurgronje reports that by the nineteenth century the very word *madrasa* had come to mean nothing more to the Meccans than a rather fine house near the *haram*.[50]

Medieval Mecca stands in sharp contrast with even secular centers in the *Dar al-Islam* in the scarcity, poverty, and impermanence of its public facilities.[51] There was a concern to supply water to the pilgrims, possibly because the water supply was a year-round problem for the permanent residents as well, but both food and lodging offered such attractive, if seasonal, prospects for a commercial windfall that their supply eventually lapsed entirely into private hands. There were other causes as well for Mecca's urban instability. Throughout most of its history the public as well as the private buildings of Mecca were made of baked brick, a material little capable of resisting the almost constant flooding that plagued the city.[52] Again, the sources of endowment were distant rulers who could exercise no supervision of their grants, while the local princes, who were in a position to do so, showed little means or even inclination toward such pious investments. As for private donations for public facilities, there were actual disincentives: anyone who wished to put up a public building in Mecca had to receive special permission from the caliph, he was not permitted to post his name on the edifice, and, finally, the prospective benefactor had to pay the sharif a sum so large that it effectively doubled the cost of the building.[53]

The *madrasa*s of Jerualem, and the same is true of those in Mecca, had no connection with the functions of the holy city as such; they were there because Jerusalem was important in a particular way to the twelfth-century rulers of the city and to many of their successors who consequently underlined that importance by causing to be built there the visible architectural manifestations of an institution that had no demonstrable relationship to the size or the needs or the desires of the population. The function of the *madrasa* was the teaching of religious law, and in particular the Shafi'ite school of Sunni law, by a subsidized elite to another subsidized elite, and so it had an intimate connection in both its function and its visible, physical presence not so much with the city as with the struggle for legal, ritual, and political supremacy within the Islamic community as a whole. How many *madrasa*s did a city of Jerusalem's size require? The question is irrelevant and perhaps even frivolous: there were as many *madrasa*s in Jerusalem as its rulers and their associates chose and could afford to construct there.

Regarded as a physical presence, the *madrasa* was a kind of ambivalent urban pseudomorph. Though Muslim iconography is far less explicit than the Christian use of symbols to post a premise, the *madrasa* was obviously a religious building since it was created from religious motives and it housed a religious activity, the teaching of the Law. And in both Mecca and Jerusalem it behaved as such. *Madrasa*s clung to the edges of the *haram*, where, facing inward, they both shared and enhanced the holiness of the primary shrine by creating a monumental frame or facade around it periphery. But *waqf* projects were also used as propaganda, as we have seen, and as advertisements of both piety and a program. These too are public functions, and they drew the endowed buildings away from their contemplation of the sanctuary and out along the commercial thoroughfares of the city. Not in Mecca, where the urban fabric was too fragile to sustain such investment, but certainly in Jerusalem, where *waqf* funds were used to buy up prime commercial property along the bazaar streets that led along the east-west axis to and from the Haram and to construct on them a dense network of *madrasa*s, *turbe*s, and *ribat*s where otherwise we might expect shops and khans.[54]

The Jerusalem *madrasa*s and *khanaqa*s have not survived into the twentieth century. Many of the splendid stone buildings erected by the Mamluks still stand, but they have long since ceased to function as either law schools or Sufi convents and either have lapsed into private occupancy, if not private ownership, or have been put to serving Jerusalem's more contemporary preoccupations: one is the headquarters of the Department of Islamic Archeology and the other is a guard post of the Israeli army. There is at present one functioning *madrasa* in Jerusalem, but its beginnings do not go back beyond the British Mandate in Palestine.

Waqf is a complex institution. It takes the income generated by property or some other form of wealth and invests it, for God's sake, in another form of property or enterprise. This transfer of income, whatever its motives or satisfactions for the donor, and whatever its social and philanthropic benefits,[55] has had incalculable economic effects in Islam, on the tax base of the Islamic polity, on the management of the "donor" property, and not least on the capital development of the Islamic city of the Middle Ages, when most of the city's "public" buildings were in fact privately initiated and funded enterprises. As a conscious instrument of urban development *waqf* was arbitrary and often willful; though they drastically reshaped the urban landscape, *waqf*-generated properties generally responded directly to the donor's intent and only peripherally and accidentally to the city's needs.

In the examples we have seen from Jerusalem and Mecca, *waqf* income invested directly into building projects was used primarily for (1) the construction or enlargement of the primary shrine and other public buildings, chiefly *madrasa*s, that possessed some religious quality, and (2) the support of the staff of those establishments, liturgical functionaries in the shrine and *ulama* in the *madrasa*s. The central shrine apart, this disposition of *waqf* funds was not altogether atypical of the Islamic city anywhere in the *Dar al-Islam*, where the bulk of such donations went into mosques and *madrasa*s.

In Jerusalem the Ayyubid and Mamluk endowment went primarily into *madrasa*s, as we have seen, building and staff, and its use for that purpose illustrates the defect in our understanding of the Islamic *waqf* as a "charitable foundation." Some of the Christian resonances of the word *charitable* are indeed discernible in the notion of "almsgiving" (*sadaqa*) encouraged by the Qur'an for the benefit of "the poor, the needy, those who collect for them and those whose hearts must be reconciled, to redeem the captives, the debtors, for God's cause [*fi sabil Allahi*] and for the wayfarer" (sura 9:60), but also present in that same verse are other elements like *ijtihad fi sabil Allahi*, "struggling for God's cause," that lead off into other, typically Muslim understandings of *sadaqa* and the works of piety. The *madrasa* was a welfare institution, but only if we understand "welfare" as the "welfare of the Islamic community," which in the eleventh and twelfth centuries was understood by many as the propagation of a Sunni and specifically a Shafi'ite version of Islam among Muslims everywhere, not excepting Mecca and Jerusalem.

But there are some important differences in the collection and disposition of *waqf* in the latter two centers. Because of their ecumenical status as holy cities, the donor properties, and so the income, of both Mecca and Jerusalem were richer and more widely distributed across the Islamic world than in other places whose *waqf* income more closely reflected the city's own wealth. Again, in the holy city rather more of the income was invested in institutions with a boarding component, like *khanaqa*s, *ribat*s, and *zawiya*s, that responded to the pilgrims' need for lodging. All of these latter institutions provided services for the community, not so directly perhaps as the immediate distribution of endowment funds to the needy citizens of Mecca,[56] but services nonetheless: the celebration of the Islamic liturgy, instruction in Islamic law, the housing and feeding of pilgrims.

But *waqf* was something more than a source of certain urban services or an instrument for the propagation of a certain religious ideology. Its income was also used for building, and the services just described were housed in edifices of more solid design and construction than the privately owned and operated buildings that surrounded them in the city. In addition, they were set down in locations determined not by commercial or economic considerations but by spiritual and, most importantly, political ones. In purely physical terms a primary use of *waqf* endowments was for the erection of public buildings. In this their donors were in fact little different from the Roman emperors subsidizing temple complexes at Baalbek or Gerasa, a wealthy and civic-minded merchant or landowner endowing a stoa at Athens or a library in Ephesus, or a pious sixth-century Christian underwriting an orphanage in Jerusalem itself. What is different is the disparity of scale in the endowment of the two holy cities and the absolute importance of *waqf* funds vis-à-vis other forms of investment in Mecca and Jerusalem. As holy cities both places were top-heavy with "social capital" converted from real wealth all over the Islamic world, but they had at the same time little commercial or administrative importance to balance that *waqf* investment, no courtly presence or secular bureaucracy to produce or require their own goods and services.

From an urban perspective, the heavy *waqf* investment in "secondary" spiritual functions like those represented by the *madrasa*—secondary, that is, relative to the principal holy place—was, like the military budgets of many contemporary states, an artificially proportioned response to a real need. That such was indeed the case appears very clearly at Mecca where the laissez-faire atmosphere of a city remote from outside political controls permitted the operation of more genuine urban forces. And those forces—the hunger of the marketplace, the ambitions and wants of the entrepreneur—quickly converted almost every piece of *waqf*-generated "social capital" back into its real wealth counterpart: *madrasa*s became rooming houses.

The lack of capital investment in Mecca, and indeed in Jerusalem too in Ottoman times, did not merely reflect local conditions; it was also the result of a change in the philosophy and policy of subsidization.[57] In the seventeenth and eighteenth centuries *waqf* funds were being used not for capital investment but for personal subsidy, and in the first instance of government and local officials. That new light is refracted from a number of different angles. The Ottomans simply stopped any significant building activity in Jerusalem in the seventeenth century, and there is no evidence from contemporary witnesses that they behaved any differently in Mecca. We see that policy shift from another perspective when we compare the Ottoman government subsidies given to Jerusalem, which had no political importance whatsoever, with the grants designated for those primary symbols of the Ottomans' Islamic legitimacy, the Holy Cities of the Hejaz; again in the case of the latter, when we note the extraordinary disproportion that began to develop between the funds for Mecca, which was merely a holy city, and Medina, where the Turkish regional administration, civil and military, was located. Looked at simply in relative terms, a typical three-way distribution in the Ottoman period allotted approximately 68 percent of the funds to Medina, 26 percent to Mecca, and a mere six percent to Jerusalem.[58] And if we look more closely at the accounts of the *Haramayn*, the grants for Mecca rose from 1.7 million silver *paras* in 1706 to 3.2 million in 1798, while for that same period Medina's subsidy exploded from 3.3 million *paras* to 16.2 million.[59]

This marked turn from buildings to people might under other circumstances be construed as a move in a more philanthropic direction if the Ottoman fiscal records did not confront us with another reality: that the stipends, gifts, grants, and endowments were going in the main into the pockets of high government functionaries, most of them remote in space and spirit from the intended destination of those moneys. The Ottoman state was in fact getting a double return on those funds: the subsidies were *seen* to be given, as indeed they were, and Mecca was so politically feeble that it did not greatly matter if the allotments were actually received. Where they did end up was far more politically useful: in the name of the *Haramayn* the Ottomans were in truth expensively underwriting the welfare of their troublesome and dangerous Mamluk military aristocracy in Egypt and the provinces.

NOTES

1. M. Shekalim 5 and 6.
2. See Josephus, *Ant.* XIV, 214, 245. In eleventh century Cairo and elsewhere the commonly held assets and property of the Jewish community was called *qodesh*, "the holy": Goitein 1971: 99, and Gil 1976.
3. Both Herod of Chalcis and Agrippa II claimed and were granted by the Romans jurisdiction over the Temple, which certainly included the allocation of its funds for public works projects (Josephus, *Ant.* XX, 15 and 223; *BJ* V, 36). This is quite different from guaranteeing the sources of such funds.
4. Schürer 1979: 280–81.
5. On the legal prohibition of exacting such payments "like taxes," *CJ* I, 3, 38.
6. Eusebius, *Life of Constantine* II, 46.
7. Jones 1964: 895–98; on the special legal provisions made for Jerusalem on the matter of alienating Church properties, Justinian, *Nov.* XL.
8. Justinian, *Nov.* LXVII, 2.
9. *Lib. Pont.* nos. 34, 35, 38, 42, 46.
10. Armstrong 1969; on the complex financial relations that developed between Church and state in this era, Armstrong 1967; Kaplan 1976; Dauphin 1979. Nor was the Church always the beneficiary: Monks 1953 (Alexandria).
11. Schwartz 1939: 177, 10–14; on the legislation concerning the private endowment (*idia dioikesis*) of public institutions, Justinian, *Nov.* CXX, 6.
12. *CJ* I, 2, 17 (Anastasius).
13. Text in Prawer 1972: 167.
14. Benvenisti 1970: 56. The "Street of Foul Smells" or "Bad Cooking" is probably a Crusader characterization of that section of the Jerusalem bazaar that specialized in "take out" food; see chapter 9.
15. On the Geniza evidence: Goitein 1971: 112–21; Gil 1976.
16. See documents 11a–c, 13 in Goiten 1971: 414–15. The designation "for the poor" does not mean that they were necessarily the first beneficiaries of the endowment, but may have been the residual beneficiaries: ibid.: 118–19.

17. Mann 1920–22: 1, 160.

18. These are not the only examples, of course. Most Muslim shrine cities were heavily endowed, and the *waqf*s at Hebron were particularly extensive and venerable, dating, according to the Muslim tradition, to the earliest days of Islam: Massignon 1951/1963: 186–89; Karmon 1975: 76, 78.

19. Cohen and Lewis 1978: 95–104.

20. The income tax on the Anastasis, which was introduced by the Ottoman Sultan Sulayman, was specifically designated for the support of Qur'an readers in the Dome of the Rock: ibid.: 95. The practice of such a "retorsive" tax is reminiscent of the Romans' diversion of the half-shekel Temple tax to the support of the pagan temples of Rome; cf. Schürer 1979: 272 and n. 58.

21. Mujir al-Din 1968: 2, 269.

22. Ibid.: 2, 41, 144.

23. See Lapidus 1967: 195–98 and cf. Burgoyne 1976.

24. The only concentration of Islamic buildings west of the old Roman *cardo* was at the Tower of David, where the civil rulers of Jerusalem have traditionally had their residence, whether they are Jewish, Christian, or Muslim.

25. On the post-Crusader proliferation of the *fada'il* literature, Sivan 1967, 1971; Hasson 1981.

26. On Nur al-Din, Elisséeff 1967, and most recently on Salah al-Din, Lyons and Jackson 1981.

27. On Nur al-Din's building program in Damascus, Elisséef 1967; al-Tabba 1982. On the similar Ayyubid program in Cairo and Damascus, Humphreys 1972; Lapidus 1972; Fernandes 1980.

28. Makdisi 1961; Humphreys 1972: 94–95; Sourdel 1976.

29. Humphreys 1972; Lapidus 1972.

30. Humphreys 1972: 86–88 for the palace and 88–93 for the obsolescence of the congregational mosque as a political symbol.

31. Drory 1981: 193–97.

32. Humphreys 1972: 98 for this characteristic of the Mamluk mosque. One interesting Mamluk "violation" of the modest flatness of the Jerusalem skyline are the two fifteenth-century minarets built, as they appear from the Haram, flanking (or guarding?) the rotunda of the Anastasis in the Christian quarter of the city: Walls 1976.

33. Cf. Burgoyne 1976.

34. Mujir al-Din 1968: 2, 41 and 47; Gabrieli 1969: 174, citing Imad al-Din. For the Salahiyya *madrasa* on the site of Saint Anne's: Tamari 1968.

35. Ayalon 1973: Drory 1981: 196.

36. Burgoyne 1976: Drory 1981: 203–08.

37. Mujir al-Din 1968: 2, 33–48, with a detailed description (2, 325–29) of the building in 1482 of the Ashrafiyya *madrasa* by engineers and craftsmen, some of them Christians, brought in from Egypt; cf. Drory 1981: 198–201. The same sultan built an equally impressive law school in Mecca; see below.

38. Wuestenfeld 1861: 184; Gaudefroy-Demombynes 1923: 145 (Zubayda) and 151–52; on the political strategy of Mu'awiya's purchase: Serjeant 1962: 54. By the 890s the *Dar al-Nadwa* was so ruined that it was no longer habitable: Wuestenfeld 1861: 206.

39. Wuestenfeld 1861: 229–30, 237, 252, 259, etc.

40. On the Jerusalem Ashrafiyya, see Tamari 1976; Peters 1985: 413–16, and n. 37 above.

41. Wuestenfeld 1861: 291–92; Gaudefroy-Demombynes 1923: 134–35; on the other *madrasa*s of Mecca: Qutb al-Din 1857: 211–12, 226, 343, 351 ff., 417.

42. Gibb and Bowen 1950–57: I/1, 77; I/2, 170–71.

43. The material on the *Haramayn waqfs* in Egypt during Ottoman times is summarized and described in Shaw 1962 : 269–71.

44. At first the fleets were maintained out of the *waqfs*' own funds as an administrative expense, but as that expense mounted the government took an increasingly large hand in defraying the fleet costs out of the imperial treasury: Shaw 1962: 270.

45. Ibid.: 270. An interesting case of pledged *waqf* shortfall is that of the "Kiswe Waqf," the endowment that had as its object the costs connected with the annual manufacture of the *kiswe*, the heavily ornamented ceremonial veil with which the Ka'ba was annually draped. The Mamluks had established *waqfs* for this purpose, and the early Ottoman Sultans, with the typical pride and generosity of new heirs to old honors, added to both the endowment and the ornamentation that it was supposed to provide, including an annual *kiswe* for the tomb of the Prophet. This too fell into arrears, and the government had to make up the deficit from imperial funds. Eventually the *kiswe* was renewed only every five years, and in the eighteenth century there was no replacement at all for almost a hundred years: Shaw 1962: 259–60.

46. One notable exception was the Sharif Hasan who was lord of Mecca from 1396 to 1426. In addition to a palace for himself, he had constructed in the holy city one new hospice and repaired another which had earlier been destroyed by fire. The famous Mustansiriyya hospital was likewise near collapse in his day, and he had this building restored as well. And finally he had repairs made on Zubayda's old aqueduct that brought in water from the "Gardens of Husayn" near Ta'if: Wuestenfeld 1861: 285.

47. Wuestenfeld 1861: 264, 284, 285, 292; on the mismanagement of endowments, Burckhardt 1829: 104–05, 154.

48. Wuestenfeld 1861: 292; Gaudefroy-Demombynes 1923: 135.

49. Burckhardt 1829: 155.

50. Snouck Hurgronje 1931: 172.

51. Burckhardt's judgment on this score (1829: 104) at the beginning of the nineteenth century is little different from Ibn Jubayr's at the end of the twelfth.

52. When Ludovico Varthema visited Mecca at the beginning of the sixteenth century, he noted that the *haram* enclosure was still constructed of baked brick: cited in de Gaury 1951: 117.

53. Ibn Jubayr 1949–51: 127 Ar./148–49 tr.

54. The tension between commercial concerns and the complex motivation that lay behind *waqf* endowments is well illustrated in the Tashtimuriyya *madrasa* of 1382, one of the westernmost of the Mamluk buildings along Muslim Jerusalem's principal commercial thoroughfare between the Jaffa Gate and the Chain Gate of the Haram. Instead of the usual blind facade, the *madrasa* was originally designed to have commercial shops along the side facing the main street. The income from these boutiques doubtless went to the support of the *madrasa* itself: Kessler 1979: 158.

55. See chapter 8 and Stillman 1975, who has reviewed the effects of *waqf enterprises* in medieval Islam; here, however, it is a matter of the effect of *waqf* income transformed into *property*.

56. Whether this pension, which might be regarded as a philanthropic dole, did more harm than good might be debated, as its Jewish analogue certainly was. The *halluka*, or "shares," were donations sent from European Jewish communities to those of their coreligionists who early in the nineteenth century had migrated to Eretz Israel's holy cities, Jerusalem, Safed, and Tiberias. Those immigrants of the so-called First Yishuv were regarded by many of their more secular successors as "spoiled" by the *halluka*, however

pious might have been the donors' intent; see Kaniel 1981: 232–35.

57. The first annual cash subsidy for Mecca appears to have been initiated by the Caliph Muqtadir in A.D. 909: Wuestenfeld 1861: 209.

58. Shaw 1962: 260.

59. Ibid.: 257.

CHAPTER VIII

For the Public Welfare

All cities possess some kind of public facilities. Those of the holy city reflect both its special religious and political importance and its peculiar urban needs. Some of the holy city's public institutions and facilities *respond to the physical and spiritual requirements of the pilgrim population, while others, like the adornment of the city's shrines, flow from a more secular impulse to enhance and glorify both the holy city and the polity of which it is part.*

If we look to the monuments recorded in our literary sources, the public facilities of Jewish Jerusalem, the Temple apart, issue from the political regimes of state and municipal government. The Hasmoneans and Herodians did build in the city, but their interests were secular and had to do with fortifications, palaces, council chambers, municipal archives, and those other inevitable corollaries of urban Hellenism, a gymnasium, theater, and hippodrome. How the community was served by Temple funds is less clear, however. The poor, we know, were recipients of the so-called third tithe, but we are not informed how it was administered or disbursed, and the same is true for the funds earmarked by religious law for the ransoming of captives and the burial of the dead.[1] The Temple's institutional outreach is, as a matter of fact, almost invisible in the sources, most of which are far more concerned with the fulfillment of the tithing *obligation* than with the actual mechanisms of the long disappeared Temple.[2]

Most of the public services described in the Mishna, which was explicating the Law for *all* Jews, none of whom actually lived in Jerusalem at the time of its redaction, are of the type that might be found in any Jewish community. Temple Jerusalem may, however, have had some privately sponsored facilities specifically for the use of pilgrims and visitors. Such at least is a plausible explanation of the inscription of "Theodotus son of Vettenus, priest and archisynagogue, son of an archisynagogue, grandson of an archisynagogue," who dedicated in the Ophel quarter of the city a synagogue that had attached to it a house, a hospice, rooms, and some kind of water installation for the use of pilgrims from abroad.[3] The same may be true by extension of other "ethnic" synagogues of Jerusalem mentioned in the Acts of the Apostles (6:9): the synagogues of the Libertines, of the Cyrenians, of the Alexandrians, and "those of Cilicia and Asia," all of which would appear to be endowed facilities for the use of particular communities of Diaspora Jews who, like the later Maghrebis in the Muslim city, were either resident in Jerusalem or had come there for one or another of the pilgrimage festivals.[4]

Though Jewish philanthropy was regular and organized in post-Exilic times, its primary locus was the synogogue, where alms were collected for the poor and strangers and a special synagogue officer supervised their distribution.[5] Our knowledge of the synagogues of Jerusalem is very scanty indeed, but what evidence there is points, as we have just seen, to Diaspora Jews who constituted "special" congregations within the larger Jewish community in the city. And if, as has been argued, the charitable efforts of those synagogues were directed toward their own ethnic constituents, then the broader and more general programs of public support in Jerusalem must have been administered by Temple treasurers, the *gazophyloi* and *gizbarim* of the sources, out of Temple funds.[6]

After the destruction of the Temple the Jews of Jerusalem, when they were permitted to reside there, returned to the synagogue-oriented system of public philanthropy, which is described in the sources almost exactly as it appears to lie behind the text of the Acts of the Apostles. According to an eleventh-century Jewish chronicle, there were in the Jerusalem two kinds of synagogues: one for the residents and another "belonging to distant congregations," that is, visitors from the Diaspora who assembled (and boarded?) in ethnic or regional facilities while they were in the holy city.[7]

Christianity, which had its own primitive welfare system on a Jewish model, inherited with Constantine's conversion the more complex Roman system of imperial and municipal philanthropy.[8] The Greco-Roman city provided a great many public services and facilities for its citizens, some of which were found, as has been remarked, in Herodian Jerusalem. They were supported in some instances from municipal revenues, sometimes by special taxes on the curial class and even by endowment. In the second Christian century those imperial and municipal services were lavishly instituted and generously maintained, but in the third and fourth they were beginning to deteriorate or were being abandoned under the trying new economic and social circumstances afflicting the Roman Empire.[9] By then, however, Christian Church and Roman state were allied in a new enterprise that included the care of the ill, the poor, the orphan, and in the case of Jerusalem, the pilgrim.

The role of the Christian Roman emperor, like that of his pagan predecessors, was to build and to bless, with buildings for public use and an extensive system of social welfare.[10] There was imperial image building in this as well, and so Constantinople was probably the chief recipient of imperial largess. But Jerusalem, the holy city where Constantine himself had set the imperial example and where the aura of Christian giving remained particularly strong, had its own monuments to public welfare and Christian charity. Justinian built an endowed hundred-bed hospital, later doubled in size, as part of a large complex attached to his church called the Nea,[11] and a similar facility with four hundred beds had been built earlier by the Empress Eudocia outside the Jaffa Gate.[12] Nor was the imperial family the only party engaged in building and maintaining public facilities in Christian Jerusalem. The city's patriarch ran his own hospital and hospice next to the episcopal palace near the Church of the Anastasis,[13] and a private donor put up an old-age home (*gerokomeion*) for indigent women.[14]

Constantine's conversion of Jerusalem into a kind of national monument to the earliest days of Christianity affected the city's hinterland and the entirety of what came to be known as the "Holy Land," an elastic denomination that extended over the Near East from Egypt (with its association with the Holy Family derived from the infancy narratives of both the canonical Gospels and the Apocrypha) as far as Ephesus in Anatolia (a city connected by tradition to both the Virgin and Saint John). And part of that broad Christian landscape from the fourth century on were the communities of monks and nuns who came to live in the wilderness but ended up being drawn into the orbit of the urban holy places as well. Some of those communities were rooted in nothing more complicated than the piety of the men and women who founded them, but others were as national and "ethnic" as the Jerusalem synagogues of the first century.[15] By the sixth some of the monasteries located south and east of Jerusalem were building and running visitors' facilities in the city itself, a number specifically for the in-city use of the monks of the founding monastery, others for visiting monks from abroad.[16]

The monasteries took care of their own finances, but otherwise Jerusalem's pilgrim accommodations were supported by the patriarch from general Church funds or by donations from individuals. Many were subsidized by the income from inalienable properties given over to and administered by the service institution itself, much in the manner of the later Islamic *waqf*.[17] By far the largest share of both gifts and endowments came from the emperor himself. Justinian in the sixth century behaved little differently in this regard from Herod in the first and the Mamluk sultans in the fifteenth when he constructed and endowed, *ad majorem Dei gloriam et imperii*, public buildings in the holiest city in his kingdom.

When the Crusaders arrived in Jerusalem in 1099 there must have been little left of the Christian charitable institutions that were flourishing there in the sixth century. Some may not have been rebuilt after the Persian destruction of 614, and those that were suffered the fatal disability of being cut off from their former imperial endowments by the Muslim conquest and probably had to rely for their support on the contributions of a much reduced number of pilgrims. The *Commemoratorium* from around A.D. 800 lists three "guestmasters" at the Holy Sepulcher and twelve clergy at what may have been the surviving hospice facilities of Justinian's Nea, but there was little else that might be construed as facilities for the pilgrim public.[18] Among the casualties of the new order may have been the first and only Latin hostel in the pre-Muslim city, that founded by Gregory the Great about A.D. 600, since we hear no more of it.[19] There was, however, another instituted by Charlemagne, who reportedly negotiated its establishment with Harun al-Rashid, and on the testimony of the Breton pilgrim Bernard it was still operating in 870 or thereabouts.[20]

Tradition connects both Western enterprises, Gregory's and Charlemagne's, with a more historically certain building, the Church of Saint Mary Latina, which stood with other ecclesiastical buildings at the site of the earlier Roman forum just to the south of the Church of the Holy Sepulcher. Saint Mary's was taken over and restored in the mid-eleventh century by Amalfi merchants who also sponsored a hospice or hospital directed by the Benedictine clergy of that church. The facility was later enlarged, and when the Crusaders took the city shortly thereafter, the hospice director and the institution itself were removed from the jurisdiction of Saint Mary Latina and given an autonomous existence, with quarters for its staff and its own church, called Saint John's. Finally in 1113 the association, hospital and staff, were constituted by papal bull as an independent religious order, that of the Knights of Saint John or, as they came to be known, the Knights Hospitallers.[21]

The Hospitallers play an important part in the military and economic history of the Latin Kingdom and of medieval Europe, but it is their specific role in the holy city of Jerusalem that concerns us here. And in that context it was an entirely new phenomenon. This was not merely a single large charitable institution—the Hospital of Saint John could handle two thousand patients on any given day—but the headquarters of a true international support network of members, associates and benefactors, independent of episcopal jurisdiction and local church tithes, and with large holdings all over Europe, one third of which was forwarded to Jerusalem.[22] Byzantine endowments and Islamic *waqf* were essentially passive instruments for the transfer of discrete income revenues from private property into the domain of material or spiritual welfare, while the Hospitallers and their public facility in Jerusalem were at the hub of an *organization* in the active pursuit of an ideal.

The Jewish philanthropic infrastructure that had once existed in Jerusalem was entirely destroyed by the catastrophes and oppression visited upon the Jews of the city by the Romans in 70 and 135 and often thereafter under Christian auspices. But the community preserved the tradition and had the means and the will to carry on those activities elsewhere in the Diaspora; when we are once again given some sense of the *structure* of Jewish communities by the Geniza documents from Egypt, the social welfare program appears to be an important element in Jewish life.[23] Jews felt responsible for their fellow Jews, wherever they were found, and not merely to individuals but to entire communities. Thus financial help was often extended, from Cairo, for example, to the Jerusalem community as a whole, and for two reasons: its greater need and its undeniable prestige. The need arose from the general poverty of the Jerusalem Jews and from their responsibility for an unusually large number of foreign visitors. Jerusalem's special status was equally apparent: the city was the seat of the gaon and the Palestinian Yeshiva; it was seen as a community of scholars, and a gift to a scholar, it was said, was the equivalent of making an offering in the Temple; and finally, Jerusalem continued to be the focus of Jewish longing for the past and hope for the future.

This recognition of the preeminence of Jerusalem did not render the Jews there either complacent or assured that their needs would be taken care of. Special collections were taken up annually for Jerusalem in the Jewish communities outside Palestine, but this activity had to be continuously encouraged and sustained by fund-raisers sent out from Jerusalem for that purpose.[24] And since then as now it was easier to raise money for specific projects than for general purposes, some of the funds were earmarked for the "ethnic" or "national" subcommunities of Jews in the Holy City, the Yemenis, for example, or the Libyans. And there were of course rewards: rich and generous benefactors could be seconded to membership in the Yeshiva or endowed with a veritable Byzantine shower of honorific titles.[25]

Not many of Geniza documents deal directly with the administration of charity and the disbursement of community funds among the Jews of Jerusalem in the eleventh century, but it seems likely that they were not very different in their general lines from what was being done at that time in Cairo, where the infrastructure was far more complete. The community chest funds, which came largely from donations outside Palestine, went in the first instance to the support of the clerical establishment that was occupied full-time with the affairs of the community: the gaon and all the judges, preachers, teachers, and cantors of the Jerusalem Yeshiva, some of whom may have lived at community expense in the Yeshiva compound or that of one of the city synagogues.[26] Another large share of the community funds went to the indigent in the form of food and even free lodging and, what was a severe problem in Jerusalem, to the payment of the alleged poll-tax arrears of the pilgrim population.[27]

All Jewish communities seem to have made a special effort on behalf of the foreigners and travelers in their midst, whether poor or not. They were fed, clothed, lodged, helped to find work, and assisted along on the next stage of their journey through a network of letters and petitions, formal and informal.[28] This must have created special problems in Jerusalem, which was often not a way station but the intended end of a journey, and that seems to have been the particular point of the special collection taken up on behalf of the Holy City in the Diaspora. It seems likely too that the Jewish pilgrim found his primary succor in his own ethnic community in the city, many of which had their own synagogues, just as they did a millennium earlier, and presumably their own social services as well.[29]

If Jewish public and social services in Jerusalem seem at least as well organized as the Muslim and earlier Christian philanthropic enterprises in the city, there were obvious and important differences. Muslim philanthropy, as we shall see, derived from both state and individual, and so was on a far more lavish scale and in the end manifested itself as much in capital investment as in the flow of cash and goods. Jewish giving and receiving was a community project, and very little of the funds raised for charitable or pious purposes went into the construction of facilities. The Christians had a surviving infrastructure of churches, convents, and hospices in Muslim Jerusalem, and they were left pretty much as they had been before the conquest; the Jews were in a sense starting over after 638, and Muslim law and custom did not much encourage the construction of religious facilities by the non-Muslim minorities under their control. The Jerusalem gaonate and its Yeshiva was certainly based somewhere in the city, but it must have been in a modest setting since it has disappeared without local trace or recollection, and there is reason to think that much of the community business of a nonliturgical type was done in the houses of either the gaon or the president of the Court.[30]

Eventually there came to be Jewish public buildings in Jerusalem. There was some kind of recovery from the setback inflicted by the Crusades, much of it now inspired and financed by burgeoning Jewish communities in Europe. In the twelfth and thirteenth centuries both Petachia of Ratisbon and the famous scholar Nachmanides report finding only a single Jew in Jerusalem, but the Aragonese Kabbalist Isaac ben Joseph, who immigrated there in 1334, was delighted to discover a prosperous Jewish community, many of them French, busily engaged in commerce, science, and the study of Torah and Kabbala.[31] Whatever it was they had built lay in ruins a century and a half later, however, but the recent past was still visible to the visitor:

> The court of the Synagogue is very large and contains many houses, all of them buildings devoted by the Ashkenazis to charitable purposes, and inhabited by Ashkenazi widows. There were formerly many courts in the Jewish streets belonging to those buildings, but the elders sold them so not a single one remained. They could not, however, sell the buildings of the Ashkenazis because they were exclusively for the Ashkenazis and no other poor had a right to them.[32]

Jewish welfare programs were limited by the size and prosperity of the community, which in the case of Jerusalem were serious limitations indeed, and more generally by the fact that such programs, though they were communal, operated entirely within the private sector. Christianity and Islam both had at their disposal the resources of a state that accepted the religious obligation to almsgiving as its own. The Muslim ruler, like the Christian emperor, was willing to divert state funds to that end as well as draw upon his own considerable crown resources.

The failure of the Crusades, though it meant an end to Christian sovereignty in Jerusalem, by no means inhibited either the urgency or the possibility of Christian pilgrimage to the Holy Land, and voyagers from Europe to Palestine persevered in their desire to visit the sites associated with the life and death of their Savior.[33] It was now a more perilous enterprise, however, and if the pilgrims did not suffer immediate jeopardy to life and limb, they did have to face a great many physical and psychological hardships without the succor of either confreres or institutions to ease the way, as they had in the past. There was a kind of Christian hostel at Ramle where pilgrims were lodged while certain formalities were arranged with the Muslim authorities, and once at Jerusalem the lay pilgrims lodged at what remained of the Hospital of Saint John across the street from the Holy Sepulcher, while the clerics among them went to live in the small Franciscan community on Mount Sion.[34] For the rest, the pilgrims bargained collectively with the local residents through their official dragoman for whatever lodging, provisions, or transportation they might need. They could expect no help from the local Christian population of the eastern rites. And little wonder since the Latins took no pains to conceal the fact that they regarded their fellow Christians in the Near East as shameless heretics and schismatics, whose chief intent was to rob them blind in every commercial transaction.

Medieval Jerusalem had, then, its social and urban problems, and all the communities that lived in the holy city shared the burden of them—whether they arose from an inept administration,[35] oppressive taxes, or, most often, from outsiders like the bedouin who raided the neighborhood in hard times, which were often, and preyed on the generally defenseless pilgrims[36]—but it normally did not lack for the necessities. There was always housing, and the nearby hinterland was rich enough to supply an adequate and sometimes, when the city and territory were not being mismanaged, even an abundant supply of food,[37] though the prices were sometimes inflated, as might be expected of a city always filled with pious visitors and tourists.[38] Jerusalem did not have much of an underground water supply, but the rainfall was plentiful and the city was well equipped with cisterns and birkehs and there was an aqueduct first built by Pontius Pilate that brought water from sources near Hebron.[39]

Mecca was not so fortunate as Jerusalem; it did not have easy access to supplementary food supplies and suffered an absolute and endemic shortage of water. The Quraysh complained about the place early on.[40] Ludovico Varthema of Bologna, who visited the city sometime between 1503 and 1508, thought that the curse of God must have lain upon Mecca since it produced neither trees nor grass and had no water at all.[41] That was not quite true since the Zamzam spring was a steady, if limited source of water, but it was hardly sufficient for the needs of a swollen population of *hajjis* who were often constrained to buy water at very high prices.[42] If the physical setting and natural gifts appropriate to vigorous urban development are a *baraka*, then indeed it must have appeared that God was sorely trying what He intended should later become the holiest of cities.

Mecca was in any event a city ill-suited to support itself in the new circumstances thrust upon it by the brilliant success of Islam. The focus of all prayers, the goal of all pilgrimage, the city required constant and considerable subsidy throughout its history, and not merely to prosper, which it never did in any recognizable urban sense, but merely to survive. Islam had in effect destroyed Mecca's economic base of caravan carriage, and it was thus Islam, or, to be more specific, the rulers of Islam who had to bear the burden, or be blessed with the privilege, of supplying the holy city with its most basic needs.

Food and water were the elemental plagues of Mecca, too little of the first and too much of the latter when it rained and too little the rest of the time. Already the second Caliph 'Umar, himself a native of the city, attempted to do something about the chronic flooding by building a dam across one of the natural sluices that dumped a runoff of water into the heart of the city after every rainstorm.[43] The first aqueduct, which was built by order of the Umayyad Caliph Sulayman in 709, carried water from the nearby hills to a basin *within* the *haram*. This was reckoned an "innovation," or, to put it somewhat differently, it undermined the privileged monopoly of the 'Abbasid family as the guardians of the Zamzam. Innovation or competition, the basin was soon destroyed.[44] Harun and his wife Zubayda, both of whom displayed a great interest in Mecca, were responsible for Mecca's most ambitious water project, an aqueduct into the city from mountain springs near Arafat,[45] and the caliph's mother Khayzuran addressed Mecca's other water problem, the periodic flooding of the *haram,* with damage to most of the city's fragile buildings, by building underground runoff channels on its western side.[46]

It was by no means the end of the matter. At the beginning of the tenth century the Meccans were reduced to renting animal transport to carry water overland from Jedda, and the Vizier 'Ali ibn 'Isa had to intervene from Baghdad. He purchased and endowed the upkeep of a herd of camels and donkeys for the purpose and tried to solve the problem permanently by opening new wells in the city and its vicinity.[47] In 1557 the water failed at Arafat, where the pilgrims were collected overnight, and once again the imperial authorities had to come to Mecca's aid. In this instance it was the Ottoman Sultan Sulayman II and his sister. A large sum of money was allocated for new water channels down from the mountains and five hundred Mamluks and engineers were brought in from Damascus, Aleppo, and elsewhere. It took fourteen years to complete the project,[48] but the problem persisted, particularly since the local bedouin were in the habit of cutting off the water supply as a form of extortion against the city.[49]

The water supply of Mecca was crucial and continually troublesome, but at least it was local. Providing the city with food, on the other hand, raised political questions of quite another order. Pre-Islamic Mecca must already have experienced grave problems feeding itself since Abraham raises the problem with God himself in the Qur'an. "Lord, I have settled some of my offspring in an unfruitful valley near Thy Holy House, Lord, so they could worship Thee properly. So incline the hearts of somebody toward them so they will be provided fruits and will be grateful" (14:37). After the conquests, however, when the Meccan caravan trade declined but the wealth and population of the city increased, the problem was even graver. And the solution was no longer prayer.

Egypt had long been the grain surplus hinterland for the entire

Mediterranean, or for whatever part of that inland sea that political necessity dictated, first Rome and then Constantinople, since both cities were incapable of feeding their own teeming and politically volatile populations. And now, in a world where neither the Old Rome nor the New was of any concern to the rulers of the *Dar al-Islam*, Egypt's assigned task was to feed Mecca. The wheat of Egypt went not as before across the Mediterranean but rather across the Red Sea, to Jedda or Yenbu, and thence into the granaries of Islam's already over-inflated holy city.[50]

What was first intended as an act of caliphal beneficence set an ominous pattern for the future, however. Mecca, it was clear, was dependent upon Egypt for its very sustenance, a fact that was recognized in Baghdad when the ninth-century vizier 'Ali ibn 'Isa, the same who had taken hold of the water problem, set up the first government ministry to regulate the provisioning of the holy city. It too was a benevolent gesture—Mecca had already become a place of exile and 'Ali passed a number of his there—and though the caliphs and sultans and princes then and later might send cash and gifts from their remote capitals, only Egypt could send grain, twenty to twenty-four ships full a year, according to one seventeenth-century report.[51] The holy city became in effect a political fief of Cairo, a token not a tributary, and after the Ottoman conquest of Egypt, the sovereignty changed but not the reality of Mecca's food supply: it was grown along the Nile.

The only practical alternative to Egyptian grain were foodstuffs carried up from the Yemen. Ibn Jubayr, who visited Mecca in 1183–84, reports on the annual visit of the bedouin with their stores of food, which they bartered against Meccan goods. The Meccans had to make do for a year on such victuals, and without them, as Ibn Jubayr dryly remarks, they would have perished.[52]

As yet it is the same Ibn Jubayr who boasts that Mecca was filled with every imaginable type of fruit and vegetable, one of the many *baraka*s given to the holy city.[53] We can guess why and how. Ibn Jubayr's litany of foodstuffs is part of a more elaborate list of products available in the markets of the city. Most of them were imported and all of them were assuredly expensive, as were the fruits and vegetables brought in at three days march from al-Ta'if. The problem of feeding Mecca was not, however, one of *delicatessen* for those who could afford it, but of bread and water for those who could not. One attempt at solving it was a soup kitchen set up next to the *haram* and supported from *waqf* funds derived in part from commercial properties in Mecca and in part from agricultural lands in Egypt.[54]

In attempting to supply these subsistence needs of Mecca, caliphs and sultan were perhaps simply fulfilling their sovereign responsibilities toward a city they could ill afford to neglect. But Islam had far deeper claims of charity on ruler and laymen alike. Muhammad's community was alms-oriented from the beginning. Whether singly or in combination, the Prophet's personal experiences as an orphan and his desire to improve the lot of the needy led him to put heavy emphasis in both his preaching and example on almsgiving as a primary religious obligation, as serious and as binding on the Muslim as the obligation to prayer: every Muslim had to tithe out of his income to supply charitable assistance to the poor, the needy, and the unfortunate.[55]

This was the obligation, but as we have seen, the matter of individual religious philanthropy, *sadaqa,* was likewise preached continuously and fervently.[56] For many the response to this divine and prophetic summons to charity might consist simply in giving alms to the poor on the street or sharing food or lodging, but for the wealthy of Islam, whether rulers, merchant princes or military grandees, this *sadaqa* was a more complex process, and one which had far-reaching and long-time effects in Islamic cities. As we have seen, the primary instrument of largescale giving in Islam was the endowment or *waqf,* an economic institution that materialized in stone and mortar in cities across the *Dar al-Islam.* But the endowed mosque, *madrasa,* or *khanaqa* did not exhaust the possibilities of pious intent. Ibn Battuta traveled over most of what constituted the "Abode of Islam" in the early fourteenth century and had probably seen most of the current manifestations of endowment charity. But he was still capable of being impressed by what he saw at Damascus, the capital of the province to which Jerusalem was then a mere appanage.

> The varieties of the endowments at Damascus and their expenditures are beyond computation, so numerous are they. There are endowments in aid of persons who cannot undertake the *hajj,* out of which are paid

to those who go in their stead sums sufficient for their needs. There are endowments for supplying wedding outfits to girls, to those namely whose families are unable to provide them. There are endowments for the freeing of prisoners, and endowments for travellers, out of which they are given food, clothing and the expenses of conveyance to their countries. There are endowments for the improving and paving of streets, because the lanes in Damascus all have a pavement on either side on which the foot passengers walk, while the riders use the roadway in between. Besides these there are endowments for other charitable purposes.[57]

These were the intentions, to come to the aid of those in need of help, to further pious enterprises, and, of course, to adorn the primary shrines of Islam and to assist those who are seeking to go there or already resided on that sacred ground. By all of the available indices, none of them very precise, Mecca and Medina, the *Haramayn*, or "Two Harams," par excellence, were endowed with income properties all over the Islamic world. Though it was in theory untaxable, it remains an open question how much of that income, which had to pass through many rapacious hands en route to its distant destinations,[58] ever reached its intended beneficiaries. Public buildings in Mecca were few and poor, as will be seen, and the populace there seemed far more engaged by the prospect of *hajj* commerce than in the arrival of large sums of alms and endowment money from abroad. Such is the picture, or at least the impression before the sixteenth century. But then with the establishment of a new Ottoman sovereignty over the Hejaz and the integration of the Holy Cities into a centralized Ottoman administration, certain details begin to emerge with great, and disturbing, detail. They have mostly to do with Egypt's contribution to the welfare of the Holy Cities, but that province had from the beginning borne the chief responsibility for that welfare, as we have seen, and so the details are not inconsequential.

When the Sultan Selim I assumed control over Egypt in 1517 he issued what was both a boast and a warning to the first governor of the new Ottoman province:

I have no desire for anything from Egypt. I have conquered only the title "Servant of the Holy Cities" and I have left as *waqf* to his Excellency the Prophet all the revenues of Egypt. Bear witness that from now on you are the agent of the *Waqf* of God, so serve it well.[59]

The warning did not long prevail, but the boast came true in the deepest and most perfect sense of irony. The Sultan in fact took no profits from Egypt, and until 1534 the surpluses of that rich province were sent directly to Mecca and Medina. Even piety has its limits, however, and the wealth of Egypt in the end exceeded that of Selim's successors: they underwrote the annual pilgrimage from Cairo to Mecca and continued to send subsidies to the *Haramayn,* but the latter became a fixed amount, to be paid out of Egypt's revenues, while the rest of that large income surplus was sent to Istanbul for deposit in the imperial coffers there.

The Ottomans kept careful records, careful enough at any rate to tell us, as it must have told them, what this pious obligation was costing the state. There was no such thing as a "fixed amount" in an Ottoman budget of state, any more than there is in a modern one. Prices rise, currencies deflate, the world changes, but nothing short of immense, unbridled and unabashed extortion can explain the explosive increases in the carefully recorded funds earmarked for the Holy Cities. The role of the *Amir al-Hajj* in this plundering of the Ottoman treasury has already been rehearsed, but the hemorrhaging of cash and foodstuffs exceeded even his large capacities for peculation.

The Ottomans had inherited or assumed a number of state obligations toward the *Haramayn.* One of them was, as we have already seen, underwriting the expenses of the *hajj* caravan that once a year left Cairo for Mecca. Another was to pay cash pensions in the form of "purses" (*surre*) to the citizens of Mecca and Medina as well as separate and special stipends to the chief sharifians in those two cities. If we take 1533 as the base year and regard only the "fixed amount" allocated to the "purses," we discover that in the course of two and a half centuries the cost had escalated an astonishing 1118%, only half of which likely even reached Mecca, while the rest remained comfortably in the pockets of Cairene officials, most notably the *Amir al-Hajj.*[60] And on a more general scale, over that same period between 1533 and 1798, the *total* cost of the *hajj* caravan and stipends to the Holy Cities went up by 587%, all but a tiny fraction of the increase to satisfying the escalating demands of the *Amir al-Hajj* and the alleged payment of pensions.[61]

This was the dimension of the *state* obligation to Mecca, a political responsibility connected with the caliphate from the beginning, inherited in turn by the ʿAbbasids, the Mamluk sultans, who ruled by license from the caliphs, and finally the Ottomans, both sultans and caliphs, and regarded by each as a pious duty, an honor, and an expensive and almost ruinous demonstration of sovereignty over the holy places of Islam. But state subsidy was only one of three distinct elements that constituted the elaborate financial counterpart of Mecca's far-flung spiritual network; there was as well the matter of private gifts and of endowment. Both were empirewide and subject to individual impulses of pious generosity, and so are difficult for us to control at this remove, but to the degree that each was state-administered in the Ottoman period, it is possible to get some idea of their extent and how they worked.

In the matter of gifts, for example, any prince or wealthy individual in the *Dar al-Islam* might pledge and deliver benefits to Mecca, but by far the most substantial, most regular, and most visible were those undertaken by the city's own sovereign, the Mamluk sultans of Egypt and their Ottoman successors in Istanbul. We know for example that the early Ottoman rulers undertook to make an annual gift of 60,000-odd gold pieces divided in quite unequal measure among Mecca, Medina, and Jerusalem. From 1668 onward the sultan in effect picked his own pocket in Cairo and ordered that sum deducted from his own Egyptian income, which would normally be sent to Istanbul, and carried in his name to Mecca and Medina in the annual *hajj* caravan. The system must have been flawed, however, since in 1714 that direct transfer was ended and the money was sent from the privy purse in Istanbul by way of the Damascus caravan.[62]

Like the state subsidy, the sultan's intervention from the *res privata* was divided into "purses" determined by a master list of entitlements kept among the accounts in the capital.[63] The protocol on the Istanbul and even the Damascus end of the transfer appears to have been relatively careful and conscientious;[64] what occurred thereafter is far less certain, however. The *surre* were distributed under the qadi's own window in the Meccan *haram* after the pilgrims had left the city, but that was the only public part of the distribution process; the sharif for his part extracted his lion's share of the gifts sent to the *haram* under far more private circumstances.[65]

The most important endowed building activity in post-Crusader Jerusalem and Mecca was undoubtedly the *madrasa,* or law school. But it was not the only type by any means, and that other group of institutions known variously as *khanaqa*s, *ribat*s, and *zawiya*s is of somewhat greater consequence in the present context since they speak more directly to the needs of pilgrims, or at least visitors to the city. The terms and the institutions they represented were not always carefully distinguished in current use, but we can see behind them quite different origins and, more to the point here, different functions that eventually run together in one and the same urban institution.[66]

To state it briefly, the *zawiya* was the residence of a Sufi master, a residence that by reason of his holiness or teaching became the resort of others who wished to hear his teaching or imitate his manner of life. At the master's death he was often buried in his *zawiya,* and so the same building might eventually become a kind of residential shrine-tomb with adepts and disciples following in the steps of the master about his grave redolent with *barakat.* While the *zawiya* was the primary institution of the Sufi "orders," those associations of ascetics and mystics united in the pursuit of a single "way" (*tariqa*) to holiness, the *khanaqa* was a more public thing, an agency of state policy, in the first instance of Ayyubid policy intent on replacing the spiritual climate of Fatimid Shi'ism in Syria, Egypt, and Palestine with *adab al-sufiyya al-sunniyya,* "Sufism Sunni-style."[67] Finally, the *ribat* was essentially a hospice that, though it had distinct Sufi overtones, was devoted to providing board and shelter for the needy, the traveler, the homeless, the divorced or widowed woman .[68]

The *ribat* and the *zawiya* responded directly to social and public needs, the first a spontaneous institutionalization of Islamic religious philanthropy and the latter a reflex of popular Muslim spirituality. The *khanaqa,* on the other hand, at least under Ayyubid and Mamluk auspices, was an institution taken up like the *madrasa* and used by the regime for its own religio-political goals: the *khanaqa* was intended to promote and stabilize spiritual Sunnism, just as the *madrasa* was intended to propagate and regularize legal Sunnism, both in the face of the Isma'ili Shi'ism of the former Fatimid domains in Egypt, Palestine, and Syria, and, one might add, to magnify the ruler-founder, whose name both *madrasa* and *khanaqa* inevitably bore.

And again like the *madrasa,* the *khanaqa* sought to achieve its end through a subsidized combination of instruction and philanthropy, *'ilm* and *sadaqa.* Both had facilities for the boarding of a permanent staff and resident "fellows," and the *khanaqa* in particular was planned, staffed, and subsidized for welfare functions. A typical *khanaqa* had quarters for its state-appointed shaykh and his family, cells for the residents, a meeting hall for common devotions, a kitchen, bathhouse, and eventually, under the Mamluks, a mausoleum to serve as the final resting place of its esteemed founder and chief benefactor.[69]

The *madrasa* and the *khanaqa* were then the chief recipients of imperial and aristocratic largesse in Jerusalem and the primary agents of a state-sponsored and -supported program of social welfare, spiritual and material, the best housed and the best administered public institutions in both Mecca and Jerusalem. Their income was endowment, and their beneficiaries were in the first instance their salaried employees, whose wages were stipulated in the charter of endowment, then, as far as the *khanaqa* is concerned, the temporary residents of the institution and the population at large of the holy city.

None of this was particular to either Jerusalem or Mecca, however; *madrasa* and *khanaqa* were from the thirteenth century onward ecumenical Islamic institutions, and to follow the steps of a traveler like Ibn Battuta across the breadth of the fourteenth-century *Dar al-Islam* is to understand the astonishing number of Muslims who were fed, clothed, and at least temporarily housed through these religious institutions and the endowments that lay behind them. In a small village in Turkey, for example, Ibn Battuta visited a *khanaqa* built in about 1300 by a certain Fakr al-Din,

> who repented before God Most High of his sins. He assigned to his son the control of the income of the *khanaqa* and the supervision of the fakirs who resided in it, and all the revenues derived from the village are constituted an endowment for it. Alongside the *khanaqa* he built a bath-house *ad majorem Dei gloriam,* which may be entered by any wayfarer without any obligation of paying, and he also built a bazaar in the village and made it an endowment source for the congregational mosque. Out of the endowment for this *khanaqa* he assigned to every fakir who should come from the Holy Cities of the Hejaz or from Syria, Egypt, Iraq, Khurasan and other parts, a complete set of clothing and a 100 silver dirhams on the day of his arrival, 300 dirhams on the day of his departure and maintenance for the duration of his stay, consisting of meat, rice cooked in ghee, and sweetmeats. To each holy man from the land of Rum [Turkey], he assigned 10 dirhams and hospitality for three days.[70]

This was *sadaqa* pure and simple, material assistance for those engaged in pious enterprise, as it was assumed the "fakirs" or Sufis of this account were. But there was more. These and other deeply staffed "public" institutions of the religious sector of the Muslim polity also provided modest but adequate livelihoods, as we have seen, for a great many people in any Islamic city, and particularly in Jerusalem where there were far fewer commercial opportunities than in Damascus. And yet there is little or no comment in the sources on the extent of *sadaqa* in the holy city. Almost everyone, Muslim and non-Muslim alike, has something to say about the endowed soup kitchens of Hebron,[71] but the visitors' wonder in Jerusalem is reserved for the Haram and the shrines. It may be a case of pure bedazzlement, the overshadowing of the ordinary by the quite extraordinary Haram, but it may also reflect a reality of sorts. There was political and symbolic capital to be made in Jerusalem, and on a far grander scale than mere *sadaqa*. The object of royal investment in Jerusalem was to establish presence and legitimacy and Sunnism, and so funds followed function into buildings rather than into services.

Where Jerusalem may have been different in its social services, and Mecca too in the same regard, was in the fact that it attracted enough foreigners to constitute within itself charitable institutions with defined *ethnic* intent, like the Jewish synagogues of that and an earlier era and like the *zawiya*s endowed specifically for visitors from Mardin and the Maghreb.[72] The village of Ayn Karim lay about five miles to the west of the city and possessed a Christian shrine of the Virgin and a Church of Saint John the Baptist. The entire village was constituted as *waqf* property in the thirteenth century by the grandson of the Algerian mystic Abu Maydan Shu'ayb (d. 1197) for the benefit of the North African community that was already well established in Jerusalem at least since the time of Salah al-Din, who had earlier made the entire quarter they inhabited at the southwest corner of the Haram into *waqf* property.[73] In the extant text of the Abu Maydan *waqf* charter, the income from Ayn Karim is allocated to the distribution of bread to poor Maghrebis recently arrived in the holy city or already resident there, to the support of those living in the community convent in the Maghrebi quarter and for the payment of their funeral expenses.[74]

The practice at Mecca shows the same tendency, though perhaps with somewhat a sectarian intent. Many of the early *madrasa*s and *khanaqa*s were specifically designated for Hanifites or Shafi'ites, though the Iranian Shah Shuja in 1369 founded a hospice explicitly for Persians, and from which Indians were just as explicitly excluded.[75] A more catholic attitude was displayed by the sultan of Bengal who in 1411 endowed a *madrasa* and hospice in which were lodged, at the founder's express wish, faculty and students drawn from all four of the legal schools, though not exactly in eqaul numbers.[76] Qa'it Bay's *madrasa* was organized along the same ecumenical lines.

Whatever the public expenditures on his behalf, whether through institutions for his welfare or in the form of an outright dole, the visitor to the holy city had largely to deal with his own needs in food, lodging, and transportation and whatever inclinations he might harbor for amusement, consolation, or edification. The post-Crusade Christian pilgrims in Jerusalem provide the most graphic illustrations of the visitor fending for himself in a sacred but unfamiliar environment, but the experience was not greatly different for all those others who essayed pious voyage to a holy city. And one and all, Jew, Christian, or Muslim, in Mecca or Jerusalem, the pilgrim was venturing onto an urban terrain that might appear alien to him but where in fact he was being eagerly awaited by the local population.

NOTES

1. For the "third tithe" see Schürer 1979: 265 n. 23 and cf. Jeremias 1969: 133; on the ransoming of captives and the burial of the dead, M. Shekalim 2:5.

2. The Mishna as we have it was edited in Tiberias sometime about A.D. 200, a century and a quarter after the Jerusalem Temple ritual had ceased and the Temple itself had been destroyed. A number of the authorities cited in and by it go back, however, to Temple times, and so at least some of the Mishnaic material is based on eyewitness accounts, though neither the intentions nor the attitudes of the transmitters is what we might call historical; see Safrai 1981: 12–13. The interval between A.D.70 and 200 was not, in any event, a very extended period for the preservation of what must have been a deeply seated oral tradition.

3. Vincent 1921; cf. Lifshitz 1967.

4. Jeremias 1969: 60–63; Safrai 1981: 69–70.

5. M. Demai 3:1; M. Kiddushim 4:5; Matt. 6:2; cf. Schürer 1979: 437.

6. M. Shekalim 5:1–2; the uses of the Temple surpluses released for community needs and described in M. Shekalim 4 cover a broad range of urban projects and even commercial investment, but pilgrim facilities are not mentioned.

7. Mann 1920–22: 1, 49 n.2.

8. Jeremias 1969: 130–32; Grant 1977: 24–45.

9. On the Roman municipal services and their decline: Jones 1964: 734–37 and Claude 1969: 107–61. Claude does note (78–81) that one type of public amenity that continued to be built right through the Arab invasion was the bath.

10. Downey 1938; Constantelos 1968.

11. Procopius, *On Buildings* V, 6, 1–26; Wilkinson 1977: 84, 23; Schwartz 1939: 175, 11–15; 177, 9–14; cf. Milik 1961: 148. The *nosokomeion,* which was actually a clinic with boarding facilities, was a specifically Christian outgrowth of the hostel and like it a direct response to the pilgrim traffic to the Holy Land: Philipsborn 1961.

12. Schwartz 1939: 204, 7–9; cf. Milik 1961: 138–39.

13. Milik 1961: 138–39.

14. Ibid.: 150.

15. Chitty 1966: 84–142, and for the "national" monasteries, Beck 1959: 206.

16. Schwartz 1939: 116, 5–25.

17. Brehier 1949: 525; Jones 1964: 897, 901.

18. Wilkinson 1977: 137.

19. Vincent and Abel 1914–26: 922–25.

20. Wilkinson 1977: 142, 10; cf. Runciman 1969: 72.

21. Riley-Smith 1967.

22. Prawer 1972: 260–64; for contemporary descriptions of the hospital: Benvenisti 1970: 59. By the fourteenth century the area had reverted at least in part to its historical Roman function as a commercial center. Isaac ben Joseph, a Jewish visitor to the city in

1334, accounts as one of the "wonders of Jerusalem" an "ancient building" called "Solomon's Palace," which is likely Saint John's hospital. "In former days," he explains, "when the uncircumcised [Christians] were in possession, this building was appointed to receive the sick of the holy city. Today a market of considerable importance is held there." (Adler 1966: 132).

23. For a general view see Goitein 1964 and 1971: 91–142; Gil 1976.

24. Mann 1920–22: 1, 162–66, Goitein 1971: 96; on the community chest drives and appeals for Jerusalem on the High Holy Days and Passover, and the familiar complaints of pledges made and not redeemed, ibid.: 106–07.

25. Mann 1920–22: 1, 277–80 and cf. Goitein 1974.

26. Goitein 1971: 124. In Jerusalem such officials had other sources of income, however. Taxes and special fees went to the gaon for ritual slaughter, and other officials collected fees for presiding at weddings or funerals, as they did elsewhere, but since the Yeshiva was in effect the chancery for all Jewish communities, there was also a considerable income that came from issuing legal documents.

27. On this problem, particularly notable in Jerusalem: Goitein 1971: 380–94.

28. Ibid.: 135–36.

29. Mann 1920–22: 1, 49, n. 2.

30. See the texts presented in Goitein 1974.

31. Adler 1966: 133.

32. Ibid. 235–36 (Obadiah da Bertinoro).

33. The greater familiarity with the Near East that the Crusaders brought to Europe may in fact have increased the urge to pilgrimage, as the former Crusader indulgences now attached to merely visiting the holy places certainly did. Christian pilgrimage to Palestine declined for other reasons, the change from Venetian to Turkish maritime control of the Mediterranean, for example, and Western Christendom's own changing post-Reform attitudes to pilgrimages, relics, and indulgences: Savage 1977: 66–68.

34. Felix Fabri 1893: 1, 246–47 (Ramle, where before the purchase of a house for them by Philip of Burgundy, the pilgrims had to stay at a public inn); 1, 285–86 (quartering of pilgrims in Jerusalem). According to Felix Fabri, writing in the late fifteenth century, the famous Saint John's Hospital was then "squalid and ruinous" and could house no more than 400 people (1, 395), while the quarters on Mount Sion, which the clerical pilgrims shared with the Franciscan community, were pleasant but cramped, and visitors were at least secure in the knowledge that the premises were protected by vicious guard dogs against "the insults and rage of the infidels" (1, 340).

35. For some contemporary reflections on the governance of the city in later Ottoman times see Peters 1985: 543–47.

36. Fraenkel 1979 for the frequent bedouin raids in the Fatimid period and Sharon 1975 for their activities in late Mamluk and Ottoman times around Jerusalem. According to Obadiah da Bertinoro, writing in 1488, the bedouin raided right up to the gates of Jerusalem, which in that era had no effective walls: Adler 1966: 241. Felix Fabri (1893: 1, 245–46, 549–51) gives a graphic account of fifteenth-century pilgrim encounters with bedouin outside Jerusalem and Bethlehem.

37. Jeremias 1969: 38–47; Muqaddasi 1963: 187; Le Strange 1890: 86–87 and 88 (Nasir-i Khusraw); Adler 1966: 194 (Meshullam ben Menachem in 1481).

38. Jeremias 1969: 120–21; Muqaddasi 1963: 188, who blames it on taxes.

39. Wilkinson 1974; Mazar 1976; Le Strange 1890: 197–202; and Bahat 1980: 118 for a plan of the aqueduct system supplying the city. Both the Christian pilgrim Arculf, who was in the city about 670, and Nasir-i Khusraw, who visited there in 1047, note the happy

effect of the rains coursing down the paved streets and washing the city clean: Wilkinson 1977: 95, 10–13 and Le Strange 1890: 88. On the quite different effect of rain at Mecca, where the streets were unpaved and the site flat, see Burckhardt 1829: 105.

40. Ibn Ishaq 1955: 134.

41. Cited in de Gaury 1951: 116; on the scarcity of food and water in Mecca from the very earliest times, Lammens 1924: 93–98, 178–95, and the pre-Islamic poet quoted by Wolf 1951: 332.

42. Burckhardt 1829: 107.

43. Wuestenfeld 1861: 120.

44. Wuestenfeld 1861: 152; cf. Kister 1972: 90–91.

45. Wuestenfeld 1861: 185–86; Burckhardt 1829: 107–08. The facility required constant repair and cleaning, and when Burckhardt visited the city in 1814, it was reported to him that the aqueduct had not been cleared in half a century.

46. Gaudefroy-Demombynes 1923: 144–45; cf. ibid.; 120–21, Lammens 1924: 103–10, and Burckhardt 1829: 93 for the flooding problem.

47. Sourdel 1959–60: 448.

48. de Gaury 1951: 129–30.

49. Ibn Jubayr 1949–51: 125 Ar./146 tr.

50. Lammens 1924: 208; Donner 1977: 252–55; Labib 1965: 53. On the size of the grain subsidies in Ottomon times, Shaw 1962: 253–71.

51. de Gaury 1951: 159.

52. Ibn Jubayr 1949–51: 132–33 Ar./155 tr.

53. Ibid.: 120 Ar./142 tr.

54. Within a century the kitchen had collapsed and the property was sold: Wuestenfeld 1861: 291.

55. E.g., Qur'an 9:60.

56. The texts are assembled in Stillman 1975.

57. Ibn Battuta 1958–62: 148–49.

58. Cf. Gibb and Bowen 1950–57: I/2, 176–78.

59. Shaw 1962: 253, citing Evliya Chelebi X, 125.

60. Ibid.: 254.

61. Ibid.: 268. These are only direct expenses. The state was also responsible for transport of the grain allotments, which required building and maintaining a special fleet on the Red Sea: ibid.: 261–63.

62. Ibid.: 260–61. The misappropriation of funds likely had something to do with the shift away from Cairo: Gibb and Bowen 1950–1957: I/2, 65. The Jerusalem share may have been picked up directly in Istanbul by that city's representatives: ibid.: I/2, 174 n. 2.

63. Wuestenfeld 1861: 301–03; on the administration of the *surre,* see Barbir 1980: 126–28; Burckhardt 1829: 156–57.

64. Barbir 1980: 126–33.

65. Burckhardt 1829: 192–93, 236.

66. The origins of the *khanaqa, ribat,* and *zawiya* are briefly set out in Trimingham 1971: 166–69, but more useful in the present context is the treatment in Fernandes 1980: 30–52, which draws more directly on endowment documents themselves and is concerned with their evolution in Cairo, the capital of the same rulers responsible for policy in Jerusalem from the twelfth to the sixteenth centuries. There is at present no parallel documentation for the same institutions in Jerusalem, and so the Cairo material, much of it endowments from the identical rulers who built in Jerusalem, is the best ground for an analogy. Soon, however, we may be able to do better. Among the documents recently

discovered in the Islamic Museum of the Haram al-Sharif (Little 1980) is at least one endowment charter, or *waqfiyya,* that gives some information on the organization of a Sufi convent in the city, in this case the Turbe of Muhammad Bey (ibid.: 212–13).

67. The phrase is Ibn Khaldun's but the intent was originally Ayyubid. Hence the insistence of Salah al-Din, who built both the first *madrasa* and the first government-endowed *khanaqa* in Jerusalem, that the latter institution was principally intended for Sufis "from abroad," that is, from the eastern or Sunni part of the Dar al-Islam: Fernandes 1980: 9, 47.

68. Ibid.: 38.

69. Ibid.: 46, 66, and in detail on the *khanaqa's* internal organization and administration, 105–83.

70. Ibn Battuta 1958–62: 464.

71. Le Strange 1890: 309 (Muqaddasi), 315 (Nasir-i Khusraw); Adler 1966: 185 (Meshullam b. Menachem).

72. Mujir al-Din 1968: 2, 42 and 45.

73. Cohen and Lewis 1978: 82–83. Nor was that all. Massignon (1951/1963: 222–24) has drawn up a list of all the Maghrebi *waqf* properties in Palestine, and they included houses and shops throughout Jerusalem and as far afield as Lydda and Jaffa. On Abu Maydan, Trimingham 1971: 46–47 and Tibawi 1978: 10.

74. The terms of the *waqf* document, its properties and endowments, are translated ibid.: 11–13. The mosque of Buraq, the nearby *zawiya,* and the entire Mahgrebi quarter closely fronted the Western or Wailing Wall of the Temple, a justaposition that led to serious tensions between Muslims and Jews in the area that began in the nineteenth century and has continued down to the present day. The history of this conflict over the Western Wall is set out by each of the parties to the conflict in Benvenisti 1976: 64–67, 305–22 and Tibawi 1978.

75. Wuestenfeld 1861: 259.

76. Ibid.: 270.

CHAPTER IX

Their Father's Business: Pilgrim Services and Industries in the Holy City

---

Among the other beneficiaries of the central shrine of the holy city are the secondary service industries whose income derives directly from providing lodging, food, and other non-sacral goods and services to the pilgrims. Some of these services remain informal in their organization, but others develop into a distinct retail trade sector *that caters specifically to pilgrims' needs and wants.*

The presence of a central shrine in a holy city affects that city in a variety of ways: in the patterns of investment by rulers and others who wish to make public display of their piety there; in the anomalous size and magnificence of its public buildings; or in the presence of a large class of priests or clerics whose livelihood is derived from service in that or other shrines. Somewhat less obvious, perhaps, though certainly no less important, are the benefits conferred on what might be called the secondary service industries of the holy city, those whose income derives directly from providing lodging, provisions, and other nonsacral goods and services for the pilgrims and visitors to the city.

These enterprises are secondary to the holy city only in that they are incremental to the normal urban functions of that time and place; they may well be primary in terms of the city's income and economic well-being. Again, some of these services remain informal in their organization, but others develop into a distinct retail trade sector that caters specifically to pilgrims' wants and needs. Thus Hasmonean and Herodian Jerusalem provided most of the goods and services associated with a developed city with a wealthy upper class in the Greco-Roman period, including wholesale and retail trade and manufacturing,[1] but there were also particular economic and commercial consequences of the city's being the site of not only the chief but the unique Jewish Temple and so the center of a broad and active pilgrimage network.

Jerusalem and Mecca are useful places to observe the growth and effect of this secondary commercial activity peculiar to the holy city. Each was an urban settlement with somewhat limited mercantile and strategic prospects during most of its history and so was more deeply and visibly affected than, say, Rome by the pilgrims and others who came there. And the numbers who did so were considerable, as we shall see. Jews of the Temple era had a religious obligation to make offering and sacrifice in Jerusalem, and Muslims from the beginning of Islam to the present are required to make at least one *hajj* or ritual pilgrimage to the Holy City of Mecca. Even after the destruction of the Temple Jews continued to visit or immigrate to their holy city in Judea, and from the fourth century onwards, when Constantine enshrined the chief holy places in Jerusalem, Christians too went there in great numbers. Thus the economies of the two cities have been substantially affected over the centuries by the need to feed, lodge, and otherwise accommodate large numbers of pilgrims.

Let us begin with the matter of moneys put into the city's economy by the pilgrims. Thrice yearly in Temple times, at the festivals of Passover, Pentecost, and Tabernacles, Jews converged on Jerusalem to fulfill their religious obligations under the Jewish Law. How many such pilgrims there were is not easy to say, but one recent estimate has placed the permanent population of the city and its environs at about 25,000–30,000 people at the beginning of the Christian era and has calculated the additional number of festival visitors at perhaps 180,000.[2] Each of those Jewish pilgrims to Jerusalem had certain needs for food and housing that had somehow to be supplied by the city, whether publicly or privately, during those sacred periods,[3] while for their part, the pilgrims brought with them the various offerings and taxes prescribed by the Law. Some of this money went directly into the Temple economy in the form of tithes, whence it was redistributed into the general economy in the form of either commercial transactions or as gifts and donations to the poor.

But at least part of the Jews' religious obligation was discharged directly into the commercial life of the city, and nowhere so obviously as in the so-called second tithe.[4] The regulations governing this tithe were complex—the entire Mishnaic tractate Ma'ser Sheni is given over to explaining them—but the general purport is clear: a certain percentage of every competent Jew's income had to be brought to Jerusalem in either money or kind,[5] not to be handed over to the Temple with the primary tithe but to be consumed in the city by the pilgrim himself in the form of either food, drink, or unguent.[6] We are uncertain of the degree of observance of this prescription or even of the numbers theoretically involved, but whatever its extent, the Ma'ser Sheni is the very paradigm of the religiously prescribed infusion of moneys into Jerusalem's commercial life by reason of the presence of the Temple and the pilgrims who came to worship there.

But there was more. The second tithe doubtless enabled Jerusalem to escape in some degree the conditions that scourged Mecca year after pilgrimage year: the descent of large numbers of pilgrims, many of them poor, some destitute, who had nonetheless to be fed and housed. The second tithe assumed, in effect, that the Jewish pilgrim coming up to Jerusalem was self-supporting, that he carried with him, in specie or kind, the means of his own subsistence in the holy city.[7] Even this modest degree of self-sufficiency likewise profited the Jerusalem merchants who provided the required goods and services. There were assuredly larger profits to be made in the scarcity markets of Mecca, but Jerusalem by way of recompense appears to have avoided the other, unhealthy consequences of the boom-and-bust economy that typified Mecca.

Retail and wholesale merchants could assist in the fulfillment of the pilgrims' second tithe obligations from their normal provisions, but other aspects of the commercial life of Jerusalem were shaped by the special requirements of the Temple ritual and those making offerings there. The priests may even have attempted to use their influence on who did business with them and on what terms.[8] The number of animals offered and sacrificed at the great feasts was pegged not to the population of the city but to the size of the entire Diaspora, and so Jerusalem had perforce to sustain an enormous market in livestock for no other purpose than for the ritual sacrifices in the Temple.[9] Even today we can localize at least one element of it: the sheep market on the north side of the Temple precinct, convenient to both the nearby city gate where the animals were brought in and the sanctuary area where they were sacrificed.[10]

Most of this Temple-connected commerce was conducted in the ordinary marketplaces of the city, but the evidence is unmistakable that some transactions were taking place within the Temple precinct itself, where money changers and even sellers of livestock had set up their tables and stalls.[11] It has been suggested too that at least some of the commercial enterprises within the Temple court were owned by priestly families, and though the evidence for that is not certain, what is better confirmed is the fact that the Temple priesthoods were engaged in commercial speculation, and sometimes at the expense of pilgrims to the holy city.[12]

In cities where extraordinarily large numbers of visitors arrived annually or seasonally, the simple matter of space for both their assembly and their lodging was obviously a matter of serious concern, if not always for the municipal authorities, then at least for the visitor himself. In one sense the holy cities' solution to this common urban problem was miraculous: embedded in both the Jewish and Muslim traditions is the divine assurance that the holy city will be capacious enough to receive all its pilgrims, no matter their number. This was one of the "ten miracles of the Temple" for Jews and a special *baraka*, or "blessing," of Mecca for the Muslim.[13] It must have been a comforting thought, since in modern terms the problem of finding lodging during the religious feasts in those earlier holy cities seems almost insoluble.

But it was somehow solved. Second Temple Jerusalem had some external options, of course. Though the rituals themselves had to be performed within the city, if not always in the Temple itself, the pilgrims could find housing in nearby villages, as Jesus did when he lodged in Bethany and then came into Jerusalem to celebrate the Passover, or possibly at one of the "ethnic" synagogues already observed. And it was always possible for the poorer pilgrims to camp in tents near the city, as they did in Jerusalem in the first century and later at Mecca during the *hajj*.[14] Finally, the ritual boundaries of Jerusalem, which were juridically—and variously—defined, could be extended to accommodate the crowds during the holy days.[15]

The Jerusalem synagogues were almost certainly endowed, but for the rest, we do not know the financial arrangements that prevailed in housing pilgrims in Second Temple Jerusalem. Jewish customary law forbade the taking of rent from Jerusalem pilgrims, and here at least the custom appears to have been generally honored in the observance,[16] and Jesus' despatching his disciples into the city and simply requesting of one of the inhabitants a place for his Passover meal was in no way untypical.[17]

Things did not work out nearly so well with respect to housing in Mecca, as we shall see, even though there was a Prophetic tradition on this very point: "Who eats of the rent of houses in Mecca," Muhammad is reported to have warned, "eats of hellfire."[18] The reasons why the warning was not often observed at Mecca are not far to seek. When Jerusalem pilgrimage was at its height, that is, in late Second Temple times, the proportionate increase of pilgrims vis-à-vis the permanent population never reached the degree it did at Mecca during the *hajj* season of a normal year. In addition, Jerusalem had a far broader base of substantial housing inside the city and in the surrounding suburbs, where it was also permitted to the visitor to reside, even though the actual ceremonies took place within the city. Mecca had no such base and no similar exurban facilities, and most of the time absolute shortages of food and water, never plentiful in the best of times, must have soon dissolved the best of generous intentions.

We have some sense of the topography of Jewish Jerusalem, chiefly from Josephus' indications, with some clues from the rabbinic literature and occasional confirmations from the Madaba mosaic map.[19] It is even possible to identify some of the commercial sites, like the Roman forum in the Upper City, where trading was still going on in the ninth century,[20] and the two great commercial thoroughfares that Hadrian turned into colonnaded avenues.[21] One of them ran down along the Tyropean valley in the Lower City and was probably the closest thing that Jewish Jerusalem had to a Sacred Way—the much later Christian Via Dolorosa had somewhat the same function—in the sense that pilgrim processions passed along it en route to the Temple and there too the city's commercial boutiques were concentrated.[22]

When Hadrian redid Jerusalem's two main commercial streets there was no longer any Temple, of course, and so the processional quality of the lower street must have disappeared as well, together with a great deal of its commercial attraction. The Romans shifted the commercial center of Aelia Capitolina into the vicinity of the forum in the Upper City, the present-day Muristan, but the market functions were not limited to that area. One description of Hadrianic Jerusalem says that in addition to other public facilities like baths, a nymphaeum, and a theater, Aelia had something built of twelve arches, formerly called *Anabathmoi,* "The Steps," which was possibly a roofed or vaulted market street that descended toward the Pool of Siloam, a popular place of pilgrimage in Christian Jerusalem, as it would be in the Muslim city.[23]

In more recent times, changes in the political fortunes of Jerusalem, with their usual religious consequences for holy cities, have forcefully illustrated the intimate and shifting relationship between a holy place, the pedestrian traffic drawn to it, and the commercial enterprises generated by such traffic. Since at least the Middle Ages, and perhaps earlier, one of Jerusalem's most important portals has been the Jaffa Gate, and after the Israeli occupation in 1967 it became the chief entrance into the Old City from the more populous, and almost entirely Jewish, West Jerusalem. The result is that King David Street from the Jaffa Gate, and its eastward extension toward the Haram, the Street of the Gate of the Chain, has become the most heavily traveled and so the most retail- and tourist-oriented street in the Old City.

But not all of it. One block short of where the Gate of the Chain gives entry into the Haram precinct, at the point where the predominantly Jewish tourist-pilgrims now turn right off the street to descend to the area of the Western Wall, the boutiques abruptly cease, and the final fifty yards of Jerusalem's old Roman *decumanus*, once the most heavily traveled and so the most valuable commercial property of all, is now almost deserted and shows obvious signs of physical deterioration.

The Muslim occupation of Jerusalem in A.D. 638 was a relatively peaceful affair and so must have had little effect on a population already decimated by the Persian bloodbath of twenty-five years earlier. Some of the richer landlords may have fled the city at the Muslims' approach, as they did elsewhere, but their number would have been more than made up by the new Muslim immigrants, officials most of them, followed by the workers recruited for the building activities connected with the Haram. The following centuries were not brilliant ones for Jerusalem, and even Muqaddasi, who saw his native city in the fairest possible light, was forced to concede that tenth-century Jerusalem was smaller than Mecca, but, he quickly adds, "larger than Medina."[24]

The Crusades and the Muslim reconquest violently shuffled both the size and composition of the population of Jerusalem, but the travelers' reports give no very reliable index of the actual number of people who lived there. The Crusader conquest we know destroyed or drove out the entire indigenous population of the city, Muslim, Jew, and Eastern Christian, and that the first Latin inhabitants of the new Kingdom of Jerusalem lived in huddled desolation in the former patriarchal quarter of the city, no more than two or three hundred of them.[25] Jews and Muslims were officially banned from returning, but by 1116 the situation had become so desperate that Baldwin I initiated a plan to transport Eastern Christians from the Transjordan to repopulate the city, and eventually some Muslims and a small number of Jews found their way back as well, until the city reached about 30,000 inhabitants.[26]

We have an extraordinarily detailed idea of the topography of Crusader Jerusalem, not so much from the physical remains as from the descriptions by chroniclers and visitors and the various documents setting out the property rights and possessions of church domains like those of the Holy Sepulcher and the Hospital of Saint John.[27] Earlier visitors from Europe—those in the fifth, sixth, and seventh centuries, for example—had apparently found little to remark upon in the urban life of Jerusalem, but by the era of the Crusades the style and manner of life in what had once been the western and eastern parts of a single Roman Empire had become so markedly different that European pilgrims were constrained to comment upon it. They noted, for example, the presence in Jerusalem of a cookery bazaar, the "Malquisinat" of the Crusaders, a facility they first assumed was for the benefit of pilgrims, though a later generation of Western visitors was somewhat more sophisticated about what was simply a regional custom.[28]

Most of what the Western travel accounts reveal in Jerusalem are simply the commercial facilities of a Near Eastern city without any appreciable importance in the international trade. The Jerusalem bazaars were for the most part retail emporia with a heavy emphasis on necessities like food and clothing. Even the money exchanges, the *Cange des Latins* and the *Cange des Syriens,* that were a legacy on the Crusades, were not foyers of international banking but more simply reflected different currencies and perhaps different tax rates in the country. Where the Christian pilgrim was more precisely served was in the street in Jerusalem where "si vent on les paumes que les pelerins aportent d'Outremer."[29]

In the post-Crusader period Western pilgrims had perforce to deal with the local population for their needs, with Muslims for the most part for transportation and lodging outside of Jerusalem and with the eastern Christians inside the holy city. They were warned at the outset that this would not be a pleasant or even an honest experience,[30] and however prejudicial the advice, it appears to have been well taken. Eastern merchants followed the pilgrims everywhere on their rounds and set up a market wherever they paused for rest or refreshment. Felix Fabri, who was on pilgrimage in Jerusalem in 1480, has left a vivid picture of pilgrims and merchants locked up together for the night inside the Church of the Holy Sepulcher:

Others spent the whole night bargaining with traders, for to every place to which the pilgrims go while they are in the Holy Land they are accompanied by Christian traders of eastern birth, most cunning and greedy heretics, who never sleep during the time that the pilgrims are in the Holy Land. Whenever the pilgrims enter the Church of the Holy Sepulcher those traders come in together with them, carrying their wares. They gain admission by payment of a great sum of money and establish themselves straight in front of the door of the church, spread out a cloth on the pavement and set out their wares upon it for sale. Some of the pilgrims, seeing that the time of their departure from Jerusalem was at hand, stayed awake all night bargaining and bought all kinds of things, for the traders there had for sale not only Pater Noster beads and precious stones, but also cloths of damask, of camlet and of silk, and round about these merchants there was much disturbance and noise, even as in a market place . . . How great a scandal it must be in the eyes of the infidels . . . is clear from the purity of their own mosques, wherein they will not for anything in the world allow buying or selling to go on, or any talk about the same . . .[31]

Two European Jews visited Jerusalem within seven years of each other in the same decades of the fifteenth century that Felix Fabri was there, and while one guesses that there were 10,000 Muslim households in Jerusalem and 250 Jewish ones, the other puts those figures at 4,000 Muslim and 70 Jewish families.[32] It is not until the sixteenth century, however, that we can quantify our impressions of the size of Jerusalem. We have by then the Ottoman tax registers, and on their testimony Jerusalem ranged in population from about 5,000 in 1525–26 to a century-high figure of about 16,000 in 1553–54.[33] Jerusalem was then, together with Gaza, the largest city in what was an economically depressed area, and the presence in it of a major Islamic shrine like the Haram al-Sharif resulted in less prosperity than did the sixteenth century change in political regimes that brought new commercial activity in its train. Two new khans opened in Jerusalem between 1552 and 1562, and the income from taxes on shops went up significantly during the same period.[34]

The city had its ups and downs surely, as the Ottoman tax registers give dramatic evidence over the brief span of twenty-five years. But from the descriptions and remarks of visitors to the city, Muslim Jerusalem seems to have had a normal commercial life for a city of the second rank with no remarkable share in the wholesale trade that made Damascus and Aleppo great metropolitan centers. There were markets in the city, notably the showplace Bazaar of the Cotton Merchants, as well as somewhat smaller markets for trade in pharmaceuticals and spices, vegetables and cloth goods, the first made over as endowment to Saladin's law school on the site of the former St. Anne's and the latter two for the benefit of the Aqsa.[35] These were all specialized bazaars in the manner of Islamic cities, a characteristic that caught the eye of a late fifteenth-century arrival from Europe who said he had never seen the like before.[36] And the Jerusalem markets were closely supervised in the ninth century, when the Christian pilgrim Bernard was there, and in the tenth, when al-Muqaddasi made his report.[37] Of goods for export there were few. There were some wealthy exporters of olive oil, which was stored in cisterns in the city, and soap made from olive oil was another substantial export item.[38]

Muqaddasi's later tenth-century reflections on Jerusalem list among its debits the fact that Christians and Jews seemed everywhere.[39] If this refers to the commercial life of the city, it may have been true of the Christians before the Crusades, but it scarcely seems likely afterward,[40] and neither the Geniza documents nor the reports of later travelers give any grounds for thinking it was ever true of the Jews in the city. There were still Christians in business after the Crusades, but they are most apparent when they are catering to the wants and needs of the Christian pilgrims, like the craftsmen who turned out miniature water jugs in Cana, oil in containers at the Anastasis, sheets and shrouds cut to the measure of the tombs of Jesus or Mary or stones from the Mount of Olives with "Pater Noster" inscribed on them for the Latin trade.[41] The Jews of Jerusalem, who seem to have played no specialized role in the economic life of the city, except occasionally as dyers, did produce calligraphic copies of the Torah, some of which fetched high prices from wealthy visitors from abroad.[42] But by and large for the Jewish immigrants to Jerusalem, and particularly those from Europe, it was not an easy matter to find a place in the commercial life of the city, as this account written by one of them shortly after 1700 vividly attests:

A few Jews have grocery shops here. Some of them have a Turk as a partner in order to protect themselves from unfair treatment. There are also a couple of Jewish spice dealers in the non-Jewish markets. There are Jews here who are called Maghrebis [Moroccans] or 'Moriscos' in their own language. They have a language of their own, but also understand Aramaic [Arabic]. They go dressed like the Arabs and it is scarcely possible to distinguish them, as the Arabs likewise follow the custom of leaving the beard uncut. These maghrebis travel on their asses from place to place with spices and other things, and in return bring wheat and barley to Jerusalem. From this they make a meager living. If they, who know the languages of the country, live in poverty, what shall we poor Ashkenazis do here when we have to pass to and fro among the non-Jews as though we were dumb? If we buy something from an Arab, he shows us the price on on his fingers and we have to answer on our fingers; so we become a laughing stock in their sight and cannot make a living.[43]

One aspect of the Jews' problem in medieval Jerusalem is revealed by Elzear Horn, a member of the Franciscan community in Jerusalem between 1724 and 1744, who describes the commercial scene in the courtyard outside the Church of the Holy Sepulcher. The church bazaar run by the Eastern Christians and described by Felix Fabri had now been closed by Franciscan pressure and one has the distinct impression that the economic life of Jerusalem was contracting:

No one of the Jews is allowed to come here, the Muslims having forbidden it under pain of death. However many other nations come here all through the winter, especially during Lent, to transact small buying and selling; the Christians exhibit for sale cloth, headgear, belts, cords, crosses, crowns of thorns and rosaries; the Muslims foodstuffs and other little things. Since many of the [Eastern] Schismatics, without any respect for that holy place, made a marketplace of the church when the door was closed, Father Boniface during his second Guardianship [Franciscan Guardian of the Holy Land, 1562–65], in his zeal for the House of God asked for and obtained a decree from the Turkish Sultan by which it was ordered that in the future nobody should dare to buy or sell anything within the church. At present, however, only a few religious objects are carried inside it by the local Christians; these are usually bought by pilgrims coming from abroad.[44]

By the end of that same century there were visitors in Jerusalem who were far more interested in the commerce of the city than the holy places. Constantin Volney, for one, made his Jerusalem "pilgrimage" in 1784 with the prototype of the social scientist's questionnaire in hand:

Jaffa is the place where the pilgrims disembark. They arrive in November and go immediately to Jerusalem where they stay until just after the feast of Easter. They are lodged arbitrarily with local families and in the cells of convents of the communions to which they belong. The religious take great pains to point out that the lodging is free, but it would be neither courteous nor a good idea to leave without making an offering which far exceeds the commercial price of such lodging. In addition, one cannot escape paying for masses, services, exorcisms, etc., which amounts to another considerable tax. Then again one must buy crucifixes, rosaries, Agnus Dei's and so forth. On Palm Sunday the pilgrims go to purify themselves in the Jordan, and this trip requires still another contribution. In a typical year it brings to the governor 15,000 Turkish sequins or 112,500 pounds, about half of which he spends to defray the expense of the escort and the passage rights demanded by the Arabs.

One can understand that the stay of this crowd of pilgrims in Jerusalem for five or six months leaves behind a large sum of money. Counting only 1500 people at 100 *pistoles* a head, it comes to a million and a half. A part of this money goes as payment for goods to the people and the merchants, who hold the pilgrims for ransom, as far as they can. Water, for example, cost in 1784 15 sous the trip. Another part goes to the governor and his employees. Finally, the third part stays in the convent. There are complaints of how the [Eastern Christian] Schismatics use it, scandalized talk of their luxury, their carpets and even of swords, kandahars and clubs that are the furnishings of their cells. The Armenians and Franks are more modest. It is the virtue of necessity for the first group, who really are poor; but it is the virtue of prudence for the second, who are not.[45]

The fact is that by the end of the eighteenth century the economy of Jerusalem had all but collapsed; by 1800 almost the only source of income for the Christians who lived there was the manufacture of religious articles; and for the Turks who ruled the city, whatever taxes they could impose on those articles or extort from the Christians who bought them. The reporter is Ulrich Jasper Seetzen and the year is 1806. We are once again in the square before the Church of the Holy Sepulcher:

The small square in front of the entrance to the Church of the Holy

Sepulcher is continuously used as a small market for a variety of souvenirs which the pilgrims take back with them to their homeland. There they give them to their families and friends who regard them as valuable and cherished presents since everything that comes from Jerusalem is believed to be holy and that possession of them confers a blessing. . . . Apart from a few merchants, there are also many individuals, men and women, who sell all manner of religious articles, especially rosaries of all kinds, some of which are made even of the bones of camels and water buffalo; there are crosses and such, crucifixes made of wood, mother of peral, etc; models of the Holy Sepulcher made wood and inlaid with mother of pearl; images of saints incised into mother of pearl; glass articles from Hebron like rosaries, bead necklaces, bracelets, rings, mouthpieces of pipes, cups of faiance and porcelain. Among the more rare religious articles are images of the saints, the Madonna, etc. carved on sheets of horn called 'Hantit Horn,' and which I make out to be rhinoceros horn. I was assured that it was brought from Ethiopia to Cairo whence it was then carried here and worked up mainly in Bethlehem. The price for a small piece some two inches in diameter and badly engraved with a saint's image is seventeen piasters . . .

Curious and almost unique of its kind is the warehouse [inside the Franciscan compound of Saint Savior's] for religious articles such as rosaries, crucifixes, Madonna's Milk, models of the Holy Sepulcher, etc., things which are made here, and particularly in Bethlehem. These are sent through agents to Italy, Spain and Portugal, and on their sale in those parts depends the well-being of all the presently existing Latin convents of the Holy Land. Perhaps there is no articles in the world traded so profitably as these and one has to concede that this convent carries on the world's most lucrative trade. The Christian inhabitants of Bethlehem are the only ones who make them . . . and so it can be said that it is the industry of the people of Bethlehem that supports all the convents from the Holy Land throughout the Levant.[46]

As might be expected of a remote city annually overrun and then just as quickly deserted by a great army of pilgrims from all over the Islamic world, Mecca had an urban life shaped to and by the *hajj*. For a few weeks every year city and pilgrim were locked in a relationship of mutual dependence: the *hajj* was the sole business of Mecca and for the *hajji* this city, of which he had so many religious expectations, was also his only source of food, water, lodging, and entertainment. Whether his religious expectations were fulfilled likely rested in the end on the pilgrim himself, but Mecca bent its every commercial energy toward satisfying those other, less spiritual needs.

Mecca was undoubtedly one of the great trading centers of the Islamic Middle Ages, not in the familiar manner of Cairo or Istanbul or Damascus, however, where commerce was part of an intricate network of wholesale and retail trade, of import and manufacture, credit and banking, and where merchant princes stored their goods in monumental khans and did their business in elegant bazaars.[47] There were wealthy Meccan merchants, to be sure, and healthy profits to be made, but the trade there was overwhelmingly retail as well as occasional and so necessarily opportunistic, and there was little in Mecca that resembled a commercial network or even a permanent economic establishment.

There was for a time just such an establishment at the nearby port of Jedda which from the era of the Crusades played an important role in Egyptian mercantile policy in the Red Sea. Jedda was opened as a port by the Caliph 'Uthman in 646, and thereafter it served as the chief Meccan access to the Red Sea and Egypt beyond. It lay a fast overnight ride or a more typical two-day caravan journey away from Mecca.[48] Mecca's chief port city may have been walled at some point, but when Ibn Jubayr was there in 1184 there remained only traces of it to be seen. This was a dangerous lapse. Even in pre-Crusader times European consumers had returned to the international marketplace and "Frankish" traders were already making their presence felt in Egypt. The Crusades made the Muslims wary of that influence and particularly of European penetration into the Red Sea, where Reynald of Chatillon had nearly gained a foothold and was contemplating an assault on Mecca itself.[49] Thereafter Salah al-Din and most of his successors in Egypt adopted a policy of mercantile protectionism toward the Far Eastern trade in general and the Red Sea in particular: the Frankish presence would be limited to Alexandria and the trans-Mediterranean routes; only Muslims would sail the Red Sea and the routes to the East.

Almost from the beginning Jedda and Aden were rivals for that new, important, and entirely Muslim thrust along the maritime roads eastward, but as long as the Ayyubids controlled both places, the rivalry could be regulated and profit taken from both places. By the beginning of the fifteenth century, however, the Yemen was under the control of a hostile dynasty, and the rivalry between the two cities and their rulers was overt and aggressive.

Jedda took profit from the declared Ayyubid and Mamluk policy of making the city their primary port in the Red Sea. As early as the thirteenth century khans, storehouses, and other commercial facilities began to be constructed in Jedda; in 1427 the harbor was enlarged and a new mosque constructed.[50] The Mamluks took over the direct administration of the city at the beginning of the fifteenth century and so put a firm restraining grip on the rapacious hand of the ruling sharifs in Jedda. As a consequence the number of Indian ships landing at the port increased dramatically until it reached an all-time high of 100 about 1500.[51] In 1426 the Sultan Barsbay announced the final steps in his attachment of this rich trade to Egypt: henceforward merchants from the East could sell their spices only in Jedda and only to Egyptian merchants going to Egypt—and after 1429, only to the sultan himself.[52]

This escalating monopoly of Cairo on the eastern spice trade had differing effects on Mecca. The emphasis on Jedda, and indeed the restriction of the eastern trade to Jedda necessarily enhanced the *hajj* caravan as the primary and most secure overland vehicle for both the spice merchants and their goods returning to Cairo. It reconverted the *hajj* itself to something close to its original function as a combined religious ritual and trade fair where merchants could convene from all over the *Dar al-Islam* and do their business in a relatively secure atmosphere. But Barsbay's declaration of his personal monopoly in 1429 effectively excluded all but the sultan's own agents from that marketplace. Thereafter there was little point of a Syrian or Iraqi or Yemeni or even an Egyptian merchant's taking the road to Mecca in pursuit of a share in the lucrative spice trade.

But the chief beneficiary in purely urban terms was Jedda. It was Jedda and not Mecca that received capital investment for khans and courts and caravanserais. Negotiations may have taken place in Mecca, where all would eventually resort, but the banking and the goods and the institutions and buildings to serve each remained close to dockside in Jedda, where they slowly crumbled into ruin once the Portuguese navigated the Cape of Good Hope and forever broke the sultan's grip on both the spice trade and the Red Sea.

Though it had no share in the great international spice trade, Mecca was from beginning to end a community of entrepreneurs, eager if occasionally amateur practitioners of a highly seasonal occupation that engaged the energies of everyone from sharif to beggar.

> The inhabitants of Mecca have but two kinds of employment, trade and the service of the Beitullah or Temple, but the former has the reference, and there are very few olemas, or people employed in the mosque, who are not engaged in some commercial affairs, though they are too proud to pursue them openly.

So Burckhardt at the beginning of the nineteenth century, and so too, it would appear, even the Mecca of the pre-Islamic *hajj*.[53]

The commercial practice in Mecca does not seem to have changed much over the centuries. Before the arrival of the great *hajj* caravans most of the population of the city went to Jedda, the sharif in the van, where at dockside they bought goods for cash from the Indiamen, carried them inland the two day march to the holy city and then sold them to pilgrims there at a retail markup of no less than 50 percent.[54] The goods were valuable and expensive, imports chiefly from India and the eastern ports, and they were sold everywhere in the city but by preference in the vicinity of the *haram*, on the adjoining Mas'a, for example, the ceremonial street where the newly arrived pilgrim performed the ritual *sa'y*,[55] and even within the *haram* itself.[56] And when the pilgrimage was over, the merchants closed their shops and spent the summer in al-Ta'if in the mountains or at their second residence in Jedda.

Mecca offered all the commercial services that might be expected in the context of the *hajj*. Bedouin sold the pilgrims sheep and goats at highly inflated prices for the sacrifice at Mina. The town itself had an abundant supply of barbers to shave or clip the pilgrims' heads; camel brokers to provide transportation to and from Arafat; loan sharks for the impecunious, pawnbrokers for the improvident, and prostitutes for the incontinent. There were even bridegrooms to let for women who wished to perform the pilgrimage but were inhibited by their unmarried state.[57]

Those occasional bridegrooms were drawn from among the ranks of Mecca's largest and most important guild industry, the corps of guides who steered the pilgrim through every step of his Meccan experience from finding lodgings to assisting in the performance of the pilgrimage ritual itself.[58] The guide (*dalil*, or, more properly, *mutawwif* or "*tawaf*-turner") was by all accounts the pilgrim's introduction and farewell to the holy city, everywhere present, always explaining, arranging, flattering, and quarreling with his sometimes ingenuous, often suspicious, and always dependent client. As such they have received predictably bad reviews,[59] and to this day the *mutawaffin* continue to pose problems for both the pilgrims and the authorities of Mecca.[60]

It is almost impossible that it should have been otherwise. Concealed under the disreputable hawker of sites and lodgings of nineteenth-century Mecca was an ancient and traditional function of the guardians of the *haram*, to guide and instruct the pilgrim through the complex ritual of the *hajj* and the *'umra*.[61] If there were guides in Muslim and Christian Jerusalem, as assuredly there must have been, they were mere cicerones, eager prototypes of their modern descendents whose self-appointed task is to point out and explain and sell in every Near Eastern city that has some claim to the tourist's attention. The Muslim and particularly the Christian pilgrim went to Jerusalem to pray, certainly, but also to see, to search out and to learn; the *hajj*, on the other hand, was a *ritual obligation*, a complicated series of liturgical acts that was performed once in a lifetime by most Muslims and was in the main foreign to the worshiper's ordinary experience in private or public prayer. The *hajji* truly needed guidance, and so the Meccan *mutawwif* responded to a real need. As his very name implies, he was a liturgical expert.

The *mutawwifs* played this role throughout their history, and the fact that it was done even by children in an accredited family suggests the almost sacramental nature of the enterprise; it was, to use one of the pilgrims' favorite words, a *baraka*.[62] But like the other traditional charges that descended from pre-Islamic

Mecca, the supervision of the Ka'ba and the Zamzam, for example, custody of a site or function at Mecca had important political and economic ramifications. A user's fee was inevitably attached, followed, equally inevitably, by the decline of the privileged charge into a franchise. The guides too became an enfranchised guild, with a jealously guarded family membership organized under a shaykh who was in turn appointed by Mecca's chief dispenser of patronage, the sharif.[63]

But the *hajji* had far more than ritual needs in Mecca, and the *mutawaffin* expanded their functions to fill them. For almost all the pilgrims Mecca would have been a spiritually familiar but culturally and socially alien place at any time, and during the pilgrimage season it became as well an unrestrained and hyperactive commercial mart where everything was in short supply and expensive. The *mutawaffin* thus became the prime agents and brokers of the holy city, sometimes helpful, sometimes as exploitive as the marketplace through which those ruined Levites were undertaking to guide their pilgrim charges.

Mecca apparently produced little or nothing of its own by way of goods: everything it sold had first to be bought, from silk to dates. The city was filled with shops, though not, as Ibn Jubayr remarked, with the kind of organized bazaars found in other commercial centers. One small section of one street was vaulted over in the traditional *suq* manner,[64] but for the rest, there were only massed shops where the pilgrims congregated, and even private homes were converted into boutiques during the *hajj* season.[65] There were no khans or factories, however. Or nearly so. Mecca did manufacture two items for the souvenir trade: the tinsmiths of the Mas'a made little metal vials in which the *hajji*s carried home a precious supply of the Zamzam's holy water and on the edge of town potters turned out a kind of local ceramic pot for the pilgrims.[66]

One occupation that engaged almost all Meccans during the *hajj* season was renting lodgings to pilgrims, and on Burckhardt's testimony, all but the wealthiest householders rented parts of their residences to pilgrims.[67] Most of the privately owned homes in the city were converted into one-and-a-half-room apartments to take advantage of the pilgrim trade, and the pressing need for lodgings also explains the persistent mixture of commercial and residential land use in Mecca in contrast to the practice of almost every other traditional Islamic city, where residential and commercial functions were as a rule sorted into different sectors of the city. It is not difficult to understand how the situation came about. Mecca had its share of public facilities, the endowed law schools, convents and hostel-shrines that testified to the piety of Muslims everywhere toward their holy city and that provided lodging for pilgrims. But all of these institutions had an extremely short life, and the abuses of the endowment system in Mecca destroyed public lodgings almost as quickly as they were built.

The wealthy *hajji* has always enjoyed special accommodations, whatever the cult and whatever the holy city. The royal house of Adiabene had its own palazzo in Jerusalem, and Agrippa II built or rebuilt for himself in that city a palace from which he could observe, and be observed from, the Temple court. The Muslims crowded even more closely about the "Noble Sanctuary" in Jerusalem, and by the fourteenth century the Haram al-Sharif was ringed on its western and northern sides with splendid schools and convents, most of them with sumptuous private quarters for their benefactors, who could look out upon the Haram through enlarged bay windows.[68] The same custom had begun even earlier in Mecca. There were private houses around the Ka'ba in pre-Islamic times, and so it is not astonishing to discover first the Umayyad and then the 'Abbasid caliphs and their relatives and viziers with their own *hajj* residences right on the *haram*.[69] And from that day to the beginning of modern times in Mecca wealthy pilgrims have found lodgings in private houses under the very galleries of the *haram* where they could, like Agrippa II, participate without always being present.[70] Even today the chief variable in rent costs for Meccan pilgrims is the distance of their housing from the *haram*.[71]

The issue of public versus private space was raised early at Mecca. In the years immediately following the death of the Prophet *hajji*s apparently set up their tents in the still abundant open space close to the sanctuary and had an acknowledged right to camp even in the courts of privately owned houses there. It was reportedly the Caliph Mu'awiya who first began buying up the open land and building on it as well as investing in a great many already existing properties in Mecca. Mu'awiya's commercial and real estate policies, which must have greatly stimulated construction in the city, found little favor among some traditionalist Muslims who feared that what had always been a free privilege would be converted into a profit-making enterprise, a fear that was rapidly realized in the holy city.[72]

If the commercial life of the holy city of Mecca sounds somewhat scandalous, it probably was. The local population had little incentive not to fleece its yearly crop of visitors from abroad, not from the sharif certainly, who was as obviously engaged in that pastime as any other Meccan. These lords of Mecca, who appropriated, as we have seen, a very large share of the city's subsidy from abroad, were not constrained to sell goods in the street; their share of the pilgrim trade was exacted in the more traditional manner of governments everywhere: they taxed the pilgrims.

As with much else that concerns Mecca, we do not know when the practice started. It was certainly in force in Ibn Jubayr's day in the late twelfth century, when the pilgrims were taxed as they landed in Jedda or, if they could not pay, were simply detained there and missed the *hajj* altogether. In 1176 Salah al-Din, now the new, if still somewhat nominal, ruler of the holy cities, put an end to the practice, though he softened the blow by reimbursing the sharif out of his own pocket.[73] But if the pilgrims could not be taxed, their personal belongings could, in the form of customs dues. In 1364 the sultan of Egypt had once more to intervene and force the sharif to remove these and other customs duties. And once again the sovereign could assure himself that his orders were being observed only by making up the shortfall to the sharif out of state funds.[74]

Despite the occasional efforts of sultans in Cairo or Istanbul, for most of its history Mecca was self-regulating when it came to the *hajj*, a freedom that was generally read in the holy city as a license to separate the pilgrim from his money and his possessions. It must not have been very difficult in an environment that was as foreign to the visitor and in which there were few commercial choices when it came to food, lodging, transportation, or even gifts for the family back home.

NOTES

1. Jeremias 1969: 4–9, 31–51. And it shows the same sorting out of trades and occupations that Wirth 1974–75: 238–50) found in the Islamic city; cf. Jeremias 1969: 5–6 on the potters, tanners and fullers of Jerusalem.

2. Jeremias 1969: 84, and compare Safrai 1981: 93–97 for a reevaluation of this tenuous evidence and of Jeremias' conclusions.

3. Ibid.: 102–04.

4. Ibid.: 134–38 and Schürer 1979: 264–65.

5. The tithe was calculated in produce but could be converted into cash, which then had to be spent in Jerusalem. If fulfilled by cash conversion, as surely it was by most Diaspora Jews, another fifth was added, though there were encouraged loopholes to that provision: M. Shekalim 4:4–5.

6. Ibid.: 2:1.

7. Safrai 1981: 148–50.

8. Levine 1978: 15–16 on what appears to be an attempt in the Temple Scroll to link permission to do business in Jerusalem with the observance of the Temple's norms of ritual purity.

9. Cf. Jeremias 1969: 46–49.

10. Avi-Yonah 1975: 240–41; cf. the "Sheep Pool" in John 5:2.

11. Jeremias 1969: 48–49; Safrai 1975: 286; cf. M. Shekalim 1:3, John 2:14, and the parallel Synoptic passages.

12. M. Shekalim 4:3, with Rabbi Akiba's condemnation of the practice.

13. M. Aboth 5:5; Ibn Jubayr 1949–51: 169–70 Ar./196 tr.

14. Jewish pilgrims in Jerusalem: Josephus, *Ant.*XVII, 9, 3; *BJ* II, 12; and Safrai 1981: 162–63.

15. Jesus in Bethany: Matt. 21:17.; on Mecca: Burckhardt 1829: 115. On the extension of the boundaries of Jerusalem: M. Menahoth 11:2, where the boundaries are extended to Bethphage.

16. So Safrai 1981: 160–61, who finds confirmation of the rabbinic prescription in the independent testimony of Josephus (*Ant.* IX, 8, 7) and Philo (*Spec. leg.* I, 70) on the general spirit of generosity that prevailed in Jerusalem during the time of pilgrimage. There are, however, other ways of compensating Jerusalem landlords: Jeremias 1969: 101–02.

17. Mark 14:12 ff. and parallels.

18. Kister 1972: 86.

19. The evidence is assembled in Avi-Yonah 1954 and Milik 1961.

20. Milik 1961: 161; the pilgrim Bernard in Wilkinson 1977: 142, 10.

21. Jeremias 1969: 18–19.

22. M. Bikkurim 3:2–4; cf. Wirth 1974–75: 244–48 on the clustering of certain retail traders along heavily traveled pedestrian thoroughfares.

23. *Chronicon Paschale* I, 474; cf. Milik 1961: 174–75.

24. Muqaddasi 1963: 188–89.

25. William of Tyre IX, 19 and Prawer 1980: 89.

26. William of Tyre XI, 27 on both the ban and the induced immigration. The population policy of the Crusaders in Jerusalem has been studied in detail by Prawer 1980: 85–101. On the Jewish and Muslim presence in the Crusader city, ibid.: 90–91, and on its estimated peak population in Crusader times, Benvenisti 1970: 26.

27. See, for example, the description of the Christian quarter in William of Tyre IX, 18; the work of Ernoul entitled *L'Estat de la Cité de Iherusalem* in Michelant/Raynaud 1882: 31–52; and the 1165 census of the properties of the Holy Sepulcher and the 1170 list of the tributaries of the Hospital in Röhricht 1893–1904: nos. 421 and 483.

28. Michelant/Raynaud 1882: 37: "Devant le Cange, venant à la Rue des Herbes, a une rue c'on apele Malquisinat. En celle rue cuisoit on le viande c'on vendoit as pelerins." Felix Fabir 1893: 2, 111:

> . . . for men do not cook in their own houses as they do in our country, but buy their food cooked from the public cooks, who dress meat exceedingly cleanly in open kitchens . . . In these parts the kitchens must needs be common walls, since owning to the dryness of the land, wood is dear, and there cannot be a kitchen in each house, as there is with us, because of the want of food.

On the cookery bazaar in Damascus, Ibn Battuta 1959–62: 143.

29. Michelant/Raynaud 1882: 34. On the palm carried back to Europe as a sign of the completion of a vow to go to the Holy Land: Brundage 1969: 18, 125.

30. Felix Fabri 1893: 1, 253, quoting from the opening instruction at Ramle:

> Let no Christian have money dealings with a Saracen except in such sort he knows he cannot be cheated; for they strive to cheat us, and believe they are serving God by deceiving and cheating us. And above all, let the pilgrim beware of German Jews and be on his guard against them, for their whole object in life is to cheat us and rob us of our money. Let him also beware of Eastern Christians when he has dealings with them, for they have no conscience, less even than the Jews and Saracens, and will cheat pilgrims if they can.

31. Ibid.: 2, 83.

32. Adler 1966: 189 (Meshullam b. Rabbi Menahcem) and 234 (Obadiah da Bertinoro).

33. Cohen/Lewis 1978: 94. Damascus and Aleppo had in the same period (1520–30) each about 57,000 residents: ibid.: 20.

34. Ibid.: 19–28, 68.

35. The "Bazaar of the Cotton Merchants" is described by Mujir al-Din 1968: 2, 50 in his general treatment of the bazaars of Jerusalem and is noted perhaps by Felix Fabri (1893: 2, 124). It has been studied by Golvin 1967.

36. Adler 1966: 236–37 (Obadiah da Bertinoro).

37. Bernard in Wilkinson 1977: 142, 10; Muqaddasi 1963: 188. Both are probably referring to some form of the Muslim office of *muhtasib*, or market inspector. The official was kept by the Crusaders and the oath and duties of the "mathessep," which are almost identical to his Muslim counterpart, are preserved in the collection known as the *Assises de la Cour des Bourgeois* (*Receuil Lois* 1841–43: 2, 238, 243–44. At the time of the Crusades the main Jerusalem bazaars were closed and vaulted (Michelant/Raynaud 1882: 43, 145, 149), as they probably had been earlier under the Muslims (cf. Richard 1965), and they were still intact and attractive in 1488 when Obadiah da Bertinoro came to live in the city (Adler 1966: 236).

38. Le Strange 1890: 88, citing Nasir-i Khusraw; on the soap industry, which bore an export tax for the benefit of the Haram, Cohen/Lewis 1968: 63.

39. 1963: 188.

40. But see Mujir al-Din 1968: 2, 50.

41. Bagatti 1949.

42.

There are also at Jerusalem excellent calligraphists, and the copies are sought for by the strangers, who carry them away to their own countries. I have seen a Pentateuch written with so much art that several persons at once wanted to acquire it, and it was only for an excessively high price that the Chief of the Synagogues of Babylon carried it off with him to Baghdad. (Isaac ben Joseph [1334] in Adler 1966: 134)

43. Gedaliah, cited in Wilhelm 1946: 79.
44. Horn 1962: 87.
45. Volney 1959: 336–37.
46. Seetzen 1854–59: 15, 17, translated by Elizabeth Koehldorfer.
47. On those more typical commercial centers of the *Dar al Islam* and their way of doing business, Wirth 1974–75.
48. Wuestenfeld 1861: 122.
49. Labib 1965: 27–28.
50. Ibid.: 55 (Ibn al-Mujawir), 380.
51. Ibid.: 378.
52. Ibid.: 381–83.
53. Burckhardt 1829: 187.
54. Ibn Jubayr 1949–51: 170 Ar./197 tr.; de Gaury 1951: 117, citing the sixteenth-century traveler Ludovico Varthema; Burckhardt 1829: 188. The condition continues: Brownson 1978.
55. Ibn Jubayr 1949–51: 107 Ar./127 tr., who called it the only organized *suq* in Mecca; cf. Burckhardt 1829: 116–17. On the religious functions of the Mas‘a; Gaudefroy-Demombynes 1923: 225–34.
56. Ibn Jubayr 1949–51: 181 Ar./210 tr.
57. On the latter; Burckhardt 1829: 195–96. Church law likewise forbade pilgrimage to Jerusalem to unattached women, and here too the prescription was often evaded: Prawer 1972: 199.
58. Snouck Hurgronje 1931: 23–36.
59. "The Idlest, most impudent, and vilest individuals of Mekka adopt the profession of guides (*metowaf* or *delyl*); and as there is no want of those qualities, and a sufficient demand for guides during the hajj, they are very numerous . . . But their utility is more than counterbalanced by their importuning and knavery." So Burckhardt (1829: 193), and the judgment is not untypical of the genre.
60. See Brownson 1978: 127–29.
61. Gaudefroy-Demombynes 1923: 201.
62. Ibid.: 203.
63. Ibid.: 201–02.
64. Burckhardt 1829: 120.
65. This mixture of residential and commercial functions was another peculiarity of Mecca; see Burckhardt 1829: 118–22 and cf. Wirth 1974–75: 237–38.
66. Gaudefroy-Demombynes 1923: 89; Burckhardt 1829: 123–24.
67. Burckhardt 1829: 105, 260.
68. Jewish Jerusalem: Jeremias 1969: 12–14; Muslim buildings around the Haram: Burgoyne 1973; 1974.
69. Gaudefroy-Demombynes 1923: 134–35, 146.
70. Ibn Jubayr 1949–51: 104 Ar./124 tr., and Burckhardt 1829: 154.
71. Makky 1978: 50; cf. Brownson 1978: 128.
72. Kister 1972: 83–89.

73. Ibn Jubayr 1949–51: 77 Ar./87–88 tr.; cf. Wuestenfeld 1861: 228–29.

74. Wuestenfeld 1861: 257. But life at Mecca was infinitely more complex than that. The personal belongings of pilgrims from Iraq were not exempted from duty, probably on political grounds, nor those of pilgrims coming from India, likely because the latter were using the occasion of the *hajj* to sell merchandise in Jedda and the Holy City.

CONCLUSION

God's Cities, Men's Abode: Jerusalem and Mecca

God knows best, as Muslim historians frequently remarked, but even holy cities, it seems, must inevitably yield to the necessity of behaving like cities. The laws of urban growth and decay may be suspended for heavenly cities of the type envisioned by the Jews after the destruction of the earthly Jerusalem in A.D. 70, but the Judean reality, like its equally terrestrial sister in the Hejaz, had to survive in a world governed by the theologically despised secondary causality: population growth and decline; shortages of food, water, and, pious traditions to the contrary, lodging; income and expenses; commercial, civil, and religious wars; natural and man-made catastrophes. Both Jerusalem and Mecca had the enormous advantage of esteem income, revenues generated solely by the status of the city and its holy place; both profited by a regular and orderly immigration in the form of pilgrims who came and never left, whether to pray or profit in the holy city or simply to die there. Each place had a leg up on urban prosperity, an opportunity to achieve success, not as God judges, but as the world does, to express in material, urban terms the glory that holiness had bestowed on each.

Preindustrial cities grew rich and prospered in a number of different ways. They dominated a rich agricultural hinterland, for example, or, more commonly, they either controlled or played a part in the international wholesale trade. Or they became objects of imperial attention. That attention was sometimes arbitrary or capricious, as when the Emperor Philip the Arab chose to promote his mean natal village in Syria into a city, or when it pleased Hadrian, a prodigious investor in cities, to honor his dead lover Antinous with an Egyptian city named after him. This is imperial self-indulgence at its most obvious, perhaps, but for every Philippopolis or Antinoopolis, there was also an Alexandria or a Constantinople, to say nothing of Cairo or Baghdad, to show the effects of imperial investment judiciously disposed and, one should add, accompanied by imperial residence.

Save for the ephemeral Crusader kings, Jerusalem had no royal presence within its walls after the last of the Herods deserted his palace in the Upper City. By then, however, all the essential components of the urban fabric were in place, and Hadrian's transient political interest in Jerusalem had something to build upon. Constantine with the fervor of the new convert and Justinian with the shrewd instincts of a ruler in trouble both took a personal interest in Jerusalem. Both were builders, understood that the holy city was important to their larger interests, and so did not hesitate to commit to it funds from the *res privata*, funds invested primarily in public buildings and facilities. And by Justinian's time there was a new political presence beside the governor of Jerusalem—*al-Batrak*, the patriarch, at the side of *al-Batriq*, the patrician, as Mujir al-Din put it—and this new Christian high priest also had at his disposal, like the Jewish high priests before him, investment capital for the benefit of the holy city.

What makes Mecca so different from even the other great centers of the medieval *Dar al-Islam* is not so much the absence of public buildings and facilities, which are after all secondary characteristics of urbanism, as the absence of political power, not simply as such but as the source and point of departure of urban investment. Kings and princes are generally the chief revenue collectors and the largest landholders in the area under their effective rule. They are as well the most prolific consumers and chief investors in the city. When the 'Abbasid caliphs decided to build Baghdad in the mid–eighth century, the suppliers were cannily present even before the royal consumers had settled upon their thrones: Baghdad's commercial suburb of Karkh was open and ready for business even before the caliph's Round City was.

It is precisely the lack of investment capital that is so striking in medieval Mecca. Rulers in distant Baghdad and Cairo and Istanbul interested themselves in their holy city no less than

Herod and Constantine had in theirs, but chiefly by committing themselves in and around the sanctuary or by sending gifts to its staff, gifts that only very occasionally passed into investment: Muslim rulers generously subsidized Mecca, but they only rarely invested in it. Or lived in it. The polarity of class and interests, political, commercial, and even religious, that so frequently converts itself into urban growth in other contexts is remarkably absent during most of Mecca's history. The *hajj* was the only enterprise of the city and pilgrims the almost unique consumers of whatever goods and services the residents had to offer. As a result, the commercial life of Mecca was flash-flood economics at its worst: three weeks of buying off the boats in Jedda; three weeks of profitable selling to pilgrims; ten months of living off the fat. Mecca was Karkh without a Baghdad.

There is another difference between the two cities, more calamitous and perhaps more fortunate than the presence or absence of political power and indirectly linked to it. Jerusalem was a contested place, Mecca generally not, though it had its occasional predators. Three religious bodies—two of them powerful in arms, all of them terrible with ideology—have claimed either the holy city of Jerusalem or its primary holy place as theirs. They have banned and proscribed each other from the city, converted each other's holy places into their own. It has been a contest sometimes fought by armies, always with words, often and most effectively with tax rates, architecture, rights of access and of property. It has been a destructive process perhaps, but it has also served to enhance the importance of Jerusalem: the city has not become, as it might have under other circumstances, a mere shrine, a mausoleum, a pilgrimage center, or a national museum; a Lourdes, a Chichen Itza, a Masada, or a Bethlehem. There is too much at stake in Jerusalem, a condition that has been apparent since the Crusades.

Before the eleventh century one might have reasonably guessed that Jerusalem's holiness was supple enough and the conditions of history sufficiently stringent to have stabilized the claims on the holy city. A politically impotent Judaism had turned its Zionist dreams heavenward; a powerful yet tolerant Islam that both permitted and protected a Jewish presence in the city; an Eastern Christendom that was forced by its Muslim masters to restrain both its missionary zeal and its occasional bloodlust toward the Jews and at the same time was itself unthreatened by Islam—all seem to come into equilibrium, if not equity, in early medieval Jerusalem.

The Crusaders destroyed that equilibrium. The political temperature of Jerusalem rose in a measurable degree from the eleventh century onward. Muslim and Christian attitudes toward the city and the possession of its holy places were altered, and not simply by the Crusades and not merely during them. Post-Crusader Jerusalem was more defiantly Muslim, and as the West's political and economic fortunes revived, increasingly and aggressively Christian as well; and it required only the nineteenth-century reconversion of Zionism to earthly and achievable goals to complete the new and ever more militant *political* enshrinement of Jerusalem.

Mecca has known civil war but never the contest of three absolutist faiths born of a single parent. Judaism and Christianity have no religious or political claims on that place, which has never been part of their world. In a sense Mecca is remote from even its own political tradition, and if the *hajj* has saved Mecca from the fate of becoming a kind of baked-brick Angkor Wat, it has not entirely saved it from a long decline toward the condition of Lourdes. From the urbanist's limited perspective, Mecca was a heavenly city fallen heavily and somewhat clumsily to earth, too esteemed and too heavily endowed to expire and yet too immature an urban organism to prosper.

Works Cited

[Classical and scriptural texts are cited according to standard divisions and formulae.]

Abel 1922: F. Abel, "Le culte de Jonas en Palestine," *JPOS* 2 (1922), 175–83.

Adler 1966: E. N. Adler, *Jewish Travellers: A Treasury of Travelogues from 9 Centuries*, 2nd ed. (New York, 1966).

Andrae 1917: T. Andrae, *Die Person Muhammeds in Lehre und Glauben seiner Gemeinde* (Stockholm, 1917)

Ankawi 1974: A. Ankawi, "The Pilgrimage to Mecca in Mamluk Times," *Arabian Studies* 1 (1974), 146–70.

Ansary 1979: A. R. al-Ansary, ed., *Sources for the History of Arabia*, vol. 1, pts. 1–2 (Riyadh, 1979).

Ansary 1982: A. R. al-Ansary, *Qaryat al-Fau: A Portrait of Pre-Islamic Civilisation in Saudi Arabia* (Riyadh, 1982).

Armstrong 1967: G. T. Armstrong, "Imperial Church Building and Church-State Relations," *Church History* 36 (1967), 3–17.

Armstrong 1969: G. T. Armstrong, "Fifth and Sixth Century Church Building in the Holy Land," *Greek Orthodox Theological Review* 14 (1969), 17–30.

Ashtor 1966: E. Ashtor, "I salari nel medio Oriente durante l'epocha medievale," *Revista Storica Italiana* 78 (1966), 321–49.

Ashtor 1976: E. Ashtor, *A Social and Economic History of the Near East in the Middle Ages* (London, 1976).

Ashtor 1981: E. Ashtor, "Muslim and Christian Literature in Praise of Jerusalem" in Levine 1981: 187–89.

Avigad 1977: N. Avigad, "A Building Inscription of the Emperor Justinian and the Nea in Jerusalem," *Israel Exploration Journal* 27 (1977), 145–51.

Avigad 1983: N. Avigad, *Discovering Jerusalem* (Hebrew original, Jerusalem, 1980; rev. English trans., New York, 1983).

Avi-Yonah 1954: M. Avi-Yonah, *The Madaba Mosaic Map* (Jerusalem, 1954).

Avi-Yonah 1975: M. Avi-Yonah et al., *The World History of the Jewish People*, vol. 7: *The Herodian Period* (New Brunswick, 1975).

Avi-Yonah 1975a: M. Avi-Yonah, "Jerusalem in the Hellenistic and Roman Period," in Avi-Yonah 1975: 207–49.

Avi-Yonah 1976: M. Avi-Yonah, *The Jews of Palestine. A Political History from the Bar Kokhba War to the Arab Conquests* (Oxford, 1976).

Ayalon 1973: D. Ayalon, "Discharges from Service, Banishment and Imprisonments in Mamluk Society," *Israel Oriental Studies* 2 (1973), 324–49.

Azraqi 1858: al-Azraqi, Abu al-Walid Muhammad, *Akhbar Makka*, ed. F.

Wuestenfeld, *Die Chroniken der Stadt Mekka*, vol. 1 (Leipzig, 1858; rpt. Khayats, 1964).

Bacht 1953–1962: H. Bacht, "Die Rolle des orientalischen Monchtums in den kirchenpolitischen Auseinandersetzung um Chalkedon (432–519)," in A. Grillmeier and H. Bacht, *Das Konzil von Chalkedon: Geschichte und Gegenwart*, 3 vols. (Würzburg, 1953–62), vol. 1, 193–314.

Bagatti 1949: B. Bagatti, "Eulogie Palestinesi," *Orientalia Christiana Periodica* 15 (1949), 126–66.

Bagatti 1962: B. Bagatti, "Il Tempio di Gerusalemme dal II all'VIII secolo," *Biblica* 43 (1962), 1–21.

Bagatti 1965: B. Bagatti, "La posizione del tempio erodiano di Gerusalemme," *Biblica* 46 (1965), 428–44.

Bagatti 1979: B. Bagatti, *Recherches sur le site du Temple de Jérusalem (Ier–VIIe siècle)* (Jerusalem, 1979).

Bagatti and Testa 1978: B. Bagatti and E. Testa, *Il Golgota e la Croce* (Jerusalem, 1978).

Bahat 1980: D. Bahat, *Jerusalem: Selected Plans of Historical Sites and Monumental Buildings* (Jerusalem, 1980).

Baldi 1955: D. Baldi, *Enchiridion Locorum Sanctorum*, rev. ed. (Jerusalem, 1955; rpt. Jerusalem, 1982).

Barbir 1980: K. Barbir, *Ottoman Rule in Damascus* (Princeton, 1980).

Baynes 1912: N. H. Baynes, "The Restoration of the Cross at Jerusalem," *English Historical Review* 27 (1912), 287–99.

Beck 1959: H. -G. Beck, *Kirche und theologische Literatur in byzantinische Reich* (Munich, 1959).

Ben-Areih 1979: Y. Ben-Arieh, *The Rediscovery of the Holy Land in the Nineteenth Century* (Jerusalem and Detroit, 1979).

Ben-Arieh 1984: Y. Ben-Arieh, *Jerusalem in the Nineteenth Century. The Old City* (New York, 1984).

Ben-Dov 1982: M. Ben-Dov, *The Dig at the Temple Mount* (Jerusalem, 1982). Hebrew.

Ben-Dov et al. 1983: M. Ben-Dov, M. Naor, and Z. Aner, *The Western Wall* (Jerusalem, 1983).

Benjamin of Tudela 1907: M. N. Adler, *The Itinerary of Benjamin of Tudela*, Critical Text, Translation and Commentary (London, 1907; rpt. New York, 1965).

Ben-Sasson 1975: H. H. Ben-Sasson, "The Image of Eretz Israel in the View of Jews Arriving There in the Late Middle Ages" in Ma'oz 1975: 103–10.

Benvenisti 1970: M. Benvenisti, *The Crusaders in the Holy Land* (New York, 1970).

Benvenisti 1976: M. Benvenisti, *Jerusalem: The Torn City* (Jerusalem, 1976).

Beugnot 1841–43: M. Le Comte Beugnot, *Assisses de Jérusalem*, 2 vols. (Paris, 1841–43).

Black 1954: M. Black,"The Feast of the Encaenia Ecclesiae in the Ancient Church with Special Reference to Palestine and Syria," *Journal of Ecclesiastical*

History 5 (1954), 78–85.
Brehier 1949: L. Brehier, *Les Institutions de l'Empire byzantine* (Paris, 1949).
Brown 1981: P. Brown, *The Cult of the Saints: Its Rise and Function in Latin Christianity* (Chicago, 1980).
Brownson 1978: M. J. Brownson, "Mecca: The Socio-Economic Dynamics of the Sacred City" in Z. Sardar and M. A. Badawi, eds., *Hajj Studies* 1 (London, 1978), 117–36.
Brundage 1969: J. A. Brundage, *Medieval Canon Law and the Crusader* (Madison, 1969).
Bulliet 1975: R. Bulliet, *The Camel and the Wheel* (Cambridge, Mass., 1975).
Burckhardt 1829: J. L. Burckhardt, *Travels in Arabia* (London, 1829; rpt. London, 1968).
Burgoyne 1973: M. Burgoyne, "Tariq Bab al-Hadid. A Mamluk Street in the Old City of Jerusalem," *Levant* 5 (1973), 12–35.
Burgoyne 1974: M. Burgoyne, "The Continued Survey of the Ribat Kurd/Madrasa Jawhariyya Complex on Tariq Bab al-Hadid, Jerusalem," *Levant* 6 (1974), 51–64.
Burgoyne 1976: M. Burgoyne, *The Architecture of Islamic Jerusalem* (Jerusalem, 1976).
Bushnak 1978: A. Bushnak, "The Hajj Transportation System" in Z. Sardar and M. A. Badawi, (eds.), *Hajj Studies* 1 (London, 1978), 87–116.
Busse 1966: H. Busse, "Zum Anschluss an jüdische Kulttraditionen," *Der Islam* (1966), 113–47.
Busse 1969: H. Busse, *Chalif und Grosskönig: Die Buyiden im Iraq* (Beirut, 1969).
Caetani 1905–1907: L. Caetani, *Annali dell'Islam*, vols. 1–2 (Milan, 1905–07).
Canaan 1927: T. Canaan, *Mohammadan Saints and Sanctuaries in Palestine* (London, 1927).
Canard 1965: M. Canard, "Le destruction de l'église de la Résurrection par le calife Hakim," *Byzantion* 35 (1965), 16–43.
Charles 1936: H. Charles, *Le Christianisme des arabes nomades sur le Limes et dans le désert syro-mésopotamien aux alentours de l'Hégire* (Paris, 1936).
Chelebi 1980: *Evliya Tshelebi's Travels in Palestine (1648–1650)*, trans. St. H. Stephan (Jerusalem, 1980).
Chevallier 1974: R. Chevallier, "Cité et territoire. Solutions romains aux problèmes de l'organization de l'espace. Problématique 1948–1973" in H. Temporini, ed., *Aufstieg und Niedergang des römischen Welt*, vol. 2, pt. 1 (Berlin, 1974), 649–783.
Chitty 1966: D. Chitty, *The Desert a City* (Oxford, 1966).
Clark 1960: K. W. Clark, "Worship in the Jerusalem Temple after 70 A.D.," *New Testament Studies* 6 (1960), 269–80.
Claude 1969: D. Claude, *Die byzantinische Stadt im 6 Jahrhundert*, (Munich, 1969).
Cohen and Lewis 1978: A. Cohen and B. Lewis, *Population and Revenue in the Towns of Palestine in the Sixteenth Century* (Princeton, 1978).

Collart and Coupel 1951: P. Collart and P. Coupel, *L'Autel monumental de Baalbek* (Paris, 1951).
Constantelos 1968: D. Constantelos, *Byzantine Philanthropy and Social Welfare* (New Brunswick, 1968).
Conybeare 1910: F. Conybeare, "Antiochus Strategos' Account of the Sack of Jerusalem in A.D. 614," *English Historical Review* 25 (1910), 502–16.
Corbett 1952: S. Corbett, "Some Observations on the Gateways to the Herodian Temple in Jerusalem," *Palestine Exploration Quarterly* 84 (1952), 7–14.
Corbo 1982: V. Corbo, *Il Santo Sepolcro di Gerusalemme. Aspetti archeologici dalle origine al periodo crociato*, 3 vols. (Jerusalem, 1982).
Coüasnon 1974: C. Coüasnon, *The Church of the Holy Sepulchre in Jerusalem* (London, 1974).
Creswell 1969: K. A. C. Creswell, *Early Muslim Architecture*, 2nd ed. (Oxford, 1969).
Crone and Cook 1977: P. Crone and M. Cook, *Hagarism: The Making of the Islamic World* (Cambridge, 1977).
Dagron 1977: G. Dagron, "Le Christianisme dans la ville byzantine," *Dumbarton Oaks Papers* 31 (1977), 11–19.
Dauphin 1979: C. Dauphin, "Church Property in the Western Galilee in the Early Byzantine Period," *Cathedra* II (1979), 57–62. Hebrew.
Davies 1982: W. D. Davies, *The Territorial Dimension of Judaism* (Berkeley and Los Angeles, 1982).
de Gaury 1951: G. de Gaury, *Rulers of Mecca* (New York, 1951).
de Goeje 1900: M. J. de Goeje, *Memoire sur la Conquete de la Syrie*, 2nd ed. (Leiden, 1900).
Delehaye 1933: H. Delehaye, *Les origines du culte des martyrs*, 2nd ed. (Brussels, 1933).
Dermenghem 1954: E. Dermenghem, *Le culte des saints musulmans dans l'Islam maghrebien* (Paris, 1954).
Dodd 1969: E. Dodd, "The Image of the Word: Notes on the Religious Iconography of Islam," *Berytus* 18 (1969), 35–79.
Donner, F., 1977: F. Donner, "Mecca's Food Supply and Muhammad's Boycott," *Journal of the Economic and Social History of the Orient* 20 (1977), 249–66.
Donner, H., 1977: H. Donner, "Der Felsen under der Tempel," *ZDPV 93* (1977), 1–11.
Downey 1938: G. Downey, "Imperial Building Records in Malalas," *Byzantinische Zeitschrift* 38 (1938), 1–15.
Dozy 1864: R. Dozy, *Die Israeliten zu Mekka* (Leipzig, 1864).
Drory 1981: J. Drory, "Jerusalem during the Mamluk Period" in Levine 1981: 190–214.
Dussaud 1927: R. Dussaud, *Topographie historique de la Syrie antique et médiévale* (Paris, 1927).
Dussaud 1942–43: R. Dussaud, "Temples et culte de la Triade Héliopolitaine à Baalbek," *Syria* 23 (1942–43), 33–37.

Eickelman 1976: D. Eickelman, *Moroccan Islam: Tradition and Society in a Pilgrimage Center*, (Austin, 1976).

Elisséeff 1967: N. Elisséeff, *Nur ad-Din, un grand prince musulman de Syrie au temps de Croisades*, 3 vols. (Damascus, 1967).

Enlart 1925–28: C. Enlart, *Les monuments des croisés dan le royaume de Jérusalem: Architecture religieuse et civile*, 2 vols. (Paris 1925–28).

Fahd 1968: T. Fahd, *Le panthéon d'Arabie centrale à la veille de l'hégire* (Paris, 1968).

Fahd 1973: T. Fahd, "Le pèlerinage à la Mekke" in Raphael et al. 1973: 65–94.

Fasi 1857: Muhammad ibn Ahmad al-Fasi, *Shafa' al-gharam bi akhbar al-balad al-haram*, ed. F. Wuestenfeld, *Chroniken*, vol. 2 (Leipzig, 1857; rpt. Hildesheim, 1981).

Fattal 1958: A. Fattal, *Le statut légal des non-musulmans en pays d'Islam* (Beirut, 1958).

Felix Fabri 1893: *The Wanderings of Felix Fabri*, trans. A. Stewart, 2 vols. (London, 1893).

Ferber 1976: S. Ferber, "The Temple of Solomon in Early Christian and Byzantine Art" in Gutmann 1976: 21–44.

Fernandes 1980: L. E. Fernandes, *The Evolution of the Khanqah Institution in Mamluk Egypt*, Ph.D. Diss. (Princeton Univ., 1980).

Finegan 1969: J. Finegan, *The Archaeology of the New Testament* (Princeton, 1969).

Fraenkel 1979: Y. Fraenkel, "The Penetration of Bedouin into Eretz-Israel in the Fatimid Period," *Cathedra* II (1979), 86–108. Hebrew.

Frend 1972: W. H. C. Frend, *The Rise of the Monophysite Movement: Chapters in the History of the Church in the Fifth and Sixth Centuries* (Cambridge, 1972).

Frolow 1953: A. Frolow, "La Vraie Croix et les Expéditions d'Héraclius en Perse," *Revue des Etudes Byzantines* II (1953), 88–105.

Gabrieli 1969: F. Gabrieli, *Arab Historians of the Crusades* (Berkeley and Los Angeles, 1969).

Gätje 1976: H. Gätje, *The Qur'an and its Exegesis: Selected Texts with Classical and Modern Muslim Interpretations*, (Berkeley and Los Angeles, 1976).

Gaudefroy-Demombynes 1923: M. Gaudefroy-Demombynes, *Le Pèlerinage à la Mekke* (Paris, 1923).

Gellner 1969: E. Gellner, *Saints of the Atlas* (London, 1969).

Geyer 1898: P. Geyer, *Itinera Hierosolymitana saeculi IIII–VIII* (Leipzig, 1898).

Gibb and Bowen 1950–57: H. A. R. Gibb and H. Bowen, *Islamic Society and the West*, vol. 1: *Islamic Society in the Eighteenth Century*, 2 pts. (London and New York, 1950–57).

Gil 1976: M. Gil, *Documents of the Jewish Pious Foundations from the Cairo Geniza* (Leiden, 1976).

Gil 1982: M. Gil, "The Jewish Quarters in Jerusalem (A.D. 638–1099) according to the Cairo Geniza Documents and Other Sources," *JNES* 41 (1982), 261–78.

Gil 1984: M. Gil, "The Origin of the Jews of Yathrib," *Jerusalem Studies in*

Arabic and Islam 4 (1984), 203–24.

Gilbert 1978: M. Gilbert, *Jerusalem: Illustrated History and Atlas*, 2nd ed. (Jerusalem, 1978).

Gilsenan 1973: M. Gilsenan, *Saint and Sufi in Modern Egypt* (Oxford, 1973).

Ginzberg 1908 ff.: L. Ginzberg, *The Legends of the Jews*, 7 vols. (Philadelphia, 1908–38).

Goitein 1966: S. D. Goitein, "The Sanctity of Jerusalem and Palestine in Early Islam" in *Studies in Islamic History and Institutions* (Leiden, 1966), 135–48.

Goitein 1971: S. D. Goitein, *A Mediterranean Society: The Jewish Communities of the Arab World as Portrayed in the Documents of the Cairo Geniza*, vol. 1: *The Community* (Berkeley and Los Angeles, 1971).

Goitein 1974: S. D. Goitein, "New Sources on the Palestinian Gaonate," *Salo Wittmayer Baron Jubilee Volume* 2 (Jerusalem, 1974), 503–38.

Goitein 1980: S. D. Goitein, "Al-Kuds: A. History," *The Encyclopaedia of Islam*, new ed. (Leiden, 1980).

Goldziher 1879: I. Goldziher, "Grabesort des Joshua—Muhammadanische Traditionen uber Grabesort des Joshua," *ZDPV* 2 (1879), 13–17.

Goldziher 1893: I. Goldziher, "La notion de la sakina chez les mohamétans," *RHR* 28 (1893); rpt. in *Gesammelte Schriften* 3: 296–308.

Goldziher 1969: I. Goldziher, "On the Veneration of the Dead In Paganism and Islam" in *Muslim Studies*, vol. 1, ed. S. M. Stern (London, 1969), 209–38.

Goldziher 1971: I. Goldziher, "Veneration of the Saints in Islam" in *Muslim Studies*, vol. 2, ed. S. M. Stern, (London, 1971), 255–344.

Golvin 1967: L. Golvin, "Quelques notes sur le suq al-Qattanin et ses annexes à Jérusalem," *BEO* 20 (1967), 101–17.

Golvin 1971: L. Golvin, *Essai sur l'architecture religieuse musulmane*, vol. 2: *L'art religieux des Umayyades de Syrie* (Paris, 1971).

Grabar 1966: O. Grabar, "The Earliest Commemorative Structures: Notes and Documents," *Ars Orientalis* 6 (1966), 7–46.

Grabar 1973: O. Grabar, *The Formation of Islamic Art* (New Haven and London, 1973).

Grabar 1980: O. Graber, "al-Kuds: B. Monuments," *The Encyclopaedia of Islam*, new ed. (Leiden, 1980).

Graindor 1927: P. Graindor, *Athènes sous Auguste* (Cairo, 1927).

Graindor 1930: P. Graindor, *Hérode Atticus et sa famille* (Cairo, 1930).

Graindor 1931: P. Graindor, *Athènes de Tibère à Trajan* (Cairo, 1931).

Grant 1977: R. M. Grant, *Early Christianity and Society: Seven Studies* (San Francisco, 1977).

Guidi 1903–1907: I. Guidi et al., *Chronica minora, CSCO, Scriptores Syri*, 3rd. ser., vol. 4 (Louvain, 1903–07).

Gutmann 1976: J. Gutmann, *The Temple of Solomon. Archaeological Fact and Medieval Tradition in Christian, Islamic and Jewish Art* (Missoula, 1976).

Hajjar 1977: Y. Hajjar, *La triade d'Héliopolis-Baalbek: Son culte et sa diffusion*, 2 vols. (Leiden, 1977).

Hamidullah 1938: M. Hamidullah, "The City-State of Mecca," *Islamic Culture*

12 (1938), 253–76.

Hamilton 1947: W. Hamilton, *The Structural History of the Aqsa Mosque* (Jerusalem, 1947).

Harawi 1957: Abu al-Hasan al-Harawi, *Guide des Lieux de Pèlerinage*, traduction annotée par Janine Sourdel-Thomine (Damascus, 1957).

Harvey 1935: W. Harvey, *Church of the Holy Sepulchre: Structural Survey, Final Report* (London, 1935).

Hasson 1981: I. Hasson, "Muslim Literature in Praise of Jerusalem: *Fada'il Bayt al-Maqdis*" in Levine 1981: 168–84.

Hawting 1982: G. R. Hawting, "The Origins of the Islamic Sanctuary at Mecca" in G. H. A. Juynboll, ed., *Studies on the First Century of Islamic Society* (Carbondale, Ill.: 1982), 25–47.

Hazzard 1977: H. W. Hazard, ed., *The Art and Architecture of the Crusader States*, vol. 4 of K. M. Setton, ed., *A History of the Crusades* (Madison, 1977).

Heffening 1925: W. Heffening, *Das islamische Fremdenrecht bis zu den islamischen-fränkischen Staatsverträgen* (Hannover, 1925).

Heyd 1975: U. Heyd, "Turkish Documents Concerning the Jews of Safed in the Sixteenth Century" in Ma'oz 1975: 111–18.

Higgins 1955: M. J. Higgins, "Chosroes II's Votive Offerings at Sergiopolis," *Byzantinische Zeitschrift* 48 (1955), 89–102.

Hill 1971: D. R. Hill, *The Termination of Hostilities in the Early Arab Conquests, A.D. 634–656* (London, 1971),

Hoade 1981: E. Hoade, *Guide to the Holy Land*, 11th ed. (Jerusalem, 1981).

Hollis 1934: F. J. Hollis, *The Archaeology of Herod's Temple, with a Commentary on the Tractate Middoth* (London, 1934).

Holmes 1977: U. T. Holmes, "Life among the Europeans in Palestine and Syria in the Twelfth and Thirteenth Century" in Hazard 1977: 3–35.

Honigmann 1950: E. Honigmann, "Juvenal of Jerusalem," *Dumbarton Oaks Papers* 5 (1950), 209–79.

Hopkins 1971: I. W. J. Hopkins, "The Four Quarters of Jerusalem," *PEQ* (1971), 68–85.

Horn 1962: E. Horn, *Ichnographiae Monumentorum Terrae Sanctae (1724–1744)*, 2nd. ed. of the Latin Text with English Version by E. Hoade and Preface and Notes by B. Bagatti (Jerusalem, 1962).

Humphreys 1972: R. S. Humphreys, "The Expressive Intent of the Mamluk Architecture of Cairo—A Preliminary Essay," *Studia Islamica* 35 (1972), 69–120.

Ibn Battuta 1958–62: Ibn Battuta, *The Travels of Ibn Battuta, A.D. 1325–1354*, 2 vols. (Cambridge, 1958–62).

Ibn Ishaq 1955: *The Life of Muhammad: A Translation of Ishaq's Sirat Rasul Allah*, with introd. and notes by A. Guillaume (London and New York, 1955).

Ibn Jubayr 1949–51: *Ibn Jobair: Voyages*, traduits et annotés par Maurice Gaudefroy-Demombynes, 2 vols. (Paris, 1949–51).

Janin 1953: R. Janin, *La géographie ecclésiastique de l'Empire byzantin*, vol. 1, pt. 3: *Les églises et les monastères de Constantinople* (Paris, 1969).

Jeremias 1958: J. Jeremias, *Heiligengräber in Jesu Umwelt*, (Göttingen, 1958).

Jeremias 1969: J. Jeremias, *Jerusalem in the Time of Jesus*, (Philadelphia, 1969).

Join-Lambert 1973: M. Join-Lambert, "Les pèlerinages en Israel" in Raphael et al. 1973: 57–62.

Jomier 1953: J. Jomier, *Le Mahmal et la caravane égyptienne des pèlerins de la Mekke* (Cairo, 1953).

Jones 1940: A. H. M. Jones, *The Greek City from Alexander to Justinian* (Oxford, 1940).

Jones 1964: A. H. M. Jones, *The Later Roman Empire*, 3 vols. (Oxford, 1964).

Jones 1971: A. H. M. Jones, *The Cities of the Eastern Roman Empire*, 2nd ed. (Oxford, 1971).

Kaplan 1976: M. Kaplan, *Les propriétés de la Couronne et de l'église dans l'empire bysantin (Ve-VIe siècles)* (Paris, 1976).

Karmon 1975: Y. Karmon, "Changes in the Urban Geography of Hebron during the Nineteenth Century" in Ma'oz 1975: 70–86.

Kaufman 1921: C. M. Kaufman, *Die heilige Stadt in der Wüste*, 3rd ed. (Kempten, 1921).

Kenyon 1967: K. Kenyon, *Jerusalem: Excavating 3000 Years of History* (London, 1967).

Kessler 1979: C. Kessler, "The Tashtimuriyya in Jerusalem in the Light of Recent Research," *Levant* II (1979), 136–61.

Khitrowo 1889: B. de Khitrowo, *Itineraires russes en Orient* (Geneva, 1889).

Kister 1969: M. J. Kister, "'You shall only set out for three mosques': A Study of an Early Tradition," *Le Muséon* 82 (1969), 173–96.

Kister 1971: M. J. Kister, "Maqam Ibrahim, a Stone with an Inscription," *Le Muséon* 84 (1971), 477–91.

Kister 1972: M. J. Kister, "Some Reports Concerning Mecca from Jahiliyya to Islam," *Journal of the Economic and Social History of the Orient* 15 (1972), 61–93.

Kister 1981: M. J. Kister, "A Comment on the Antiquity of Traditions Praising Jerusalem" in Levine 1981: 185–86.

Knudstad 1977: J. Knudstad, "The Darb Zubayda Project: 1396/1976 4. Preliminary Report on the First Phase," *Atlal: Journal of Saudi Arabian Archaeology* 1 (1977), 44–68.

Kortepeter 1979: C. M. Kortepeter, "A Source for the History of Ottoman-Hijaz Relations: The *Seyahatname* of Awliya Chalaby and the Rebellion of Sharif Sacd b. Zayd in the Years 1671–1672/1081–1082" in al-Ansari 1979: 229–46.

Kraeling 1938: C. H. Kraeling, *Gerasa, City of the Decapolis* (New Haven, 1938).

Krautheimer 1965: R. Krautheimer, *Early Christian and Byzantine Architecture* (Baltimore, 1965).

Kriss and Kriss-Heinrich 1960: R. Kriss and H. Kriss-Heinrich, *Volksglauben im Bereich des Islam*, vol. 1: *Wallfahrtswesen und Heiligenverehung* (Wiesbaden, 1960).

Labib 1965: S. Labib, *Handelsgeschichte Aegyptens im Spätmittelalter* (Wiesbaden, 1965).

Lammens 1924: H. Lammens, *La Mecque à la veille de l'Hégire* (Beirut, 1924).

Lammens 1926: H. Lammens, "Les sanctuaires pré-islamites dans l'Arabie occidentales," *MUSJ* II (1926), 39–173.

Lammens 1928: H. Lammens, "Le culte des bétyles et les processions religieuses chez les Arabes préislamites" in *L'Arabie occidentale avant l'Hégire* (Beirut, 1928), 100–80.

Lapidus 1967: I. Lapidus, *Muslim Cities in the Later Middle Ages* (Cambridge, Mass., 1967).

Lapidus 1972: I. Lapidus, "Ayyubid Religious Policy and the Development of the Schools of Law in Cairo" in *Colloque international sur l'histoire du Caire* (Cairo, 1972), 279–86.

Lassner 1980: J. Lassner, *The Shaping of Abbasid Rule* (Princeton, 1980).

Lassus 1947: J. Lassus, *Sanctuaires chrétiens de Syrie* (Paris, 1947).

Le Strange 1890: G. Le Strange, *Palestine Under the Muslims* (London, 1890).

Levine 1963: B. L. Levine, "The Nethinim," *JBL* 82 (1963), 108–10.

Levine 1978: B. L. Levine, "The Temple Scroll: Aspects of Its Historical Provenance and Literary Character," *BASOR* 232 (1978), 5–23.

Levine 1981: L. Levine, ed., *The Jerusalem Cathedra*, vol. 1 (Jerusalem, 1981).

Levine 1982: L. Levine, ed., *The Jerusalem Cathedra*, vol. 2 (Jerusalem, 1982).

Lewis 1950: B. Lewis, "An Apocalyptic Vision of Islamic History" *BSOAS* 13 (1950), 308–38.

Lewis 1974: B. Lewis, "On That Day: A Jewish Apocalyptic Poem on the Arab Conquests," *Mélanges d'Islamologie . . . Armand Abel* (Leiden, 1974), 197–200.

Lifshitz 1967: B. Lifshitz, *Donateurs et fondateurs dans les synagogues juives* (Paris, 1967).

Little, 1980: D. Little, "The Significance of the Haram Documents for the Study of Medieval Islamic History," *Der Islam* 57 (1980), 189–219.

Lueling 1977: G. Lueling, *Der christliche Kult an der vorislamischen Kaaba als Problem der Wissenschaft und christlichen Theologie* (Erlangen, 1977).

Lyons and Jackson 1981: M. C. Lyons and D. Jackson, *Saladin: The Politics of the Holy War* (Cambridge, 1981).

Mackowski 1980: R. M. Mackowski, *Jerusalem, City of Jesus: An Exploration of the Traditions, Writings and Remains of the Holy City* (Grand Rapids, 1980).

Mader 1957: A. E. Mader, *Mambre: Die Ergebnisse der Ausgrabungen im heiligen Bezirk, Ramat al-Halil in Süd-Palästina* (Freiburg in Breisgau, 1957).

Makky 1978: G. A. Makky, *Mecca: The Pilgrimage City. A Study of Pilgrim Accommodation* (London, 1978).

Mann 1920–1922: J. Mann, *the Jews in Egypt and in Palestine under the Fatimid Caliphs*, 2 vols. (Oxford, 1920–22; rpt. Oxford, 1969).

Mantel 1975: H. Mantel, "The High Priesthood and the Sanhedrin in the Time of the Second Temple" in M. Avi-Yonah, ed., *The World History of the Jewish People*, vol. 7: *The Herodian Period* (New Brunswick, 1975), 264–83.

Ma'oz 1975: M. Ma'oz, ed., *Studies on Palestine during the Ottoman Period* (Jerusalem, 1975).

Marmadji 1951: A. S. Marmadji, *Textes géographiques arabes sur la Palestine* (Paris, 1951).

Massignon 1908/1963: L. Massignon, "Les saints musulmans enterrés à Baghdad," *RHR* "1908", 329–38; *Opera minora* (Beirut, 1963), 3: 94–101.

Massignon 1951/1963: L. Massignon, "Documents sur quelques waqfs musulmans . . ." *REI* (1951), 74–120; *Opera minora* (Beirut, 1963), 3; 181–232.

Massignon 1958/1963: L. Massignon, "La cité des Morts au Caire (Qarafa, Darb al-Ahmar)," *BIFAO* 57 (1958); *Opera minora* (Beirut, 1963), 3; 233–85.

Matthews 1932: C. D. Matthews, "The Wailing Wall and al-Buraq: Is the 'Wailing Wall' in Jerusalem the 'Wall of al-Buraq'?" *The Moslem World* 22 (1932), 331–39.

Matthews 1936: C. D. Matthews, "A Muslim Iconoclast: Ibn Taymiyyah on the 'Merits' of Jerusalem," *JAOS* 56 (1936), 1–21.

Matthews 1949: C. D. Matthews, *Palestine, Mohammedan Holy Land* (New Haven, 1949).

Maundrell 1963: Henry Maundrell, *A Journey from Aleppo to Jerusalem in 1697*, with a new introd. by David Howell (Beirut, 1963).

Mazar 1969: B. Mazar, *The Excavations in the Old City of Jerusalem: Preliminary Report of the First Season, 1968* (Jerusalem, 1969).

Mazar 1971: B. Mazar, *The Excavations in the Old City of Jerusalem: Preliminary Report of the Second and Third Seasons, 1969–1970* (Jerusalem, 1971).

Mazar 1976: A. Mazar, "The Aqueducts of Jerusalem" in Yadin 1976: 79–84.

Michelant and Raynaud 1882: M. Michelant and G. Raynaud, *Itineraires à Jérusalem et descriptions de Terre Sainte redigés en francais* (Geneva, 1882).

Milik 1960: J. Milik, "Notes d'épigraphie et de topographie palestiniennes IX Sanctuaires chrétiens de Jérusalem à l'époque arabe," *Revue biblique* 67 (1960), 354–67, 550–86.

Milik 1961: J. Milik, "La topographie de Jérusalem vers la fin de l'époque byzantine," *MUSJ* 37 (1961), 127–89.

Monks 1953: G. R. Monks, "The Church at Alexandria and the Economic Life of the City," *Speculum* 28 (1952), 227–45.

Mujir al-Din 1968: Mujir al-Din al-Ulaymi, *Al-Uns al-jalil bi-ta'rikh al-Quds wal-Khalil* (Najaf, 1968).

al-Muqaddasi 1963: *al-Muqaddasi: Ahsan at-Taqasim fi Ma'rifat al-Aqalim*, traduction partielle, annotée par André Miquel (Damascus, 1963).

Musil 1928: A. Musil, *Northern Negd* (New York, 1928).

Nau 1933: F. Nau, *Les Arabes chrétiens de Mesopotamie at de Syrie du VIIe au VIIIe siècle* (Paris, 1933).

Netzer 1981: E. Netzer, "Herod's Building Projects: State Necessity or Personal Need?" in Levine 1981: 48–61.

Noeldeke 1909: T. Noeldeke, *Das Heiligtum al-Husains zu Kerbela* (Berlin, 1909).

Noth 1973: A. Noth, *Quellenkritische Studien zu Themen, Formen und Tendenzen frühislamischer Geschichtsüberlieferung* I *Themen und Formen* (Bonn, 1973).

Ovadiah 1970: A. Ovdiah, *Corpus of Byzantine Churches in the Holy Land* (Bonn, 1970).

Paret 1958: R. Paret, "Les villes de Syrie du Sud et les routes commerciales d'Arabie à la fin du VI siècle," *Akten des XI Internationalen Byzantinisten Kongresses* (Munich, 1958), 438–44.

Pedersen 1953: J. Pedersen, "Masdjid" in *Shorter Encyclopaedia of Islam* (Leiden, 1953), 330–53.

Peeters 1947: P. Peeters, "Les ex-voto de Khosrau Aparwiez à Sergiopolis, *Analecta Bollandiana* 65 (1947), 5–56.

Peeters 1950: P. Peeters, *Le tréfonds oriental de l'hagiographie byzantine* (Brussels, 1950).

Pesikta Rabbati 1968: *Pesikta Rabbati*, trans. William G. Braude, 2 vols. (New Haven and London, 1968).

Peters 1977: F. E. Peters, "The Nabateans in the Hawran," *JAOS* 97 (1977), 263–77.

Peters 1982: F. E. Peters, *The Children of Abraham: Judaism, Christianity and Islam* (Princeton, 1982).

Peters 1983: F. E. Peters, "Who Built the Dome of the Rock?" *Graeco-Arabica* 2 (1983), 119–38.

Peters 1985: F. E. Peters, *Jerusalem: The Holy City in the Eyes of Chroniclers, Visitors, Pilgrims and Prophets from the Days of Abraham to the Beginning of Modern Times* (Princeton, 1985).

Peters 1985a: F. E. Peters, "The Procession That Never Was: The Painful Way in Jerusalem," *The Drama Review* 29:3 (1985), 31–41.

Philipsborn 1961: A. Philipsborn, "Der Fortschritt in der Entwicklung des byzantinischen Krankenhauswesens," *Byzantinische Zeitschrift* 54 (1961), 338–65.

Pinkerfeld 1960: J. Pinkerfeld, "David's Tomb: Notes on the History of the Building," *Bulletin Rabinowitz* 3 (1960), 41–43.

Pixner 1976: B. -G. Pixner, "An Essene Quarter on Mt. Zion?" *Studia Hierosolymitana* 1 (1976), 245–84.

Prawer, J., "The Friars of Mount Zion and the Jews of Jerusalem in the Fifteenth Century," *Bullentin of the Jewish Palestine Exploration Society* 14 (1948), 15–24.

Prawer 1972: J. Prawer, *The Latin Kingdom of Jerusalem. European Colonialism in the Middle Ages* (London, 1972).

Prawer 1980: J. Prawer, *Crusader Institutions* (Oxford, 1980).

Price and Trell 1977: M. J. Price and B. Trell, *Coins and Their Cities: Architecture On Ancient Coins of Greece, Rome and Palestine* (Detroit, 1977).

Qutb al-Din 1857: Qutb al-Din, *Kitab al-i'lam bi a'lam bayt allah al-haram*, ed. F. Wuestenfeld, *Chroniken der Stadt Mekka*, vol. 3 (Leipzig, 1857; rpt. Hildesheim, 1981).

Rahman 1976: F. Rahman, "The Pre-Foundations of the Muslim Community in Mecca," *Studia Islamica* 43 (1976), 5–24.

Raphael et al. 1973: F. Raphael et al., *Les Pèlerinages: De l'antiquité biblique et classique à l'occident médiévale* (Paris, 1973).

Rapp 1973: F. Rapp, "Les pèlerinages dans la vie religieuse de l'Occident médiévale aux XIVe et XVe siècles" in Raphael et al. 1973: 117–60.

Receuil Lois 1841–43: *Recueil des Historiens des Croisades . Lois*, 2 vols. (Paris, 1841–43).

Richard 1965: J. Richard, "Sur un passage du *Pèlerinage de Charlemagne*: le marché de Jérusalem," *RBPH* 13 (1965), 552–55.

Riley-Smith 1967: J. Riley-Smith, *The Knights of Saint John in Jerusalem and Cyprus, 1050–1310* (London, 1967).

Röhricht 1893–1904: R. Röhricht, *Regesta Regni Hierosolymitani*, 2 vols. (Innsbruck, 1893–1904).

Romani 1948: M. Romani, *Pellegrini e viaggiatori nell'economia de Roma dal XIV al XVII secolo* (Milan, 1948).

Rubin 1982: Z. Rubin, "The Church of the Holy Sepulchre and the Conflict between the Sees of Jerusalem and Caesarea" in Levine 1982: 79–105.

Runciman 1969: S. Runciman, "The Pilgrimages to Palestine before 1050" in K. M. Setton, ed., *A History of the Crusades*, vol. 1: *The First Hundred Years* (Madison, 1969), 68-80.

Safrai 1975: S. Safrai, "The Temple and the Divine Service" in M. Avi-Yonah, ed., *A World History of the Jewish People*, vol. 7: *The Herodian Period* (New Brunswick, 1975), 284–338.

Safrai 1981: S. Safrai, *Die Wallfahrt in Zeitalter des Zweiten Tempels* (Neukirchen, 1981).

Sauvaget 1947: J. Sauvaget, *La mosquée omeyyade de Médine: étude sur les origines architecturales de la mosquée et de la basilique* (Paris, 1947).

Savage 1977: H. L. Savage, "Pilgrimages and Pilgrim Shrines in Palestine and Syria after 1095" in Hazard 1977: 36–68.

Schaefer 1985: K. Schaefer, *Jerusalem in the Ayyubid and Mamluk Era*, Ph.D. Diss. New York Univ., 1985.

Scholem 1954: G. Scholem, *Major Trends in Jewish Mysticism* (New York, 1954).

Schmidt 1933: H. Schmidt, *Der heilige Fels in Jerusalem—eine archäologische und religionsgeschichte Studie* (Tübingen, 1933).

Schuerer 1973: E. Schuerer, *The History of the Jewish People in the Age of Jesus Christ*, rev. and ed. G. Vermes and F. Millar, vol. 1 (Edinburgh, 1973).

Schuerer 1979: E. Schuerer, op. cit., vol. 2 (Edinburgh, 1979).

Schur 1980: N. Schur, *Jerusalem in Pilgrims' and Travellers' Accounts: A Thematic Bibliography of Western Christian Itineraries, 1300–1917* (Jerusalem, 1980).

Schwartz 1939: E. Schwartz, *Kyrillos von Skythopolis* (Leipzig, 1939).

Seetzen 1854–1859: U. J. Seetzen, *Reisen durch Syrien, Palästina, etc.*, 4 vols. (Berlin, 1854–59).

Serjeant 1962: R. B. Serjeant, "Haram and Hawtah, the Sacred Enclosures in Arabia" in A. Badawi, ed., *Mélanges Taha Husain* (Cairo, 1962), 41–58.

Seyrig 1929: H. Seyrig, "La triade héliopolitiane et les temples de Baalbek,"

Syria 10 (1929), 314–56.

Seyrig 1934: H. Seyrig, "Bas reliefs monumentaux du temple de Bel à Palmyre," *Syria* 15 (1934), 155–86.

Seyrig 1941: H. Seyrig, "Inscriptions grecques de l'agora de Palmyre," *Syria* 22 (1941), 223–70.

Seyrig 1970: H. Seyrig, "Les Dieux armés et les Arabes en Syrie," *Syria* 47 (1979), 77–112.

Sharon 1975: M. Sharon, "The Political Role of the Bedouins in Palestine in the Sixteenth and Seventeenth Centuries" in Ma'oz 1975: 11–30.

Shaw 1962: S. Shaw, *The Financial and Administrative Organization and Development of Ottoman Egypt, 1517–1798*, (Princeton, 1962).

Shinar 1977: P. Shinar, "Traditional and Reformist Mawlid Celebrations in the Maghrib" in M. Rosen-Ayalon, ed., *Studies in Memory of Gaston Wiet* (Jerusalem, 1977), 371–414.

Silberman 1982: N. A. Silberman, *Digging for God and Country: Exploration, Archeology and the Secret Struggle for the Holy Land, 1799–1917* (New York, 1982).

Simon 1962: M. Simon, *Recherches d'histoire Judéo-Chrétienne* (Paris and the Hague, 1962).

Simon 1973: M. Simon, "Les Pèlerinages dans l'antiquité chrétienne" in Raphael et al. 1973: 97–115.

Sivan 1967: E. Sivan, "Le charactère sacré de Jérusalem dans l'Islam aux XIIe-XIIIe siècles," *Studia Islamica* 27 (1967), 148–82.

Sivan 1968: E. Sivan, *L'Islam et la Croisade. Idéologie et Propagande dans les Réactions Musulmans aux Croisades* (Paris, 1968).

Sivan 1971: E. Sivan, "The Beginnings of the *Fada'il al-Quds* Literature," *Israel Oriental Studies* 1 (1971), 263–71.

Smith 1894: C. R. Smith, *The Religion of the Semites: The Fundamental Institutions*, 2nd ed. (London, 1894; rpt. New York, 1972).

Snouck Hurgronje 1888: C. Snouck Hurgronje, *Mekka*, vol. 1: *Die Stadt und ihre Herren* (Leiden, 1888).

Snouck Hurgronje 1931: C. Snouck Hurgronje, *Mekka in the Nineteenth Century*, translation by J. H. Monahan of *Mekka*, vol 2 (Leiden, 1931).

Soucek 1976: P. Soucek, "The Temple of Solomon in Islamic Legend and Art" in Gutmann 1976: 73–124.

Sourdel 1959–1960: D. Sourdel, *Le Vizerat Abbaside de 749 à 936*, 2 vols. (Damascus, 1959–60).

Sourdel 1976: D. Sourdel, "Réflexions sur la diffusion de la Madrasa en Orient du XIe au XIIe siècle," *Revue des études islamiques* 44 (1976), 165–84.

Sourdel-Thomine 1952–54: J. Sourdel-Thomine, "Pèlerinages damascains: Les anciens lieux de pèlerinage damascains d'après les sources arabes," *BEO* 14 (1952–54), 65–85.

Starcky 1964: J. Starcky, "Petra et la Nabatène" in *Supplément au Dictionaire de la Bible*, fasc. 39 (1964), 886–1017.

Stillman 1975: N. Stillman, "Charity and Social Service in Islam," *Societas* 5

(1975), 105–15.

Stratos 1968: A. N. Stratos, *Byzantium in the Seventh Century*, vol. 1: *602–634* (Amsterdam, 1968).

Tabari 1879–1903: Muhammad ibn Jarir al-Tabari, *Kitab akhbar al-rusul wa al-muluk*, ed. M. J. De Goeje et al., 13 vols. (Leiden, 1879–1903).

Tabba 1982: Y. al-Tabba, *The Architectural Patronage of Nur al-Din (1146–1174)*, 2 vols., Ph.D. diss. New York Univ., 1982.

Tamari 1968: S. Tamari, "Sulla conversione della chiesa di Sant'Anna a Gerusalemme nella Madrasa as-Salahiyya," *Rivista degli Studi Orientali* 43 (1968), 327–54.

Tamari 1976: S. Tamari, "Al-Ashrafiyya—An Imperial Madrasa in Jerusalem," *Memorie Accademia Nazionale dei Lincei* 15.5 (Rome, 1976), 537–68.

Tamari 1982: S. Tamari, "Darb al-Hajj in Sinai. An Historical-Archaeological Study," *Accademia Nazionale dei Lincei: Memorie* 25 (1982), 431–525.

Tchalenko 1955–1958: G. Tchalenko, *Villages antiques de la Syrie du Nord. La Massif du Bélus à l'èpoque romain*, 3 vols. (Paris, 1955–58).

Tibawi 1978: A. L. Tibawi, *The Islamic Pious Foundations in Jerusalem. Origins, History and Usurpation by Israel* (London, 1978).

Tobler and Molinier 1872: T. Tobler and A. Molinier, *Itinera hierosolymitana et descriptiones Terrae Sanctae . . .* (Geneva, 1872).

Torrey 1946: C. C. Torrey, *The Lives of the Prophets* (Philadelphia, 1946).

Tresse 1937: R. Tresse, *Le pèlerinage syrien aux villes saints de l'Islam* (Paris, 1937).

Trimingham 1971: J.S. Trimingham, *The Sufi Orders in Islam* (London, 1971).

Tsafrir 1975: Y. Tsafrir, "Jerusalem" in *Reallexikon zur byzantinischen Kunst*, vol 3. fasc. 20 (Stuttgart, 1975), 544–52.

Tsafrir 1977: Y. Tsafrir, "Muqaddasi's Gates of Jerusalem: A New Indentification Based on Byzantine Sources," *Israel Exploration Journal* 27 (1977), 152–61.

Tushingham 1968: A. D. Tushingham, "The Armenian Garden," *Palestine Exploration Quarterly* 100 (1968), 109–11.

Vilney 1973: Z. Vilney, *The Sacred Land*, vol. 1: *Legends of Jerusalem* (Philadelphia, 1973).

Vincent 1921: L. -H. Vincent, "Découverte de la 'Synagogue des Affranchis' à Jérusalem," *Revue biblique* 30 (1921), 247–77.

Vincent 1954: L. -H. Vincent, "Le temple hérodien d'après la Mishna," *Revue biblique* 61 (1954), 5–35, 398–418.

Vincent and Abel 1914–26: L. -H. Vincent and F. -M. Abel, *Jérusalem nouvelle*, 4 fasc. (Paris, 1914–26).

Vincent et al. 1923: L. H. Vincent et al., *Hébron: Le Haram al-Khalil, Sépulture des Patriarches* (Paris, 1923).

Vogt 1967: E. Vogt, "Das Wachstum des alten Stadtgebietes von Jerusalem," *Biblica* 48 (1967), 337–58.

Vogt 1974: E. Vogt, "Vom Tempel zum Felsendom," *Biblica* 55 (1974), 25–64.

Volney 1959: C. F., Comte de Volney, *Voyage en Syrie et en Egypte pendant les années 1783, 1784 et 1785*, 1st ed. (Paris, 1787; repub. with introd. and notes by Jean Gaulmier, Paris, 1959).

von Grunebaum 1951: G. B. von Grunebaum, *Muhammadan Festivals* (New York, 1951).

von Schoenborn 1972: C. von Schoenborn, *Sophrone de Jerusalem* (Paris, 1972).

Walls 1976: A. Walls, "Two Minarets Flanking the Church of Holy Sepulcher," *Levant* 8 (1976), 159–61.

Wardi 1975: C. Wardi, "The Question of the Holy Places in Ottoman Times" in Ma'oz 1975: 385–93.

Wellhausen 1897: J. Wellhausen, *Reste arabischen Heidentums* (Berlin, 1897).

Wellhausen 1899: J. Wellhausen, *Prolegomena zur ältesten Geschichte des Islams* (= *Skizzen und Vorarbeiten* 6) (Berlin, 1899).

Wensinck 1916: A. J. Wensinck, "The Ideas of the Western Semites concerning the Navel of the Earth," *Verhandelingen der Koninklijke Acad. van Wetenschappen*, 1916.

Wensinck 1927: A. J. Wensinck, *A Handbook of Early Muhammadan Tradition* (Leiden, 1927).

Widengren 1955: G. Widengren, *Muhammad, the Apostle of God, and His Ascension* (Wiesbaden, 1955).

Wilhelm 1946: K. Wilhelm, *Roads to Zion: Four Centuries of Travelers' Reports* (New York, 1946).

Wilkinson 1974: J. Wilkinson, "Ancient Jerusalem: Its Water Supply and Population," *Palestine Exploration Quarterly* (1974), 33–51.

Wilkinson 1975: J. Wilkinson, "The Streets of Jerusalem," *Levant* (1975), 118–36.

Wilkinson 1977: J. Wilkinson, *Jerusalem Pilgrims Before the Crusades* (London, 1977).

Wilkinson 1978: J. Wilkinson, *Jerusalem as Jesus Knew It: Archeology as Evidence* (London, 1978).

Wilkinson 1981: J. Wilkinson, *Egeria's Travels in the Holy Land*, rev. ed. (London, 1981).

Windisch 1925: D. H. Windisch, "Die ältesten Palästinapilger," *ZDPV* 48 (1925), 145–58.

Wirth 1974–1975: E. Wirth, "Zum Problem des Bazars," *Der Islam* 51 (1974), 203–60; 52 (1975), 6–46.

Wirth 1975: E. Wirth, "Die orientalische Stadt: Ein Überblick aufgrund jungerer Forschungen zum materiallen Kultur," *Saeculum* 26 (1975), 45–94.

Wolf 1951: E. Wolf, "The Social Organization of Mecca and the Origins of Islam," *Southwestern Journal of Anthropology* (1951), 330–77.

Wuestenfeld 1857–58: *F. Wuestenfeld, Die Chroniken der Stadt Mekka*, 3 vols. (Leipzig, 1857–58; rpt. Hildesheim, 1981).

Wuestenfeld 1861: F. Wuestenfeld, *Geschichte der Stadt Mekka nach den Arabischen Chroniken bearbeitet* (Leipzig, 1861; rpt. Hildesheim, 1981).

Yadin 1976: Y. Yadin, ed., *Jerusalem Revealed: Archaeology in the Holy City, 1968–1974* (Jerusalem, 1976).

Yadin 1977: Y. Yadin, *The Temple Scroll*, 3 vols. (Jerusalem, 1977). Hebrew.
Zander 1971: W. Zander, *Israel and the Holy Places of Christendom* (London, 1971).

Index